The Handloom Industry of Begampur in Transition

The Handloom Industry of Begampur in Transition

Technology, Disjuncture, and Development

Abhradip Banerjee

LEXINGTON BOOKS
Lanham • Boulder • New York • London

Published by Lexington Books
An imprint of The Rowman & Littlefield Publishing Group, Inc.
4501 Forbes Boulevard, Suite 200, Lanham, Maryland 20706
www.rowman.com

86-90 Paul Street, London EC2A 4NE

British Library Cataloguing in Publication Information Available

Library of Congress Cataloging-in-Publication Data

Names: Banerjee, Abhradip, author.
Title: The handloom industry of Begampur in transition : technology, disjuncture, and development / Abhradip Banerjee.
Description: Lanham : Lexington Books, [2024] | Includes bibliographical references and index.
Identifiers: LCCN 2024028556 (print) | LCCN 2024028557 (ebook) | ISBN 9781666960587 (cloth) | ISBN 9781666960594 (ebook)
Subjects: LCSH: Handloom industry–India–Begampur.
Classification: LCC HD9866.I43 B42 2024 (print) | LCC HD9866.I43 (ebook) | DDC 338.4/767754552–dc23/eng/20240812
LC record available at https://lccn.loc.gov/2024028556
LC ebook record available at https://lccn.loc.gov/2024028557

Dedicated to Our Beloved Daughter Yoshita Banerjee (Rai)

Contents

List of Illustrations

FIGURES

TABLES

Foreword

Gopalkrishna Chakrabarti

To the people of West Bengal and also in the tourist map of India, Bishnupur—a small town in the district of Bankura—has an indelible mark for its terracotta temples (built between 1622 and 1758 A.D.) founded by the regional principality of Malla kings (late-sixteenth-century onward) as a sign of their embracing Bengal Vaishnavism. These terracotta temples witness the development of a unique style in temple architecture of Eastern India. The other reason is the silk saree (drapery) called *baluchari* that the weavers of Bishnupur have been producing for the last one hundred years and more though it is not the unique production of Bishnupur. The colorful motif or design on the body of the saree, its borders, and its end has drawn the attention of wealthy consumers as well as appreciation from the national and international markets.

Bengali litterateur Samaresh Basu published a fiction titled *Tana-Poren* (warp and woof) on the life of handloom weavers of a village near Bishnupur of West Bengal, India, in 1961. His vivid narration of the life of the weavers around Bishnupur has been painted around the central character of the novel. Panchu is a *nakshadar* (designer/pattern maker), who learned the art of designing and weaving a saree from his mentor who earned the name and fame in the region and beyond. The story of his success has been orchestrated by a *mahajan* (financer and entrepreneur) who introduced *Baluchari* bearing his design in big markets of India and Mumbai. Panchu is a worthy disciple of his mentor for his two designs had earned appreciation in the *Baluchari* market of India. His family, friends, and neighbors take pride in him, and at the same time, he has earned envy from his brother and a rival competitor of the same village. This rival competitor is a well-to-do farmer and a disciple of a discarded designer who was also a rival of Panchu's mentor. Panchu is a familiar householder in his village with a humble earning from his own pair of handlooms. An affectionate father of four children, he lives with his wife, children, and father and holds his family in high esteem. Currently, he is busy creating designs after successive failures to get his designs passed by his mentor, although his mentor considers him as his son. Finally, Panchu's third design gets approval from his mentor with unexpected applause. He calls on his patron *mahajan* whose family business of manufacturing and trading of textiles has been much benefitted from his designs of *baluchari*. After a prolonged wait the *mahajan* visits Panchu's mentor relieving their tension regarding the fate of the design. He immediately granted the design since it has been approved by the master designer, handing over an advance to Panchu for commencing work and cautions him of his bad habit of drinking. The narration would have ended here, but the anticlimax is still at large. The fiction ends with the death of Panchu's mentor after a few days he starts weaving his dream. The *mahajan* discards the order on the plea that the market is not favorable to the expensive saree like *Baluchari*. He could not do so earlier as his father was indebted to this master designer for his success in the trading market. A mentally shattered Panchu returns to the loom again with all of his existence, his hope, and his dream. Samaresh Basu has sketched the life of the people belonging to the weaver caste group, their occupation, hereditary practice, inheritance of tangible and intangible property, economic competition and rivalry, marital practices, and exposure to the outside world including the national market scenario. His portraiture of the community of weavers is generally covered by the term "culture" in a different writing enterprise of ethnographers. Anthropology writes the culture of a community. In this way, ethnography and literature tend to share many common grounds.

Abhradip Banerjee's anthropological study of the weaving community in Begampur unravels the complexities involved in the production of sarees. These complexities on the one hand narrate the struggle of the resourceless weavers and the desperate efforts of the master weaver to combine multiple resources against the dominant forces of market regulators on the other. Plenty of studies dealing with the ecstatic motif and design of saree produced in Bengal handloom, its history, and technology are available in print. Most of them bypass the complex interrelations among the various grades of producers and laborers, technology, regulators of the market for the supply of raw material, and disposal of the finished product as well as consumers let alone the social bonding among the laborers. The ethnography of Banerjee is probably the first of its kind in eastern India that also delves into theoretical discussion over the issue of industrialization in India. Conceptually, the weavers are not a uniform or homogenous community of artisans, nor are their social relations of production and marketing of products. It varies as the history of the country, or the regional histories vary to produce different sets of norms and values around the production and marketing of handloom products. Banerjee's attempt bridges a gap in ethnographic research on the artisan community in West Bengal and Eastern India.

In the context of West Bengal an ethnographer identifies *Tanti* as the weaver caste group of the Hindu, whose members are supposed to engage themselves in weaving dress material and related items like that of other regions and states in India. All the weaver caste groups are not necessarily known by the same name and enjoy the same social status in the regional caste rankings. Having different ways of life, they are necessarily dependent upon the market networks and their regulators for the supply of raw materials and disposal of the produced fabrics. The market regulators may or may not belong to the same community or region and state. In these asymmetric economic relations, the skills and domestic labor of the weavers' families remain unrecognized, unpaid, and invisible. Similarly, all of the weavers of a locality or region may not belong to the weaver caste group. The entry of non-weaver caste people in this occupation is an adjustment with historical and other local or regional factors.

In Uttar Pradesh (erstwhile United Provinces in British India), Rai (2011) narrates how in a desperate effort to gain control over the market, the Muslim weavers of Uttar Pradesh leaned toward the radical ethnocentrism during the period of freedom movement. *Julaha*, low caste but semi-urban weaving artisans of Uttar Pradesh who were converted to Islam in the fourteenth to the seventeenth century, are distributed in the most important weaving centers of Uttar Pradesh. Their adoption of the term *grihasta* from the Hindu usage to mean the householder points out the Hindu-Muslim antagonism to have cultural control over the trade. But this adoption finally resulted in the creation of a hierarchy among the laborers and traders when the East India Company attempted to monopolize control over the entire textile production of eastern India. Though East India Company's interaction with the South Indian weavers occurred in the seventeenth century, it had no legal authority to control the production and trading of Banaras in the late eighteenth century. But by introducing one rule for Bengal Presidency (that included Banaras) East India Company began to pay in advance to the *grihasta* or the resourceful master weavers to get the entire production of the region. Taking advantage of the Company, in the long run, transformed them into supervisors of production only at the cost of losing control over the production and marketing of textile products. Their sole duty was to ensure that the East India Company received the supply of entire fabrics produced regionally in due time. Finally, Rai observes that the contest among the regional players in marketing the handloom products, underutilization of traditional technology and skill, import of new technology, change in consumption pattern of textile fabrics, new market, and labor relations paved the way for the new capitalistic regime from the colonial period. If the ethnography is placed within the context of history, we find the "community" in "community of weaver," therefore, is a multilayered economic connotation having heterogeneous cultural tradition in their practices of social life (Rai, Santosh Kumar, "Becoming a *Grihasta*: Hierarchies of Work among Handloom Weavers in Early Twentieth Century United Provinces, India." In Rana Behal, Alice Mah, and Babacar Fall (Eds.) *Rethinking Work: Global Historical and Sociological Perspective*, 2011, pp. 73–88).

Historical complexities narrated by Rai (2011) in his study of the weavers of early twentieth-century Uttar Pradesh (erstwhile United Provinces) show that weaving was not an occupation confined to the Hindu caste group only, and therefore, the marketing of the produced fabrics witnesses the intense competition among the producers of different communities. East India Company took the multicultural market practices to their advantage. Historical studies on the production and marketing of handloom products put a question mark on the idea that caste is a unique system in India that integrates economic, social, and religious systems. In another landmark ethnographic study on the South Indian caste system in a village of Thanjavur (formerly Tanjore) district of Tamilnadu Province, Gough (1955a, 1955b, 1962) has discussed the historical aspect of village foundation and, therefore, the commencement of caste group's functioning as early as the late eighteenth century. The Maratha king brought four exogamous patrilineal family clusters of Smartha Brahmans to settle in the village having usufructuary rights over the agricultural land and no right to sell the same to outsiders. Other cultivator caste groups settled here to cultivate the land and had the right to get a share of the crops. The king used to get a substantial share of the produced crop while the Brahmans themselves did not take part in the cultivation, and their role in controlling the village economy was limited to supervising the production and administration (Gough, E. Kathleen, "The Social Structure of a Tanjore Village." In M.N. Srinivas (Ed.) India's Villages. Calcutta: West Bengal Development Department, 1955a; "The Social Structure of a Tanjore Village." In McKim Marriott (ed.) Village India: Studies in the Little Community. Originally published as Memoir No. 83 of American Anthropological Association; "Caste in a Tanjore Village." In E.R. Leach (ed.) Aspects of Caste in South India, Ceylon and North-West Pakistan. Cambridge: Cambridge University Press, pp. 11–60). From the perspective of economic anthropology Indian castes as occupational groups have been intensely debated among the adherents of two theoretical schools, namely, ecological anthropology originated through the works of L.A. White and the other substantivist approach to economic analysis derived from the studies of K. Polanyi. Critically discussing the study of E. Kathleen Gough and W.C. Neale, the student of Polanyi, Morton Klass

(Caste: The Emergence of South Asian Social System. New Delhi: Manohar, 2004) asserts that the caste system originally derived from the exchange of brides among the fixed exogamous marriage circles that further articulated to the controlling of access to certain commodities and services among the dominant castes (Klass, 2004, pp. 105–134). That might have led the ethnographers to assume the caste as a hereditary vocation-based endogamous social system. N.K. Bose's observation on castes in Bengal as occupational groups practicing hereditary vocations in a non-competitive market system ("Some Aspects of Caste in Bengal," *Man in India, 1958, 38:2:73–97*) and its subsequent changes due to the process of modernization ("Modern Bengal," *Man in India, 1958, 38:4:229–295*) ignores the fact that the concept of Indian caste system having hereditary guild is actually imposition of an image of European guild system by the colonial administrators and surveyors (Klass, 2004, pp. 70–72). Why the caste question should necessarily be addressed is supposed to be answered here. Studies on the regional social transformation in historical periods and the diversities evidenced in the caste system in different parts of India from the anthropological studies have led scholars in Indian history to think that the discourse on caste as a social system, as we know it today, is the gift of the British colonial rule and its cultural project of modernizing the non-European societies like that of India (Dirks, Nicholas B. Castes of Mind. Delhi: Permanent Black, 2001).

Again, on the question of whether the weavers should be regarded as belonging to caste or community, one can only point out the loose concept or definition of caste and community. Both of the terms are used in anthropology and sociology in a somewhat vague manner. While the conceptual association of caste and occupation is on the wane, Dipankar Gupta summarily disagrees with the anthropological characterization of the Indian caste system as a homogenous pan-Indian social system. The "reason" that the high caste groups provide for the low-ranking of some caste groups in the system is not acceptable to the people belonging to the same caste groups of different regions (Interrogating Caste. Penguin Books. 2001, p. 1). Instead of having a unified social system, as it appears, regional systems have developed a parity or tacit understanding among the different communities over the social and cultural transactions. In this context, each and every region of India has developed (social and cultural) "knowledge" to resolve the problem of living on the earth that is specific to the region.

Like Dirks (2001), Bernard S. Cohn (Colonialism and Its Forms of Knowledge. Oxford: Oxford University Press, 2002) has also studied the historical development of different institutions in India that were regarded so far as traditional. He affirms that the cultural project of colonialism has invented the term "traditional" and imposed it on many indigenous regional practices so that they may appear as immutable and ahistorical and thereby caused the decay of regional indigenous knowledge beholden by the low caste group paving the way for supremacy of high caste group. The dominance of colonial power concealed the regional and even local variation of castes as an economic system flagged off the introduction of industrial capital that imparted the flow of capital and labor beyond the regional markets. This has unsettled the occupational or job security at the village level. Individuals are now free from the regional social system to begin with moving from one region to another in search of livelihood with the increasing economic and social insecurity.

Colonial rule disrupted the artisans, traders, and the like system of practicing and disseminating traditional knowledge. Though the caste system has been despised by humanist scholars and philanthropists, some social scientists opine that every aspect of the system is not an instrument of oppression. Vaidyanathan (2023) opines that each caste group itself is social capital if we agree with the concept of the Organisation for Economic Co-operation and Development (OECD). Social capital entails the network of shared norms, values, and understanding of cooperation among people themselves. He draws our attention to the "economic cluster"—the rising phenomenon in the sphere of Indian economic development. Such economic clusters are organizations that put together "similar or related goods or services," "financial capital," and forward and lateral linkages of distributors, customers, and related companies. A group of specialists including academicians, businessmen, chartered accountants, and others examine the validity of economic clusters developed in the states of Tamilnadu, Gujarat, Punjab, Karnataka, and erstwhile Andhra Pradesh in 2000. One of the most interesting findings is that "clusters specialized in a particular economic activity are run by specific caste groups". There are approximately 7000 clusters in traditional handloom, handicraft, and modern Small and Medium Enterprise (SME) segments with the existence of another "2500 unmapped rural industry" clusters (R, Vaidyanathan, Caste as Social Capital. Gurugram: Penguin Random House, pp. 46–56, 68–79).

In the neorealism genre in Bengali literature, the said novel of Samaresh Basu's *Tana Poren* has earned a special place. It has lifted the struggling life of a rural community along with its local dialects on the printed pages of the novel. Like a master designer, he has weaved the characters in such a way that the readers would feel that they are present within the context of the novel. The neorealism genre in Bengali literature like that of Basu presents people's unhappiness with the post-independent unexpected economic, social, and cultural scenarios of the country. After independence, democratically elected governments have failed to ensure the livelihood of the common people, and the political practice of the unrepentant concerned stakeholders are using the pillars of democracy to uproot it from the foundation. Economic and social insecurity is not only abundant in India but also in the majority of the countries of the world, particularly those who were once the colony. Discussion on the economic and social insecurities of any country necessarily requires looking into its democratic practices. The condition of democracy in the majority of the countries is in a languishing state—reports Pranab Bardhan citing a report of the V-Dem Institute at the University of Gothenburg published in 1921 (A World of Insecurity: Democratic Disenchantment in Rich and Poor Countries. Cambridge etc.: Harvard University Press, 2022). His critical analysis draws emphatic relations between economic insecurity and democratic practices. The mentioned report specifically mentions that India, the largest democracy of the world, has turned into a country of shrinking democratic space through "electoral autocracy" that hardly addresses the most important issues of the country like livelihood security. The case of Begampur as narrated in Abhradip Banerjee's ethnography is a sorry victim of unabated capitalistic growth in India and the world.

Dealing with people belonging to a well-defined time and place is not the only similarity the fiction writer and ethnographer share; they are concerned with the existential problems of people's lives. *Tana Poren*—the fiction referred to in the text—the lexicon itself has a number of meanings and nuances. Ups and downs (in life), continuity, pattern, design, etc. are a few that have reference in the semantic field of both the fiction writer and ethnographer. The only difference is that they have to safeguard their boundary while the fiction writer develops the characters of the fiction to their full realization of meaningful existence in their course of life, the ethnographer searches for the people's understanding about the meaning of their lives culminated through complex interpersonal and extra-personal relations. While the litterateur finds for himself/herself an existence through the created characters by transcending the time and space, an ethnographer discovers himself/herself while doing fieldwork beyond his/her own cultural boundary or interacting with the people of the same culture. Both of the litterateur and ethnographer always belong to a fuzzy area of knowing and not knowing the existential problems of human beings. An ethnographer is credited when he/she is able to make a balance between knowing and not knowing the group of human beings under research. Abhradip Banerjee has done his task to keep the required balance in his ethnography.

Acknowledgements

First and foremost, I should thank Eric Kuntzman, acquisitions editor, history, asian studies, and slavic studies, Lexington Books, who after reading my article "Understanding Some of the Key Factors Responsible for Transition within an Indian Cotton Weaving Tradition," published in *Asian Journal of Social Sciences* in 2016, became interested in knowing whether my work "relates to a larger, book-length project" back in 2018. This initiated the conversation between me and Lexington Books. Due to being part of my PhD thesis, I always had the empirical data to convert this work into a book. However, despite having the materials to write, I was overloaded with teaching and fieldwork assignments. Hence, I dropped the idea at that point in time. But Eric kept being persistent, as he checked in once again with the same proposal in 2022. And this is how the journey of writing this book started.

As I have mentioned already, this book contains portions of my PhD dissertation. Therefore, I must also acknowledge the role of my PhD supervisor Dr. Gopalkrishna Chakraborti, former professor, in the Department of Anthropology, University of Calcutta, and anonymous examiners of my PhD thesis who first instilled the idea that my work could be converted into a book. I must also thank my co-supervisor Dr. Arnab Das, associate professor, Department of Anthropology, University of Calcutta, and Subha Ray, professor, Department of Anthropology, University of Calcutta, who have extended their support beyond academics, and all the faculty members, and staff of the library at the department, students, and research scholars of the Department of Anthropology, University of Calcutta, from where I have carried out my doctoral research.

My stint in the Department of Anthropology, University of Calcutta, as a research fellow was for five years, during which the University Grants Commission (UGC) provided me a fellowship, initially as a junior research fellow for two years and then as a senior research fellow for three more years. Therefore, I need to express my gratitude to the University Grants Commission (UGC) for providing me with funds to carry out my PhD research in the first place, without which this book wouldn't have materialized.

I must also thank Shri Kartik Chakrabarty, assistant professor, Post-Graduate Department of Anthropology, Bidhannagar College, Kolkata, and Dr. Sankha Priya Guha, associate professor and head, Post-Graduate Department of Anthropology, Bidhannagar College, Kolkata, for inviting me to look over the works of a group of post-graduate students of Bidhannagar College back in 2021, who incidentally were working on the weavers of Begampur. I saw many new developments in the handloom industry in Begampur region which re-spurred my interest and provided me a new impetus to carry out fieldwork afresh. I also must thank Dr. Pinaki Ghosh, IPR-chair professor, Department of Law, National University of Juridical Sciences (NUJS), Kolkata, for inviting me to talk on the prospect of GI and the handloom industry of Begampur region. It opened a new horizon of research with which I was not familiar previously.

Next, I must thank all my respondents in Begampur who have tolerated me for all these years. Despite knowing that my research may not bring any radical change to their economic and social situation, most of the respondents were welcoming, patient, and generous. Not only they provided me with the in-depth information, but they inquired about my problems and goals in life and at times looked after me as a human being. I would like to express my gratitude to Shri Samir Dey especially, who introduced me to the villagers, and Shri Madan Dey who helped me understand many important aspects of the handloom industry of this region back in 2004. I would also thank my former student, Sri Kiran Ghosh, for helping me out during my most recent stint of fieldwork in Begampur who incidentally is an inhabitant of Kharsarai (the neighboring village of Begampur). He helped me find the leads regarding the data collection on the life-cycle ritual and religious life of the handloom weavers in Begampur region. In this regard, I must also mention Dr. Biswanath Gan, cultural research officer, Cultural Research Institute, Backward Classes Welfare Department, Government of West Bengal, for his generous help in providing important documentary leads regarding the ethnic background of the weaver population in Begampur region. I also need to thank Shri Saila Kundu, Manager, Begampur Cluster Development Society, for providing important leads regarding ongoing welfare efforts that have been taken for the handloom weavers of this region. It is he who took the initial burden of providing the information regarding the changes that have taken place in the handloom industry of Begampur region.

Last but not the least, I also need to mention the help and guidance that I received while writing, rewriting, and copyediting right from the very beginning. In this regard, I must mention the name of Megan White who took over the role of associate acquisitions editor, anthropology, Latin American and Caribbean studies, linguistics, and economics section of Lexington Books from her predecessor, Alexandra Rallo, while I was preparing to submit the book proposal to Lexington Books for consideration. Apart from charting out the academic prerequisites, she helped me in understanding the nuances and some of the basic minimum requirements of the printing and publication process at Lexington Books. This eventually pushed me to expand my horizon and modify my initial ideas by incorporating the overlooked areas regarding the handloom weavers of Begampur region under the purview of this book. I must also thank the anonymous reviewer who took the burden of reading the entire manuscript and providing constructive comments for its betterment. Subsequently, I received tremendous support from Courtney Morales during the process of peer review, as she took over the role of associate acquisitions editor, anthropology, Latin American and Caribbean studies, linguistics, and economics section of Lexington Books, from Megan White. Her precise, focused, and clear instructions helped complete the necessary modification within the stipulated time. A big thanks is also due to Linda Kessler, Associate Production Editor, Rowman and Littlefield Publishing, Akshaya Ravi Pemmasani, Project Manager, and the entire team at Deanta Global Publishing Services who arranged, formatted, extensively copyedited, and made the entire manuscript ready for publication.

Introduction

Why Handloom? Excavating the Trope

The answer to the question of why one needs further research on Indian handloom is manifold. In fact, this is true for any kind of research. Understanding the rationale behind the choice of a particular research problem requires the churning of many related issues and their adequate analysis. And this stands true in the case of this particular research as well. I am realizing it more as I am in the process of writing this book.

To be honest, if anyone asks me why I chose to work on handloom weavers I would not be able to answer him/her in clear terms. Right at the initial stage, it came to me more as a convenient proposal rather than a well-researched problem based on which usually any researcher carries out his/her research. However, understanding the prerequisites of carrying out meaningful research among the handloom weavers started to come along as I delved into this topic more and more in due course of time.

HANDLOOM INDUSTRY AND THE INDIAN ECONOMY

While studying literature the first information that I noticed is the unique position that the handloom industry held within the Indian economy. The literature revealed that throughout the year the handloom sector played quite a pivotal role in the contribution of India's industrial output, employment generation, and export earnings. Figures show that in the year 2009 the Indian handloom industry contributed to over 22 percent of India's total cloth production, about 14 percent to industrial production, 4 percent to the Gross Domestic Product (GDP), and 17 percent to the country's export earnings (Ministry of External Affairs of India 2009; Sinha et al. 2006). Moreover, by either directly or indirectly engaging more than 6.5 million people with weaving or any of its allied activities, the handloom industry also played a crucial role as one of the largest livelihood providers, only after agriculture (Ministry of Textile, Annual Report 2007–08).

Needless to say, the Indian handloom still plays a crucial role as an employment provider and significantly contributes to India's economic growth and export earnings. As per the estimates of the Fourth All India Handloom Census 2019–20, there are 2.82 million handlooms across India, 2.52 million of which are located in rural areas and only 0.29 million in urban areas. With over 2.6 million people associated with the job of weaving and another 0.84 million with allied activities, the handloom industry still holds considerable economic importance (Ministry of Textile, Handloom Census 19–20, 11). The magnanimity of this industry can be estimated easily from the fact that hand-woven fabric production from India constitutes 95 percent of total global production. Currently, 15 percent of the total cloth production in India comes from handlooms. The textile sector, including the handloom industry, contributes 7 percent of the industrial output in value terms, 2 percent of GDP, and 15 percent of India's export earnings (Ministry of Textile, Annual Report 2017–18, 1; Ministry of Textile, Annual Report 2020–21).

I have also noticed that the rise and decline in total production of handmade items depend upon the changing export policies and demands in the international market. Industrial Development Services (IDS) (1985), using census reports and export figures, has estimated the rise in the total production of handicrafts between the years 1961 and 1984. Total production of handicrafts grew from rupees 2,533 million in 1961 to rupees 37,500 million in 1983–84. The trade figures, which are far more reliable, also show that exports of Indian handicrafts rose from $40.4 million in 1961–62 to $1495.8 million in 1984–85 (Cable, Weston and Jain 1986). Despite the imposition of quotas on the amount that developing countries could export in the form of yarn fabric and clothing to developed countries through Multi-Fiber Arrangement (MFA)[1], which was introduced in 1974 and was active till 2004, handicrafts emerged as one of the major exportable commodities during the 1990s and in subsequent years. In eight years, between 1993 and 2000, the scale of handicraft and handloom exports increased from about Rs 30 billion to Rs 100 billion (Liebl and Roy 2004: 5336). Recently, India exported handloom products of US$319.02 million and US$ 223.19 million for the financial year 2020 and 2021, respectively (Kumar et al. 2021). The major importer of these products is the United States with US$83.11 million trade, followed by the United Kingdom (US$18.99 million), Australia (US$10.7 million), Germany (US$9.94 million), and France (US$9.73 million).

However, along with the emergence of free trade opportunities in the post-Multi-Fibre Agreement (MFA) environment, there is growing competitiveness in the textile industry both in the national and international markets. Factors such as increasing international trade, rapid economic growth, and the growing dependency on exports of craft objects, which now have become so crucial for its survival and growth, are also pushing the handloom industry toward abrupt industrialization and commercialization. In fact, these factors are providing further impetus to many recurrent problems like sturdy inequality, poverty, and massive reduction of jobs (Roy 1993; Basu 2001; Murshed 2004, 312), which are ultimately bringing transition within different craft traditions. A number of policies, projects, and aspirations have risen out of various quarters of the Indian population to save the handloom industry from the ill effects of growing mechanization and steep competition related to free trade opportunities. Nonetheless, reviving this heritage craft tradition remains to be one of the toughest challenges today.

PERSPECTIVES ON INDIAN HANDLOOMS AND THE DE-INDUSTRIALIZATION DEBATE

Over the years Indian handlooms have been studied from diverse perspectives. Historians (e.g., Specker 1984; Chatterjee 1987; Roy 1989; Hossian 1988; Harnetty 1991; Haynes 1996; Roy 1999) have tried to illustrate the role and the proceedings of Indian handlooms during both the Mughal and Colonial periods. Meanwhile, cultural history scholars (e.g., Barnes 2005; Wild and Wild 2005; Ray 2005; Riello and Roy 2009) have viewed and analyzed Indian handloom differently. Based upon the movement of "textile as a major commodity of trade" between cultures, these scholars have tried to address varied issues like status, wealth, and identity transformation around Indian Ocean regions. Finally, present-day empirical issues (Mehta 1953; Sinha 1989; Srinivasulu 1994; Das 2001; Khasnabis and Nag 2002; Niranjana 2004) surrounding production (Kundu 1980), marketing (Goswami 1985; Banerjee 1995), and development (Jain 1980, 1983, 1985; Saha 1982; Goswami 1990a; Goswami 1990b; Mishra 1993; Abdul 1996; Mukund and Syamasundari 1998; Roy 1998) of the Indian handloom industry have also received considerable scholarly attention.

Despite the availability of a multitude of issues for analysis, historiographic scholars have predominantly examined Indian handlooms through the lens of de-industrialization. Influenced by the anti-imperialist sentiments of the Indian Art and Craft Movement (e.g., Birdwood 1880; Havell 1986; Coomaraswamy 1909), several researchers have sought to assess the impact of colonialism on Indian craft traditions (Guha-Thakurata 1992; Mitter 1997). Handloom was often considered a political symbol within the growing tension between Indian nationality and the process of industrialization (Cohn 1996, 147; Ramagundam 2004, 54).

However, with this predominant emphasis, scholars delving into the subject of "de-industrialization" (e.g., Thorner 1962; Harnetty 1991; Mohamad 1996; Clingingsmith and Williamson 2008) have presented their diverse perspectives that have sparked an intense debate among Marxist and non-Marxist scholars. Followers of both Marxist and Dependency school theories attributed the arrival of Europeans in the nineteenth century as the principal catalyst for the significant decline of Indian handlooms (Antlöv 1997; Parel 1997, 107). These scholars aimed to elucidate how Britain initially gained control over India's export market and eventually dominated a substantial portion of its domestic market, leading to the decline of the handloom industry. On the contrary, non-Marxist scholars often challenge this notion. They contend that the primary cause of the decline lies in the proliferation of capital-intensive technology (Roy 2002, 507; Prasad 2001, 281), which has substituted human labor with machinery.

This ongoing debate has had a profound impact on perceptions regarding whether the Indian handloom industry has genuinely undergone the phenomenon of "de-industrialization." Daniel Thorner (1962, 70), one of the earliest scholars to investigate this alleged phenomenon, has viewed it as a global trend affecting different countries at various junctures. He goes on to explain that minimal decline occurred during 1881–1931. However, others (e.g., Bagchi 1976, 136; Roy 1999; Specker 1988), considering the broader economic context of the country, contend that the growth of the Indian handloom industry stagnated during this period. These scholars stress the need to evaluate how the Industrial Revolution differentially impacted metropolitan nations and their colonial counterparts before arriving at conclusions. Additionally, they advocate considering the workforce's size and the time frames involved in both cases. In contrast to Thorner's perspective, another group (Nehru 1947; Krishnamurty 1989; Clingingsmith and Williamson 2008, 210) underscores the issue of absolute decline in terms of both scale and vitality.[2]

Notwithstanding the array of explanations, historical studies have failed to provide a definitive answer as to why India has maintained greater continuity in handloom cloth production and trade compared to other Asian regions. Relying exclusively on quantitative metrics like the count of looms, weavers, cloth volumes, or export values proves insufficient to elucidate India's domestic market dynamics in response to British manufactured goods (Wendt 2009, 196). Furthermore, the continued involvement of handloom weavers in the "mixed" mechanized textile industry from the nineteenth century through the twentieth and into the twenty-first centuries has prompted significant criticism of the "de-industrialization" thesis.

WITHIN A MAZE: MY EARLY RESEARCH AND INVOLVEMENT

My involvement with handloom weavers of Begampur region started when I began research for my MSc dissertation entitled "The Changing Cotton Weaving Tradition in West Bengal: An Anthropological Case Study" back in 2004. As prescribed in our syllabus, I carried out this fieldwork in Begampur region for over two months and collected information on population composition, technology, organization of production, etc. Needless to say, my understanding regarding the technicalities of cloth production and the looms especially was not as solid as required for academic writing and publication. Being completely unaware of these lacks I presented my findings in a couple of seminars and conferences. The criticism received during these sessions made me realize the naivety of my research approach. To fill up these gaps, I visited Begampur time and again during the course of 2006 and 2007. Thereafter, starting from 2008 up to the end part of 2012, I did a four-year-long, in-depth, and intense fieldwork on the weavers of Begampur region for my doctoral thesis entitled "Craft, Culture, and Economy of the Traditional Weaving in West Bengal." However, my PhD research was not solely centered on Begampur. For portraying the culture and economy of the handloom industry of West Bengal I had to work on the cotton weavers of Dhaniakhali in Hooghly district and silk weavers of Bishnupur in Bankura District during these four years. And I started to experience the intellectual turnaround from this point onward. Working as a UGC-research fellow in the Department of Anthropology, University of Calcutta, freed me up as I didn't have to worry about money or attending classes; all I had to do was to read relevant literature, think and strategize about my own research. It was a perfect opportunity for me to carry out ethnographic research among these different handloom weaver communities in West Bengal in the true sense of the term. Furthermore, my exposure to other weaver communities in West Bengal helped me to understand the tiny little details of handloom cloth production which I lacked earlier. The first thing I have tried to find out is the anthropological aspects of the study of craft.

ANTHROPOLOGY OF CRAFT AND CRAFTSMEN: CONCEPTS, DIMENSIONS, AND THEORETICAL PERSPECTIVES

With its rich cultural and historical tapestry and conceptual diversity surrounding the term "craft", deriving a workable definition of the term became a matter of utmost importance. Because the meaning of the term "craft" fundamentally has changed at least three times in the last two centuries which varies from nation to nation even within the Western world (Victoria and Albert Museum 2013). Earlier, especially during the Middle Ages, the term was usually applied to people engaged in small-scale production of goods. The modern English term craft is often used interchangeably with terms such as arts, artisans, and technology. The etymological closeness between the English term craft and the German "kraft," the Latin term "ars" and the Greek term "techne" was quite evident. I noted that the German term "kraft" has a broad meaning that includes power, and physical strength along with art, and artifice (Kluge 1999, 481). The Latin term "ars" also had a broader meaning including science, skill, virtuosity, craftsmanship, and trade, as well as artifice. Meanwhile, the Greek term "techne," the root of technology, is often translated as craftsmanship, craft, skill, ability, or art. Invariably I had to settle for the broad working definition of the term "craft" which meant trade, skill, artisanry, ability, dexterity, and guild, mostly relatable with an occupation in which skill in the use of the hands is needed, especially when most traders and arts and crafts producers choose to produce items by hand even amid the availability of industrially produced substitutes (Oxford Advanced Learners Dictionary 1987, 200; Greiner and Pröpper 2016, 215).

While finding anthropology in the study of craft, I observed that craft objects present an image which is local and global at the same point in time. Moreover, the relationship between the different dimensions of craft like "means" including materials, technology, and objects is intrinsic and is directly connected to the manual side of production. Meanwhile, the meaning that craft objects attain depends upon the particular context or culture that needs to be grasped and understood from a socioeconomic relationship (Moore 1988, 48–49). Because, technology and social relationships surrounding a craft often intermingle with one another and are articulated by several aspects such as "apprenticeship of skill and transmission of embodied knowledge," and the inequalities and despotisms of production, distribution, and consumption. However, despite having such varied dimensions, the study of craft within social-cultural anthropology has maintained a sort of shadowy existence. Apart from those social anthropologists inclined to study craft from the material culture, educational anthropological, and labor historical perspectives, the ethnographic analysis of crafts or craftsmen mostly remained secluded within standard discourses of other major subfields such as economic anthropology (Clammer 1978; Hann and Hart 2011; Lang 2010; Narotzky 1997; Plattner 1989; Rössler 1999; Wilk 1996), anthropology of art (Gell 1998; Marcus and Myers 1995; Morphy and Perkins 2006), and already marginalized subfield of anthropology of technology (Pfaffenberger 1988; Schiffer 2001a, 2001b; Suchman 2001).

Meanwhile, the particular domain of the study of craft continued to receive a strong impetus from independent domains such as "art history" and "museology," "technology," and "design studies" other than disciplines like political science, sociology, economics, and anthropology. Due to this, I found the cultural and historical boundaries between the domain of craft studies and other fields such as industry, technology, and art to be fuzzy and permeable, to say the least. Interestingly, I also found that interest toward studying craft/craftsmen gradually became diffused, the effect of which can be witnessed even within the discipline of anthropology. Eventually, this has resulted in the emergence of specialized subfields like museum anthropology, visual anthropology, anthropology of art, and anthropology of work (DeNicola and Wilkinson-Weber 2016, 12).

Due to this reason, I found the concepts, perspectives, and dimensions within anthropological studies of crafts and craftsmen incredibly hard to pin down to any single unitary theoretical framework. Over the years anthropologists have studied craft and the society of craftsmen from diverse perspectives (see Goody 2000). Anthropological studies of craft and craftsmen first came to the fore with the efforts of late-nineteenth-century and early-twentieth-century "material culture scholars and folklorists" who were interested in the detailed "description and mapping of material culture, with a view of preserving a record of rapidly disappearing 'early' forms of society." Then, craft and craftsmen grabbed the attention of the "mid-twentieth century ethnographers" (e.g., Nadel 1942; Miner 1965; Goody 1982; Bernstain 1996, 181; Argenti 2002; Simpson 2006, 51) who with their focus on issues like "apprenticeship of skill and transmission of embodied knowledge," "division of labour," "hierarchy, authority and patronage" became inclined in explaining the correlation between these issues with several social institutions.

During the post–Second World War period when industrial mass production started replacing craft objects, understanding the differential impact of the process of industrialization on craft communities living in the Western- and the non-Western world became one of the areas of anthropological concern (see Gluckman 1961; Holzberg and Giovannini 1981; Ferguson 1999; Mollona, De Neve and Parry 2009). Invariably, anthropologists became interested in exploring issues like the quality and design of the craft objects (e.g., Stromberg-Pellizi 1993), the correlating pattern of value distribution (e.g., Cook 1993), the intergenerational social mobility (Linton, 1987; Miner 1973) along with the impact of industrialization on households' subsistence and consumption patterns, and structure and division of labor (Nash 1993; Parry 2005). Later, anthropological studies of craft witnessed another major shift from their usual focus of studying "modes of production" (that include natural, material, and technical productive forces and social relationships) along with the emergence of a "neo-Marxist perspective" (Seddon 1978; Kahn 1980; Ennew, 1982; Coy 1989). That invariably pushed many ethnographic studies to explore issues like "reallocation and migration of labour to the factories," "emerging new labour ethics," "workers' resistance" (Ong 1987), and "shopfloor organisation" (Burawoy 1979) to explain the correlation between technology, market, and the organization.

Nonetheless, the process of technological transformation leading to the "redistribution of skills and power" and "taking away of the immediacy and autonomy of individual craft production" remains one of the most prominent themes (Dormer 1997a: 102). Invariably, this led anthropologists (e.g. Pfaffenberger 1988; 1992, 497; Pinch and Bijker 1984; Keller 2001) to study crafts as a form of technology itself—a perspective in which instead of assuming technology to be a dehumanized, disembodied, and autonomous agent responsible for social change, often producers' perspectives and relationships through which technology operates, impacts, and obtains different social meaning for different social groups are taken into account and analyzed for their social embeddedness. Crafts from this perspective have been analyzed as a part of a "socio-technical system" which is connected through "seamless webs," including manual labor, skills, artistic imagination, precision, and entrepreneurial skills, along with the successful mediation of several actors (Pinch and Bijker 1984; Pfaffenberger 1992, 498).

However, despite their valiant efforts, the scholars studying craft from a technological perspective faced criticism for distinguishing the "human" and "non-human entities" in the sociotechnical system and especially for their "excessive agency-centric" approach (Pinch 1996). Finally, this led to the reemergence of material cultural perspective (e.g., Appadurai 1986) among anthropological studies of craft. However, unlike the earlier hollow cultural ones, recent material culture scholars have become interested in understanding the meaning and experiences surrounding the production, distribution, and consumption of craft objects. Some of the more recent anthropological studies exploring issues of apprenticeship, dexterity, ingenuity, and intelligence that lie at the heart of craftwork (e.g., Marchand 2021), utilization of the local and transnational networks, based on identity, religiosity, and affective circulations, to access resources, support, and forms of mutuality among the migrant north Indian Muslim woodworking population (e.g., Chambers 2020), dichotomies of clothing choices between colonizers and the colonized during the colonial and postcolonial periods (e.g., Tarlo 1996), and the preservation efforts involving craft producers and government and nongovernmental agencies (e.g., Venkateshan 2009) perfectly align with this particular theoretical tradition.

THE BACKDROP OF THE PRESENT RESEARCH

In the meantime, a lot of things have begun to change both on my personal and professional front. I joined the Cultural Research Institute, Backward Classes Welfare Department, Government of West Bengal, in 2013 and worked there as a research investigator, I was awarded a PhD in anthropology by the University of Calcutta in the year 2015, and then I switched to join as assistant professor of anthropology under the Higher Education Department, Government of West Bengal, in 2015. I wrote and published a few articles on the handloom industry of Begampur region in journals of national and international repute. However, due to my busy work schedule, I was not able to revisit Begampur as a researcher any further. The opportunity came along when, because of my familiarity with handloom weavers of Begampur region, I was invited to help and look over the fieldwork affairs of a group of post-graduate students of Bidhannagar College, Kolkata, who required that information for a project in the year 2021. To be honest, I was astonished to see the changes that have taken place in Begampur region. It planted the seed in my mind regarding the prospect of carrying out fieldwork on the handloom industry of Begampur region all over again. This seed germinated when on the occasion of World IP Day 2022, I was invited to speak on the "Future of Geographical Indication (GI) Registration and Social Impact on Begampuri Saree" for an international workshop on "Intellectual Property Rights for Society & Youth" organized by DPIIT IPR Chair, West Bengal National University of Juridical Sciences (WBNUJS), Kolkata.

THE HANDLOOM INDUSTRY OF BEGAMPUR IN TRANSITION: TECHNOLOGY, DISJUNCTURE, AND DEVELOPMENT

Based on the empirical exposure gathered during my first phase of research and involvement with handloom weavers of Begampur region between 2004 and 2012, I already knew that the handloom industry in Begampur region, due to the technological mediocrity, use of a coarser variety of yarns, and average kinds of hand-woven items, was not that renowned compared to other developed centers of handloom weaving in India and West Bengal. Even the historical records offered scant evidence of cotton cloth production in Begampur around the 1860s. O'Malley and Chakravarti (1912) indirectly alluding to weaving activities in the adjacent Kharsarai is the only substantive piece of historical reference that I could gather. Moreover, the comparison of my empirical findings and almost elusive historical accounts regarding the efforts of technological upgradation except for the case where fly-shuttle-frame-looms were introduced from *Farashdanda* during the 1860s (O'Malley and Chakravarti 1912) led me to believe that the handloom industry in Begampur region remained technologically stagnant for a long period.

Due to my first field exposure, I also knew that the handloom weavers of this region generally produced particular kinds of hand-woven items which they catered to a particular section of local clients. However, due to the technological mediocrity and lack of aesthetic finesse in their woven products, the situation was exacerbated and the handloom weavers of Begampur region had to face the repercussions of the technological transition. The process of technological transition has often adversely impacted the handloom weavers of this region which otherwise had impacted different handloom weaving traditions in different manners altogether. While handmade items from other developed weaving centers in West Bengal remained relatively insusceptible to steep competition from mill-made items, handloom items from Begampur region became easy prey in this competition. The introduction of power-looms in Begampur region only worsened the situation of handloom weavers further by offering more lucrative avenues for making a profit. Eventually, this attracted investors toward powerlooms and that subsequently resulted in irregular work assignments, underpayment, and unemployment (Banerjee, Chakrabarti, and Das 2010). The informal organizational setup of handloom cloth production and marketing where individual entrepreneurs (*mahajans*) exercised their control over different activities of production and marketing also played its part in this regard. However, despite the frequent concerns regarding income inequality, low social status, and exploitation, artisans are left with no choice but to operate under these *mahajans* as they were often constrained by their lack of resources (Banerjee 2016).

Then the landscape of cotton cloth production and marketing in Begampur region began to witness a gradual change from the 1970s along with the introduction of handloom weavers' cooperatives. Supported by government-backed initiatives, these institutions, at least during the initial period, were able to impart a sense of security to the economically disadvantaged weavers. However, in due course of time, issues like scarcity of working capital, corruption, politics, and especially the lack of technological innovation started making considerable impact on the proceedings of these institutions and at times held them back from attaining their intended objectives (see Banerjee, Chakrabarti and Das 2011). The efforts of technological upgradation within the handloom industry of Begampur region began from around 2010 onward along with the implementation cluster development program. Both the state and the central government took several steps for the revival of handlooms in this region. To improve the quality and designs within woven items many local weavers received training in both *dobby*[3] and jacquard looms. Moreover, jacquard fly-shuttle frame looms were introduced through Kharsarai Madhyampara Samabai Samity with which the local handloom weavers started producing high-quality cotton items.

All of these changes became more evident during my second stint of fieldwork in Begampur from 2021 onward. I saw visible improvements in aesthetic elements within the hand-woven items of this region, which has been able to rekindle a separate identity for Begampuri saree in the world of handlooms. So much so that it has led a group of these weavers to file for Geographical Indication (GI) registration of Begampur Cotton Handloom Saree in the year 2022. This is when I realized the prospect of re-studying the handloom industry in Begampur region which is in the process of transition concerning technology, welfare measures, and the efforts of development. I realized that with my earlier exposure and prior knowledge of the handloom weavers of Begampur region, I could easily shed light on the reasons, rationality, and feasibility of the technological transition along with its social and cultural impacts. My keenness to doing a comprehensive portrayal of this ongoing shift encompassing the what, why, and how in the context of the Begampur region was also triggered by the fact that I saw considerably less academic attention excluding my own (e.g., Banerjee, Chakrabarti, and Das 2010, 2011; Banerjee 2014, 2016) despite ample opportunities of studying the interrelationships between technology, "organization," "relations in production," "marketing mechanism," welfare measure, and development along with their social and cultural impacts for an enhanced understanding regarding industrialization and class formation in India (De Neve 2001, 134).

METHODOLOGY

Obviously, for a longitudinal study, spanning over almost 20 years, of a handloom weaving tradition that is in the process of transition, I needed a suitable theoretical perspective first that allows me to see and analyze the interplay and interrelationships among macroeconomic forces, actors, structures, and the flow of social interactions and exchange which were affecting cloth-making practices at ground level in Begampur region (see Wherry 2008). Because of my particular focus on understanding the impact of ongoing technological innovation and the effect of changing developmental and welfare measures within the handloom industry of Begampur region, I realized that my theoretical approach needs to be quite close to both the "Marxist Anthropologists" (see Burawoy 1979; De Neve 2001) who have often studied the "modes of production" (that include natural, material, and technical productive forces and social relationships) and "Industrial Anthropologists" (see Goody 1982; Cook 1993; Nash 1993; Stromberg-Pellizi 1993) who tried to understand how industrial mass production is replacing craft objects and its impact on households' subsistence, consumption patterns. Yet at the same time, I also needed to remain cautious as I could not afford to make the same mistake of assuming technology to be a dehumanized, disembodied, and autonomous agent responsible for social change as has often been done under these two aforementioned theoretical perspectives. I realized that such a blindfold "technological determinism" (see Downey 1992, 3) would restrict my ability to see and analyze the interrelationships between technology, work coordination, relations in production, products and their market, welfare measures, and development. Eventually, that will increase my inability to understand the role of social and economic contexts based upon which the process of technological transition and changing scenario of developmental and welfare measures have brought differential impacts for different social groups and given rise to several disjunctures and juxtapositions in Begampur region.

Due to this reason, rather than mere hollow cultural description and documentation of the handloom industry in Begampur region as a disappearing craft or a community of craftsmen like the late-nineteenth-century and early-twentieth-century material culture scholars and folklorists (Washburn 1991; Miller 1998), or dwelling upon any forms of "technological determinism," I have tried to view and analyze the handloom industry of Begampur region as a form of sociotechnical system (Pinch and Bijkar, 1984; Pfaffenberger 1992, 498)[4] by incorporating social, cultural, and economic nuances along with people's felt experiences, their concerns, enthusiasms, ambivalence, and the diverse forms of human relationships and behavior surrounding this ongoing transition (McCarthy and Wright 2004, 49; Baudrillard 1996, 5). I have tried to focus on the diverse pathways that Appadurai (1986) calls "value regime" through which handloom objects mediate and become partly constitutive to everyday social interactions (Schneider 1986, 1987; Weiner and Schneider 1989; Dant 2005).

I also had to struggle a little while choosing a suitable method. I knew that I would be dealing with a considerable number of historical stats and figures along with a lot of qualitative information for this particular kind of research problem of deciphering this ongoing transition surrounding the handloom industry of Begampur region. Therefore, striking the right balance between qualitative and quantitative invariably became very important. Due to this reason, I have adopted a particular kind of ethnographic research method, which is predominantly qualitative, with a right balance for its reliance on numeric information and the inclination toward qualitative data collection and analysis (Creswell 2006; William and Pearce 2007). While mediating through different contexts/sites or the varied arena of the craft world, I also realized that I would require more than mere description and analysis of the interrelationship between capitalist hegemony, the exploitation of indigenous people, and technological development from a self-conscious critical perspective (see Hymes 1972; Ulin 1991, 63). Turning back upon my own self-awareness, self-understanding, self-reflection, and (partially) self-emancipation (Scholte 1972, 448) regarding both the research problem and research process became invariably important. Hence, I have employed a "self-reflexive," narrative ethnographic strategy (e.g., Tedlock 1991) in order to showcase the entire process right from my initial conceptual framework regarding Indian handlooms, my early interactions with handloom weavers of Begampur region, the time when I attained theoretical reorientation regarding the anthropology of craft to reasons and rationale of doing the second stint of fieldwork in Begampur, which eventually pushed me to pursue this particular research problem.

The process of data collection for this particular study never posed any serious challenges as half of my job was already done and I already had a solid first-hand ethnographic database on several aspects of the handloom weavers of Begampur region. For example, I already had information on the history of Begampur as a place, its population and ethnic composition, technology, skill, and knowledge surrounding different stages of cloth production, division of labor, persisting forms of relation in both organization of production and marketing, handloom weavers cooperative, which I have collected using known anthropological tools and techniques such as mass interviews, case studies, life histories, in-depth interviews, and participant observation (see Holstein and Gubrium 1997; Bernard 2011). During my second stint of fieldwork in Begampur, I collected information on some of these aforementioned aspects all over again using similar known anthropological tools and techniques. Eventually, that allowed me to make comparisons as well as to explain some of the areas of transformation.

The comparison between the large pool of secondary information available in the form of books, district gazetteers, journal articles, websites, and news information and my own first-hand empirical observations during both stints of fieldwork in Begampur region proved quite a handful in explaining the relevance and history of this region as a place, more specifically the course of the handloom industry's transformation in India, West Bengal, and Begampur region. Further, the comparison of secondary information on the social and religious life of these handloom weavers along with fresh first-hand ones that I collected during my last field visit also proved to be quite useful for explaining important areas of transformation regarding family, marriage, kinship, life-cycle rituals, religious ceremonies, and festivals. Again, the comparison of first-hand information on some of the old cloth-making techniques with the new ones, both of which I have collected at different points in time, became important parameters for understanding the psyche and the social and economic situations based upon which people made decisions in either accepting or rejecting technological transformation and their consequent impacts. The comparison of information on the old and emerging forms of cloth-making technologies, and the informal and formal system of cloth production and marketing further helped in understanding some of the key juxtapositions and a few important sources of disjuncture in the life of these handloom weavers. Finally, a comparison of first-hand information on the initial failure and the relative success of the Begampur Handloom Cluster in recent times played a key role in explaining people's changing perception toward welfare and development.

However, I must also admit the fact that this study is not free from limitations. Because of being ethnographic in nature, data collection and analysis for this book took a lot of time, which at times was quite painstaking, to say the least. Due to this reason, the view of all the stakeholders, especially those government officials, who stay far away from these handloom weaving centers, but are responsible for either sales and export or policy-making and their implementation that greatly influence the lives and world of these poor artisans, could not be incorporated within the purview of this study. Looking at the analytical requirements, I have tried to supplement the views of these important stakeholders by studying literature, which revealed a lot regarding the overall scenario, but literature didn't provide me with a chance to grasp what was not written, the unspoken empirically observable things those stayed between the lines. And this certainly is one of the core limitations of this research.

STRUCTURE OF THE BOOK

In this book, I have tried to provide the overall scenario in the handloom industry through six chapters. In chapter 1, "The Setting: People, Place, the Economy, and Lives," I provide an overall glimpse regarding the Begampur region as a "field site." Hence, invariably I touch upon the historicity of Begampur as a place and provide brief accounts regarding the geographical location of Begampur, its geology and the climate, and the flora and faunas available in this region. In this chapter, I also describe the ethnic composition of this region and try to explain how it is correlated to aspects such as education and occupation. Finally, I provide a brief overview of the healthcare facilities and the infrastructure available in this region to project the overall picture regarding the living conditions.

In chapter 2, "Tracing the Historical and Cultural Landscape of Handloom Industry in Begampur: From Past to the Present," I provide a detailed account of the historical, cultural, and geographical landscape under which the "Indian handloom industry," "handloom industry in West Bengal," and "the handloom industry in Begampur region" came into existence, flourished under the Mughal patronage, and eventually started to face several issues during the colonial and postcolonial period through three subsections. I provide an account of how the Indian handloom industry went through this transition in the first subsection. Then I provide an account regarding the transition of the handloom industry in West Bengal in the second subsection. Finally, I try to trace the origin of the handloom industry in Begampur region and subsequently how it went through a transition in the third subsection.

In chapter 3, "The Social and the Religious Life of Handloom Weavers in Begampur Region," I explore the intricate threads of the social and religious life that define the existence of cotton cloth weavers in Begampur region. Here I explore some aspects starting with their ethnic origin and religious cohabitation up to the role and functionality of some of the primary social institutions such as family, marriage, and kinship to understand how they play an important role in the sustenance of social and economic existence of these handloom weavers. Then I provide a detailed description of the life-cycle rituals of the handloom weavers of Begampur region, especially concerning "birth," "marriage," and "death" rituals as they reflect some of their unique identity, beliefs, and practices as a group. Finally, I describe the major religious ceremonies and festivals observed by the handloom weavers of Begampur region to explain how these beliefs shape their daily lives, their artistry, and their collective identity.

In chapter 4, "The Craft of Handloom Weaving: Technology, Work Coordination, Products, and Their Market" I delve into the nitty-gritty of cotton cloth production in Begampur region through four subsections. I provide a detailed description of the looms and other implements that are used for cotton cloth production in the first subsection. Then I provide a detailed step-by-step description of the stages of cotton cloth production in the second subsection. Thereafter, I provide an account of inter-group work coordination in the third subsection. Finally, I also provide a descriptive account regarding practices of using certain kinds of raw materials and how eventually it determines the quality and designs of different types of products.

In chapter 5, "The Disjuncture and Juxtapositions of Cloth Production, Organization, and Marketing," I touch upon the disparities and inequality that define the life and world of the handloom weavers of the Begampur region through six subsections. First and foremost, I explain how the issue of individual creative identity and community-level collective production creates juxtapositions in the first subsection. Then, in the second subsection, I look closely into the dichotomy of traditional artisanal craft and technology-driven commercialized mass production which perhaps is one of the biggest sources of disjuncture among the handloom weavers of this region. Here I explain the social and economic nuances based upon which people choose to opt for a particular form of technology or reject another one. Then I move my attention toward some of the organizational issues. In the third subsection, by providing a comparative account of "the formal and the informal organizational set-up," I show how these two different types of institutional setups stand in stark juxtapositions that we often get to see all across India and West Bengal. While exploring how handloom weavers act upon the issue of dependence and relative independence, I also show how the disparity in the proceedings of these two different organizational setups tremendously impacts poor artisans and the situation in Begampur is no different in this regard. In the fourth subsection, I provide an account regarding the types of contracts and the relations in production. By unraveling some nuances of most preferred forms of labor contracts, I show the disparity, inequality, and hierarchy that exist between groups involved with cotton cloth production and marketing and how these different groups adapt to the issue of empowerment and exploitation. Here I explain how and under what circumstances despite having different life experiences and intentions, these different sets of groups involved with cloth production and marketing come together to provide a character to cloth production and marketing in the Begampur region. In the fifth subsection, I explain how due to the persisting situation the local weavers, entrepreneurs, and philanthropists often face difficulty while making the choice between utility products and items with high aesthetic content. Finally, in the sixth subsection, I explain the dilemma that the local weavers encounter while retaining their local identity amidst the ongoing process of homogenization.

For the revival of the handloom industry in the Begampur region historically both state and central governments have taken and are still taking many measures through the implementation of welfare policies and programs. The introduction of handloom weavers' cooperatives and handloom clusters in the Begampur region are a few of them. Through chapter 6, "Handloom Weavers' Cooperative Societies in Begampur: A Failed Experiment?", I provide a brief evaluative account regarding the success and failure of these welfare measures in three subsections. In the first subsection, I briefly touch upon the issues based on which handloom weavers' cooperatives were introduced in India. In the second subsection, I look into the historical causes based upon which handloom weavers' cooperatives were introduced in the Begampur region. Then I critically gauge why the handloom weavers' cooperatives in the Begampur region haven't been able to meet their primary objectives. In the third subsection, I do a detailed case analysis regarding the rise of Begampur Handloom Cluster and its initiative for the revival of handloom weavers. Here I try and explain the differences between the handloom cluster and handloom weavers' cooperative in terms of structure and consortium, funding and support, and activities and proceedings. Finally, I evaluate the efforts undertaken by the Begampur Handloom Cluster for the revival of handloom weavers to chart out how they are bringing the difference.

In the concluding section, I try to explain the uneasy balance between "technology" and "developmental efforts" that has been persisting within the handloom industry of Begampur region for a long time. In so doing, I show how technological choices are deeply embedded within historicity of Begampur as a separate handloom weaving tradition, how the sociotechnical system of cloth production in this region is largely driven by a somewhat coercive interplay between "capital" and "labor relationship," and the reasons of initial failure of handloom weavers cooperative and the emergence of handloom cluster in this region. Finally, I show why, despite having all these differences, dispositions, disjuncture, and juxtaposition, different groups of people come together to struggle and at times compete with one another within this uncertain and negligible world of craftsmanship.

NOTES

1. Multi-Fiber Arrangement (MFA) is an international trade agreement that was introduced in the year 1974 and was active till 2004. The task of this agreement was to regulate the affairs regarding the export and import of clothing objects between developing and developed countries. This agreement imposed quotas on the amount that developing countries could export in the form of yarn fabric and clothing to developed countries.

2. These scholars indicated several correlated factors such as (i) eighteenth-century political chaos, economic decline sandwiched between the stable and prosperous Mughal and British hegemonies, (ii) India's nineteenth-century progressive ruralization and destruction of artisanal employment by British factory-made goods, and lastly (iii) slump in agricultural productivity following deterioration in climatic conditions and the eighteenth-century dissolution of Mughal hegemony that led to aggregate supply-side problems for Indian manufacturers as factors which caused the decline.

3. It is one of the most traditional designing apparatuses found in this region. This designing apparatus is quite simple in structure. It looks like a wooden box where there are several wooden rids cyclically arranged one after another. During the time of weaving as these rids rotate they facilitate the process of design formation.

4. A sociotechnical system may broadly be defined as a system with a particular configuration where technology, regulations, actors, services, and infrastructure all play their respective roles in the sustenance of the system. See Pinch and Bijker (1984) and Pfaffenberger (1992, 498) where they explain how the sociotechnical system is connected through "seamless webs," including manual labor, skills, artistic imagination, precision, and entrepreneurial skills, along with the successful mediation of several actors.

Chapter 1

The Setting

People, Place, the Economy, and Lives

The present-day Begampur is relatively modern in its outlook. However, along with the rest of the Bengal, Begampur and its adjacent areas underwent many important historic events. First, it remained under Muslim rule for over 500 years—starting from the time of Baktiar Khilji in 1204 AD till the East India Company got the Dewani rights in 1765 AD. Second, this region, especially Baksa (adjacent to Begampur), was heavily influenced by the establishment of a Portuguese port around 1530 AD. Torture, rape, and forceful marriages were quite common phenomena during this period (Sur 1986). Nonetheless, apart from some of the old names which might have remained as reminiscent of its past, and quite a large number of Muslim populations living in different parts of this region, today's Begampur hardly represents any resemblance to such historic events. A large number of people move out of the area for their livelihood activities. Facilities of communication that over the years have improved immensely and especially the constant influence that the working people have carried back along with them definitely have played a part in this regard. Furthermore, the growing infrastructural facilities in the form of schools, banks, playgrounds, modern gymnasiums, hospitals, markets, and well-connected roads provide a perfect suburban feel to the area.

In this chapter, I will discuss the people, place, and overall economy of this region along with some of these developments in detail. In so doing, I provide a brief outline regarding the history and geographical location of Begampur in the first subsection. Then in the second subsection, I look into the geology and climate of Begampur. After that, I provide a brief overview of flora and fauna and population and ethnic composition in the third and fourth subsections, respectively. Then I provide overviews of the educational and occupational scenario of this region in the fifth and sixth subsections, respectively. Finally, I discuss about the development of infrastructure and healthcare facilities and the transforming literary and cultural traditions of this region in the seventh and eighth subsections.

HISTORY AND GEOGRAPHICAL LOCATION OF BEGAMPUR REGION

Begampur is a census town. It is situated in Hooghly district in the state of West Bengal, India. The exact geographical location of the town of Begampur is 22.74° North and 88.24° East at an elevation of 15 meters (49 feet) above sea level. It is included under the Chanditala police station in Serampore subdivision (see figure 1.1 A, B, and C). It is approximately ten minutes away from the Begampur railway station on the Howrah-Bardhaman chord line which is part of the Kolkata suburban railway network. Bus service from Srirampur to Domjur connects this place with the subdivision. The area is surrounded by villages like Kharsarai, Chhotatajpur (in the North), Borotajpur (in the Northeast), Jaykrishnapur and Panchghara (in the Eastern side), Adan and Baksa (in the Southern side), and Madhabpur and Monirampur (in the Western side).

Begampur is quite an important town of the Hooghly district laced with its pristine nature and rich ethnicity. The administrative headquarters of the district is located at Chinsura. Despite not being too far away from Kolkata, the impoverished slow-moving lifestyle of the majority of inhabitants is one of the first things that catches the eye. The narrow alleys, number of small ponds (*pukurs*), toddlers playing in the streets, children going to a nearby school in their untidy uniforms, a mid-aged person passing by in his worn-out bicycle, colorful dyed cotton hanging from the bamboo poles, wives/mother/unmarried teenage girls either starching or rolling dyed yarns in *chakras*, and finally the rhythmic gentle clacking of looms coupled with old-Hindi/Bengali film song takes you miles away from the imageries that we often encounter in any bustling metropolitan city.

Begampur's history can be traced back to ancient times when it was part of the broader Bengal region. The region was known as Vardhamana Bhumi in the ancient Indian texts, and it played a crucial role in the trade and commerce of the Mauryan and Gupta empires. The strategic location along the banks of the Ganges made it an important center for agriculture and trade.

During the medieval period, Begampur was part of the Gauda Kingdom, the capital of which was in the present-day Malda district in West Bengal. Gaud was subsequently ruled by various dynasties, including the Pala and Sena dynasties. These rulers left their mark on the region in the form of

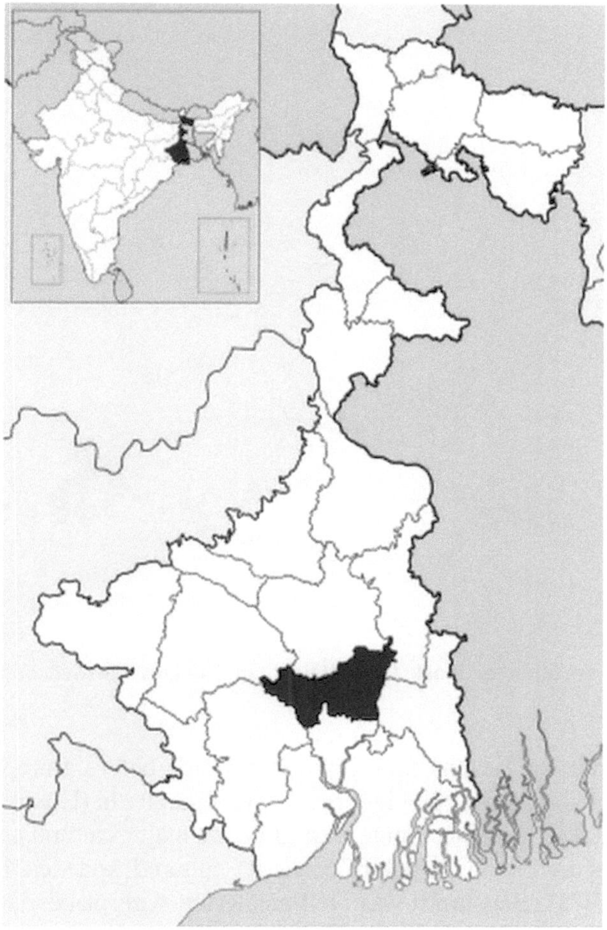

Figure 1.1A Location of Hooghly District in West Bengal. *Source:* Author's Photo.

magnificent temples and palaces, many of which still stand as a testament to their architectural prowess. The Gauda Kingdom was also known for its flourishing arts and culture, with poets, scholars, and artists thriving in the region.

The arrival of the Mughals in India marked a significant turning point in the history of Begampur. It is believed that the region got its name from Begum, the wife of Mughal Emperor Jahangir, who is said to have visited the area. The Mughals brought with them a blend of Persian and Indian cultures, which left a lasting impact on the region's architecture and cuisine. Names of several places and tombs in and around Begampur bear testimony to this influence.

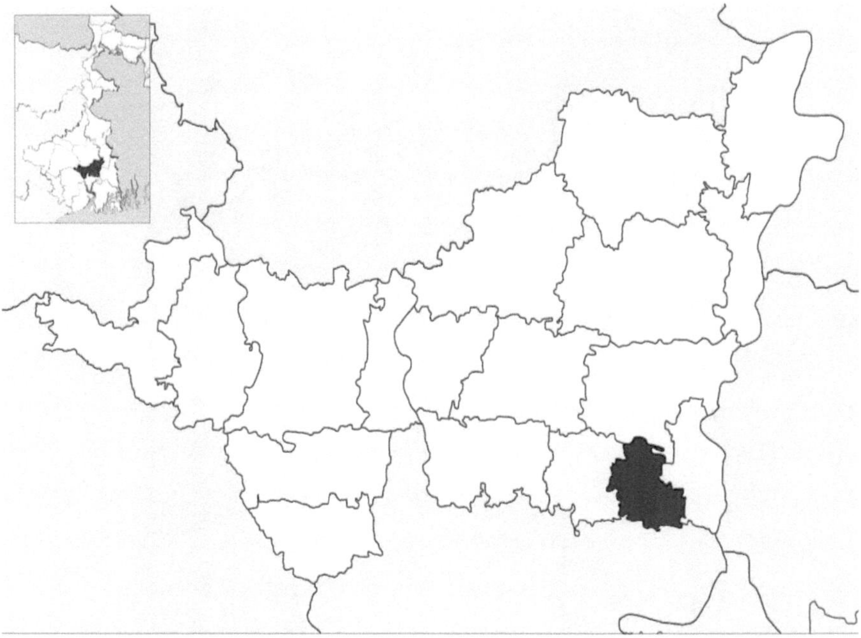

Figure 1.1B Location of Block Chanditala II in Hooghly District. *Source*: Author's Photo.

From about the seventeenth century onward, before European traders started establishing their colonies around river Bhagirathi (Hooghly), villages like Janai, Baksa, and Begampur used to be the major cultural trade centers. These places used to be the hub of educated, cultured, and wealthy individuals (Mitra 1975). Begampur was well connected with places like Chandernagar, Chinsura, and Srirampur, which all are the neighboring settlements of river Baghirathi. Historically, because of its geographical location adjacent to river Saraswati (that once used to be the main flow of river Bhagirathi) and Saptagram[1] (an inland port) that gained importance along with the decline of Tamralipta[2] (modern Tamluk), this place was quite an important trade root. But, as river Saraswati became less navigable due to the poor flow of water, some of these places started losing their importance. This is also one of the reasons why Begampur and adjacent places like Adan, Baksa, Madhabpur, and Manirampur haven't achieved so much in the sphere of agriculture.

With the advent of the British East India Company in the eighteenth century, Begampur, like the rest of Bengal, became a part of the British Empire. The British era brought about significant changes in the region's economic and administrative structure. The construction of railways and the development of industries transformed the landscape of Begampur, making it a hub of trade and commerce.

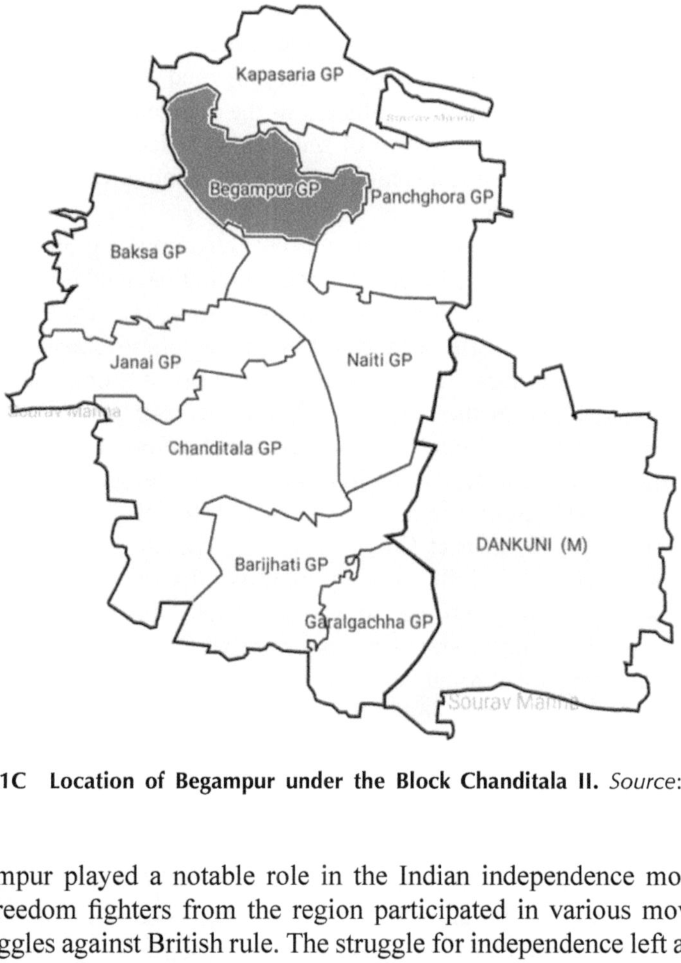

Figure 1.1C Location of Begampur under the Block Chanditala II. *Source*: Author's Photo.

Begampur played a notable role in the Indian independence movement. Many freedom fighters from the region participated in various movements and struggles against British rule. The struggle for independence left an indelible mark on the collective memory of Begampur's residents.

Post-independence, Begampur continued to evolve. The region saw significant developments in infrastructure, education, and healthcare. Today, it is a thriving part of West Bengal, contributing to the state's cultural and economic vibrancy.

GEOLOGY AND CLIMATE

The geological characteristics of Begampur, like many regions in the district and the country, played a crucial role in shaping its landscape, soil composition, and natural resources. New alluvium top layer and clay subsoil are the most common forms found throughout the district of Hooghly. The size of the area is about 2.32 square kilometers. Because of its position beside river Saraswati, which now has become a small channel without any outlet, Begampur is much closer to what Ray (1962) mentions as "marshy depressions" seen more frequently between Hooghly and the Saraswati rivers. Originally, much of Begampur is situated in the Gangetic Plain, a vast alluvial plain formed by the deposition of sediments carried by the Ganges and its tributaries. This alluvial soil is highly fertile and conducive to a wide range of agricultural production.

The geological substrata of the present-day Begampur region nonetheless are composed of various sedimentary rocks, including sand, silt, clay, and gravel, which have been deposited over millions of years. Needless to mention it has affected the fertility of the soil in this region. Present-day Begampur is much more a village site formed over silted-up beds of a small stream. Quite naturally, it serves the purpose of homestead rather than agricultural land. Moreover, shreds of evidence indicate the development of metal clay (*enlel mati*) over this silt deposition in Begampur and its surrounding region.

The climate in Begampur region is not much different from what one gets to see in the Hooghly district (Ray 1962). The climate of Begampur, like much of West Bengal, is influenced by its proximity to the Bay of Bengal, the Himalayan foothills, and the tropical monsoon climate. The climate in this region is often characterized by an oppressive summer, profuse rains, and high humidity all through the year. Begampur experiences a tropical monsoon climate, characterized by distinct wet and dry seasons. The climate is influenced by the seasonal monsoon winds, which bring heavy rainfall during the wet season and dry conditions during the dry season.

Ideally, there are six seasons in a year as per the calendar. Depending upon their location in different parts of West Bengal and India people experience at least five of these seasons, namely, summer, monsoon, post-monsoon, winter, and spring. However, the climate and the weather conditions of Begampur region, in general, can be categorized into four seasons.

A hot summer starts from March and lasts till the end of May. Often the highest temperature is recorded in May when it goes beyond 45 degree Celsius. The monsoon starts around the middle of June and stays till September. The months of July and August receive the most rainfall with a precipitation count of 384.07 millimeter. During this time, the region receives the majority of its annual rainfall. The southwest monsoon winds carry moisture-laden air from the Bay of Bengal, leading to heavy rainfall. This is crucial for agriculture in the region. Begampur receives a significant amount of rainfall during the monsoon season, which is essential for rice cultivation and other crops. The annual average rainfall in the region can vary, but it generally ranges from 1,500 to 2,000 millimeters. The autumn/post-monsoon starts from October and lasts only up to the first half of November. During this period, Begampur region weather-wise experiences a transition as temperatures gradually begin to drop, and the weather becomes more pleasant. The winter—that starts at the end of November—intensifies from the middle of December to the middle of January, during which the average temperature stays around 16 degree Celsius or less than that. Finally, the winter fades away from the end of January till about the middle of February. These two months are most pleasant as one gets to see days with bright sunshine and the average temperature stays around 26 degree Celsius.

FLORA AND FAUNA

Begampur region is devoid of any dense forest, nor it is characterized by swampy rice fields that one gets to see in other parts of Hooghly district (Ray 1962). Whatever little agricultural activities that take place in this region are performed at the outskirts much away from the settlements. Generally, paddy is cultivated within these agricultural fields during the monsoon. Jute also plays a significant part in the agricultural production of this region. West Bengal is a major jute-producing state in India, and Begampur contributes to this industry. Jute is used in making textiles, bags, and various other products. In dispersedly forested areas around Begampur, you can find Teak and *Sal* trees. These trees are valuable for their timber and are also important for local ecosystems. Furthermore, there is a preponderance of weeds, shrubs, and smaller plants, belts of bamboo, coconut, palm, mango, fig, and jack, and other trees around the human settlement. Bamboo grows abundantly in the region and is used for various purposes, including construction, handicrafts, and as a source of food for some wildlife. Moreover, the Saraswati riverbank areas are lined with fruit-bearing trees like mango, guava, jackfruit, figs, tamarinds, and date palms with thick undergrowth. All of which provide a source of food and livelihood for the local population.

The scenario is quite similar in terms of fauna that one gets to see all over the Hooghly district. Monkeys, for example, especially the hanuman or langurs, which are found all over the district, are quite commonly found in Begampur region. Besides jackals and other common mammals, the muskrat, common rat, mouse, small gray-striped squirrel, civet cat, and mongoose are also found in this region. Begampur and its surrounding areas are home to a diverse range of bird species. Common birds include sparrows, pigeons, mynas, and kingfishers. Additionally, migratory birds visit the region during the winter months, making it a popular spot for birdwatching. The rivers and water bodies in Begampur teem with various fish species, including catfish and varieties of carp. Fishing is an essential economic activity for many locals. Snakes, turtles, and various lizard species are found in the region. Some snakes, like cobras and vipers, are venomous. The presence of agricultural land and forested areas attracts various mammal species. Common mammals in the region include wild boars, Indian civets, and various species of bats. Insects are abundant in Begampur, and they play a crucial role in pollination and the overall ecosystem. You can find butterflies, bees, and other pollinators throughout the region. Besides, the domestic animals of the region include cows, buffaloes, bullocks, ponies, goats, sheep, pigs, cats, dogs, fowls, ducks, and pigeons.

THE POPULATION AND ETHNIC COMPOSITION

As per the report released by Census India 2011, Begampur has a population of 10,487 of which 5,405 (51.54%) are males while 5,082 (48.46%) are females. The sex ratio is slightly lesser, that is, 940 than the state average, that is, 950. Schedule Castes (SCs) constitute 10.58 percent while Schedule Tribes (STs) constitute 0.08 percent of the total population in Begampur.

In Begampur region, the Hindu population forms the majority. As per the Census 2011, the Hindu population is 9,055, that is, 86.34 percent of the total population. However, as mentioned earlier this region has been under Muslim influence. Due to this, one gets to see names of villages like Chhotatajpur and Borotajpur which still hold a considerable proportion of the Muslim population. The total Muslim population in Begampur is 1,412, that is, 13.46 percent of the total population.

During the sixteenth century, Rarhi *Brahmins* and the Dakshinrarhi *Kayashya*s (people associated with documentary and clerical works) were the dominant caste groups in Begampur region. However, things have changed along with prolonged Muslim and colonial rule. Today, most of these villages in Begampur area are quite similar in terms of caste composition. Along with a considerable amount of Muslim population, there are various other caste groups such as *Tanti* (weavers), *Karmakar* (blacksmith), *Brahmin* (priest), *Tili* (oil-presser), *Barujibi* (betel-leaf growers), *Napit* (barber), and *Kumor* (potter) which form the other considerable part of the population.

Except for the Muslims, all of the caste groups in the village live alongside each other. Muslims live in a particular portion of the village. Generally, all the Hindu caste groups live in small nuclear families. The weaver caste group (*Tanti*) in this regard is no different. With their low level of income, these caste groups hardly manage to accumulate enough resources to support an extended family. Due to this reason, the Hindu caste groups started showing their inclination toward nuclear families. In most cases, families have separated along with the marriage of one of the earning male members. And as a result, the extended families of this region have transformed into a large number of small nuclear families. However, the kin bond remained intact as these families often live within close quarters.

EDUCATION

The scenario of education in Begampur, West Bengal, reflects both the challenges and opportunities that many regions of our country and state are facing currently. While infrastructure, quality, and access remain concerns, the determination of the community and the support of government initiatives offer hope for a brighter future. The key lies in sustained efforts to address these challenges, enhance the quality of education, and ensure that every child in Begampur, especially those weaver caste young boys and girls, has the opportunity to fulfill their educational aspirations. As the town continues to evolve, its commitment to education will undoubtedly be a crucial factor in shaping its future.

The overall scenario of education in the Begampur region is quite good in comparison to the regional standard. The literacy rate of Begampur Census Town (CT) is 87.81 percent, higher than the state average of 76.26 percent. The standard of literacy among men is slightly better than that of women. The male literacy rate is around 91.06 percent while the female literacy rate is 84.36 percent. Moreover, except for the secondary and to some extent in the higher secondary level—where the participation of girls is higher than boys—men are ahead of women in all other categories. For example, men show a higher frequency in the primary, graduate, and postgraduate levels. One of the most important reasons is that after a certain age, male members from the weaver caste and the Muslim families of this region tend to prioritize their working career over education. Only the men and women from higher caste families such as *Brahmins* or *Karmakars* tend to continue higher level education.

In fact, the standard of literacy has increased in the last few years. My field observations regarding age-group-wise comparison (see Banerjee 2014) show that it has increased from 68.96 percent in the age group "60+" to 88.15 percent in the age group "45–59" to 91.85 percent in the age group "30–44" to ultimately reach 98.02 percent in the age group "15–29." The emergence of educational institutions like Begampur High School (for boys) and Begampur Girls High School has played an important part in this regard. But, still, the number of highly educated people in this region is quite low. Most of the people in this region tend to continue their education only up to primary and secondary levels. Thereafter, they get into the struggle of securing bread and butter for their family and themselves. The only exception is the high caste people (such as *Brahmin*)—who tend to continue their education up to higher secondary, graduate, and postgraduate levels.

Even the standard of education among the weaver caste population has improved along with the overall improvement in this region. There are instances of people from weaver caste families continuing their education up to the postgraduate level. It proves the fact that even the weaver caste people have started showing an inclination toward having higher education. Nonetheless, the general and more common trend of getting an education up to primary, secondary, and higher secondary levels before pursuing a working career still holds its forte.

Several factors hindered the growth of education in Begampur region. For example, the lack of adequate infrastructure is one of the major challenges. Many schools in this region still suffer from dilapidated buildings, insufficient classrooms, and a dearth of essential facilities such as libraries, laboratories, and sports. Ensuring a high standard of education remains another challenge. While there are dedicated educators in the region, the quality of teaching often varies. The absence of standardized teaching methods in some schools further exacerbates this issue. Accessibility to quality education can be a hurdle in some parts of Begampur, especially for underprivileged, impoverished children of weaver caste households. Distance from school, a lack of transportation, and socioeconomic disparities often deter students from pursuing their education. There is also a shortage of trained and qualified teachers in the region, particularly in subjects like mathematics and science. This shortage hinders the delivery of quality education.

Understandably, the government of West Bengal has launched several educational initiatives to address these issues. Schemes like "Kanyashree" for girls' education and "Sabuj Sathi" for bicycles to school-going children have made a positive impact. The community's active involvement in education is another bright spot. Local Nongovernmental Organizations (NGOs) and nonprofit welfare organizations have been working tirelessly to bridge gaps in education, providing resources, scholarships, and academic support to students. The advent of digital learning has opened up new avenues for education in Begampur. Access to online resources and digital platforms has enabled students to overcome geographical barriers and access quality educational materials.

OCCUPATIONS

The scenario of occupation in Begampur region reflects the town's dynamic blend of tradition and modernity. While traditional crafts and agriculture continue to play a vital role, the town has diversified its economic activities, embracing education, commerce, and emerging industries. This diversity not only sustains the livelihoods of its residents but also contributes to the vibrant cultural and economic landscape of Begampur.

The census data of 2011 shows that, out of a total of 10,487 people living in Begampur, 4,510 are working and 5,977 are non-working population. Like what is found in different parts of West Bengal and in the country, the proportion of males (82.66%) among the total working population is considerably high compared to females (17.34%). Again, out of the total population who are engaged in some sort of livelihood activities, 3,886 (86.16%) are main workers, that is, who earn or engaged with any sort of livelihood activities for more than six months. The rest 624 (14%) of the people are marginal workers, that is, those who are engaged in livelihood activities for less than six months.

Begampur is not known for agriculture. There is not enough cultivable land or facilities of irrigation required for an extensive scale of cultivation. Even the census data of 2011 substantiate this fact. Out of this total working population, only ten people are owner cultivators while fifty-three earn their livelihood as agricultural laborers. But, generally, these people, who are engaged in the cultivation of rice, jute, and various seasonal crops, contribute significantly to the region's food supply and economy. The specialty of this area lies in other fields such as the cultivation of betel-leaf and fishery along with the task of handloom weaving. My field observations (see Banerjee 2014, 2016) reveal that around 55.94 percent of the total working population of this region is associated with weaving and its allied activities. The other major section of the population of this region, that is, 31.23 percent, are engaged in business and unskilled work. Begampur's strategic location has made it a hub for trade and commerce. Local markets and shops offer a wide range of goods, including textiles, spices, and agricultural products. Trade plays a pivotal role in the town's economy. Historically, the town's vibrant cultural scene offered opportunities for artists, musicians, and performers. Cultural events and festivals apart from being a means of celebration also provided livelihood avenues for those involved in the arts. With economic development, Begampur has seen the emergence of small-scale/cottage and modern industries, which subsequently led to the creation of job opportunities such as rope making and the making of collars for T-shirts through manufacturing units and technology-based enterprises. These provide a contemporary employment landscape and contribute to the town's industrial growth. Besides, employment in government offices and agencies remains a stable source of livelihood for many residents. Government jobs span various sectors, including administration, education, and healthcare.

Cumulatively, the weaver caste (*Tanti*) male and female members form one of the major chunks of the total earning/working population. Interestingly, the participation of women in weaving and its allied activities (86.57%) is much higher compared to men (37.61%). These people collectively perform their respective roles and duties in the handloom production system. The other major chunk includes Muslim male and female members who are inclined more toward the collar machine[3] and embroidery work, respectively. Due to their prolonged stay in weaving quarters members of other caste groups have adopted these skills quite successfully. Apart from the *Brahmins* (priests) who constitute only a small portion of the total working population, members from nearly all other caste groups are associated with handlooms. The involvement of *Barujibis* and the *Karmakars* are perhaps two of the most prominent examples.

However, despite the long history of handloom in the Begampur region, the scenario has begun to change in recent times. Nowadays many people meet their livelihood activities through "business and unskilled work." Most of these people have taken up small businesses like making collars

Figure 1.2 The Collar Machine of Begampur Region. *Source*: Author's Photo.

for T-shirts, unskilled work, business, shopkeeping, and sales and vending. Moreover, many people have shifted toward different sorts of "skilled works" where these people have either taken up goldsmithy, blacksmithy, carpentry, or chosen to be electricians or mechanics. Many others have shifted to making ball pens or cloth production in powerlooms, whereas only a few people meet their livelihood as service holders, teachers, doctors, and people who independently provide private tuition to others.

The comparative picture of peoples' age-wise participation in "weaving and its allied activities" reveals that the rate of participation has gradually decreased from 83.47 percent in the age group "60+," to 61.28 percent in the age group "45–59," to 54.39 percent in the age group "30–44," to ultimately only 43.13 percent in the age group "15–29" (Banerjee 2014). People's life experiences reveal that around this region quite a large number of people, especially the younger generations, have taken up making collars for T-shirts as their alternative mode of earning. Most of the average weavers in Begampur are shrunken, over-aged, or hardly equipped to take on the physical hardships required for handloom weaving. One can readily find them working on their fly-shuttle frame looms in work sheds which are often built just outside their household. Most of the time, thinly built walls (either by bricks or bamboo splits), tiled roofs, and the specific position of these work sheds add to their weird looks. Those who do not even possess any such work sheds plant the loom inside their household. In most cases, one or two of such looms—worked upon by the man and his wife with the children—takes up almost the majority of space within the household. Nonetheless, despite such a gradual decline, handloom weaving still holds the key to the local economy.

In the last few years especially, either the manually operated collar machines or their power-driven versions have captured the attention of the majority of the labor force in Begampur region. It's the Muslim males in general who have popularized the collar machines in this region. With their tenacity and ability to work hard for a long period, they have initiated the trend of using collar machines among various other inhabitants. Whereas, Muslim women have stuck to their somewhat familiar task of embroidering finished clothes. A few Muslim women are also engaged in seizing and rolling of pirns.

Many weaver households are now shifting toward collar machines which cost about rupees 20,000 to 30,000 each. Moreover, some of them started showing clear signs of growing interest. As one of the aged weavers has stated—"look my nephew has moved into collar making . . . considering the time and labour he invested since morning; he may have earned around hundred rupees already . . . and that too being naive in the field. Experienced workers often earn between hundred and fifty to two hundred per day." Often people ask the most impregnable questions:

> tell me who will be working for over eight hours when he would get only rupees fifty to sixty? Indeed, it is very demoralizing for a person to be engaged in weaving when one knows that he/she won't be able to accumulate rupees one hundred to one hundred and twenty per day. And look at the irony, even the common labourers working on a petty project of mandatory hundred days work earn that much amount quite easily.

For this reason, even the resourceful people of this region now have started opting for the power-driven models of collar machines which cost about 0.15 to 0.20 million rupees. It provides them with a reasonable amount of profit, much more than the handlooms. Moreover, the powerlooms also played its part in this regard. Often entrepreneurs don't feel very enthusiastic about the handlooms anymore. As one of these entrepreneurs has expressed,

> The golden days are not likely to come back . . . there used to be both gains and losses in business, previously we have earned a lot of profit along with the usual evils associated with the trade. There used to be a design once in every ten to fifteen years that used to eradicate all our losses in previous ventures . . . but it is highly unlikely in the present scenario, and we are not expecting it either.

It reflects the situation in this region.

INFRASTRUCTURE AND HEALTHCARE FACILITIES

With basic infrastructure and amenities such as a nearby railway station, one primary health center and three subcenters, a post office, one cinema hall, nine primary and two secondary and higher secondary schools for both boys and girls, office of electricity supply, a few banks, market, three well-developed playgrounds, gymnasiums, and constant supply of running water from the Public Health Engineering (PHE) department, Begampur is a considerable place to live in.

Begampur falls under the jurisdiction of Chanditala police station (PS) of Hooghly district. Presently Chanditala PS comes under the Chandannagar Police Commissionarate. With its jurisdiction spreading into eight unions, namely Seakhala, Akuni-Ichapasar, Nababpur-Kumirmora, Janai, Begampur, Chanditala, Monoharpur, and Krishnarampur, Chanditala PS was established in 1872. Begampur union is formed by localities like south-Naity, Chikrand,

Bankagacha, Adan, Begampur, Panchghara, Kharsarai, Tisa, Chhotatajpur, Baratajpur, Jaykrishnapur, and Kapasharia. In 1964, this union was further divided into four groups, that is, Naity, Panchghara, Kapasharia, and Begampur. During this period, no separate Panchayat was formed despite having separate Panchayats for Naity, Panchghara, and Kapasharia. Begampur Panchayat used to be known as Begampur Union Board. The name of the first president of the Begampur Union Board was Seikh Sobhan Baks. People like Amulya Das and Keshab Dey were elected as the president of this Union Board later. The office of the Union Board used to run from the present Panchayat building which is located just beside the Begampur railway station (Das 2002b, 2).

Begampur was very much a part of "Howrah-Burdwan Chord Line" since its inception in 1914. However, due to the heavy influence of the Muslim League (a Muslim-dominated political party of the pre-independence period that operated in India before the partition) in this region, today's Begampur railway station used to be known as Borotajpur during this period. Even the names of present railway stations like Baruipara and Mirjapur-Bankipur used to be known as Mamudpur due to such heavy influence of the Muslims. The names of the present-day Gobra and Janai railway stations were Aakhdanga and Fuldanga, respectively. Understandably, the mode of communication was not as developed as one gets to see presently. Depending upon the distance and preference, people used to use Fuldanga (present-day Janai) or Borotajpur railway stations (Das 2002a, 4).

The name Borotajpur was altered to Begampur during the 1950s when one of the cabinet ministers of the then West Bengal government came to visit the house of his relative in Begampur. Seeing the unjust naming of the station he proposed for the alteration and that is how the railway station was renamed. Over the years facilities of communication have improved immensely, especially the constant influence that the working people have carried back has played crucial a part in this regard. Today, Begampur is well connected to the sub-divisional headquarters Srirampur, district headquarters Chinsura, and Kolkata through either railway or bus services. Moreover, people easily roam around short distances in their motorcycles and private vehicles.

Both *Chatuspathi* and *Pathshala* were the common avenues through which people attained education in the medieval period. *Chatuspathis* were more traditional where only the male students used to learn *Smritishastras* (oral scriptures that are passed on from one generation to another) apart from astrology, logic, drama, mathematics, grammar, etc. from the *Pandits* (teachers). Meanwhile, *Pathshalas* were more lenient in their approach to imparting education as it allowed both boys and girls to learn reading and writing from the appointed *Gurumosai* (teacher). Historical records suggest that there were many such *Pathshalas* in Begampur region. Gradually, many of these *Pathshalas* were closed due to lack of financial aid, and a few of them were converted into primary schools. Annapurna Prathamik Vidyalaya is one prime example that has been converted from a Pathshala during the 1950s. Amritamoyi Balika Prathamik Vidyalaya that has been established in the year 1942 is another example of such conversion. Earlier, it used to be a *Pathshala* devoid of any separate buildings. Girl students from affluent Muslim families also used to take education from this *Pathshala*. Later, under the leadership of Roysaheb Jogindramohan Singh and with financial aid from Shri Aashutosh Pal it was converted into a primary school. It was named after Anadamoyi Devi mother of Shri Aashutosh Pal (Das 2002c, 2).

Despite all these reforms in the sphere of primary education, the people of Begampur region didn't have any secondary and higher secondary schools where they could send their children to have secondary and higher secondary levels of education. Invariably, young boys and girls had to go to Adan, Baksa, and Janai for higher education. However, the establishment of Begampur High School completely changed the scenario after the independence. The local landlords gave the land for the establishment of the school building. Today, there are two separate higher secondary schools, one for boys and another for girls. Begampur Girls High School is one of the top and renowned educational institutes in this region. Yet there is still scope for further improvement. For example, to date, no college has been established in this region. For graduation, boys and girls of Begampur region generally take admission either in colleges of Kolkata or in Uttarpara. Very few go to Government General Degree College, Singur, Chandernagore College, and Hooghly Mohsin College for their graduation.

The market in Begampur region is situated just beside the railway station. This market consists of a few banks, automated teller machines (ATMs), garment, grocery, and pharmaceutical shops. Besides there are additional shops for stationaries, fruits and vegetables, fish and meat from which people procure according to their daily requirements. Apart from playgrounds attached to the school compounds, there are three dedicated playgrounds in Begampur region, one of which is located near Begampur Hospital. People play football, cricket, volleyball, and badminton matches on this ground. This ground is also used for different charitable and welfare programs. Over the years the healthcare facilities in this region have improved reasonably. Besides the Begampur Public Health Centre which used to serve people's immediate needs, a few private and aided healthcare institutes have come up in recent years. Village Health Care—a multispecialty healthcare institute that was established by Begampur Regional Rural Development Society during the late 1980s—is one of the prime examples. Besides, in case of medical emergencies people also go to healthcare institutes like Chanditala Rural Hospital, Medisky Hospital and Diagnostic (in Chanditala), Seven Rangers Private Nursing Home (in Dankuni), and We Care and Arogya Niketan (in Uttarpara).

LITERARY AND CULTURAL TRADITIONS

The contribution of Begampur is immense in the sphere of literary traditions. Both the renowned writer, Shri Avatar Chandra Laha, contemporary of Shri Bankimchandra Chattopadhyay, and Shri Sailendra Krishna Laha, the associate editor of Prabashi (a well-known Bengali Magazine) hails from Begampur. Besides, celebrated writer Smt Ashapurna Devi, recipient of Gyanpith and Rabindrasmriti awards was also born in Begampur region. A few individuals have made a concerted effort by writing and running wall magazines like Probohan, Kolom, Bikash, etc. Undoubtedly this has helped in generating literary interest among the inhabitants of this region.

The tradition of *song-saja* (enactment as a clown) was perhaps the most renowned cultural tradition that was found in Begampur region. People from nearby places used to visit Begampur for this sole reason. Besides, theatre and drama troops were also quite common apart from cultural programs and recitation—where local inhabitants used to practice and perform. Sometimes the professional and amateur groups used to perform for the people of Begampur region which entertained and educated the locals about the developments outside their region.

Begampur is also known for music. The tradition of Hindustani classical music in this region started to develop when due to the Hindu-Muslim riot in Kolkata (then Calcutta), the renowned classical musician Shri Dulal Chand Sen came and settled in Begampur during the 1950s. Shri Rabindranath Dutta, a local inhabitant, started learning classical music from Shri Dulal Chand Sen. Later, Shri Rabindranath Dutta also took lessons from Sarafat Hossain (Agra School of Hindustani Classical Music) and Atahar Hossain Khan (Atouli School of Hindustani Classical Music). Gradually this tradition of classical music in Begampur region grew and became prominent during the 1960s and 1970s which began to fade away slightly along with the passing away of the pioneers (Das 2002d, 4).

CHAPTER SUMMARY

This chapter paints a holistic picture of Begampur in terms of how multiple factors such as geology and climate, flora and fauna, economy, education, infrastructure, and healthcare facilities collectively contributed to the social construction of Begampur as a place. The analysis of the historical trajectory of this region reveals the process of transformation in Begampur region. It shows how Begampur as a place has transformed from being a mere rural setting to eventually becoming a suburban town in the recent past. It shows how Begampur's well-developed connection with the district administrative headquarters Chinsura and particularly its nearby location (around 30 km away) from Kolkata (i.e., the capital city of the Indian state West Bengal) played a crucial part in this development. Subsequently, this has also brought in developmental efforts in the areas of education and infrastructure. Many secondary and higher secondary schools were established in Begampur apart from the radical development of roads and the emergence of modern amenities like banks, cinema halls, playgrounds, and gymnasiums.

This broad overview regarding Begampur as a place and available occupational choices should help readers understand the backdrop based upon which the handloom weavers of this region have made and are still making their economic choices. The chapter shows how due to the nonavailability of suitable arable land and particularly because of the soil composition agricultural activities in Begampur region in general never took center stage despite being surrounded by settlements that were quite prominent in terms of their Agricultural production. Factors such as the insipid climate, lack of rainfall, and lack of irrigation facilities may have also played a part in this regard. Eventually, all of these didn't provide handloom weavers of Begampur region an opportunity to shift to agricultural activities during times of turmoil, much like what handloom weavers did in other prominent centers of handloom weaving in the district.

The chapter shows that the handloom industry in Begampur region had a blurry beginning, especially prior to the period when the handloom weavers and the general inhabitants of this region came under Mughal, European, and British influence subsequently. The historical evidence also indicates that throughout the course of history, people of this region have lived with naturally available fruits, vegetables, and marine creatures. Findings show that handloom weaving as an occupation has never been a lucrative option in Begampur region. Invariably this made a lasting impact on people's perception—as one gets to see people with hopes, despairs, longings, and frustrations of generations at the same point in time, many of whom hardly see any future in this occupation. Despite this, a section of the population of this region is still clinging on with the job of handloom weaving. For these people, handloom weaving is more than just an occupation. It's an integral part of their identity and culture.

NOTES

1. Sur (1986, 257) has mentioned the meeting point of seven villages, namely Bansabati, Krisnapur, Basudebpur, Nityanandapur, Sibpur, Sambokara, and Baladmat, which in those days cumulatively known as Saptagram.

2. It was quite an important center of the seaborne trade of Bengal until Emperor Sahajahan destroyed the Portuguese colonies at Hooghly and Saptagram (Banerjee 1972, 285).

3. These machines are quite small and portable. Often these machines are used for making collars of T-shirts. These machines are a one-time investment as they don't require constant maintenance. Raw materials for these machines are easily available, and they present the possibility of earning instant cash. Therefore, they have gained popularity among the common weavers.

Chapter 2

Tracing the Historical and Cultural Landscape of Handloom Industry in Begampur

From Past to the Present

India is known for its rich traditions, spirituality, ethnicity, and most importantly, cultural, economic, and geographical diversity. Home of many unique things, India, historically has attracted the attention of travelers/explorers, intellectuals/thinkers/spiritual leaders, and foreign warlords who came intending to conquer this land thriving with cultural and economic prosperity. A number of them have conquered and gone back to their homeland, and others who stayed back and got immersed in the beauty and serenity of the land and the people themselves. Undeniably, all of them have left a lasting impression on the Indian people at large, their economy, the rich culture, and traditions.

Indian handloom industry today stands as a heritage and the timeless facet of India's rich cultural history. Apart from being the epitome of unparalleled and exclusive craftsmanship that has amazed the world for a long period of time, handloom items perfectly reflect the diverse ethnic, cultural, and technological influence that it withstood as a subservient to the Indian economy. The influence of Persian art and Buddhist iconography as main sources of inspiration can be found in Indian handmade items. Some of these features are still prevalent among contemporary handloom items as decorative motifs of flora and fauna that are still used in forming exotic designs show marked resemblance (see Banerjee and Chakrabarti 2020, 64).

Right from its inception as a subsidiary occupation, which mostly thrived in clusters in specific parts of villages or cities and where handloom weavers mostly produced utility products from hand-spun cotton yarn for the local market, to its flourishment under the Mughal patronage to its struggle due to changing export policies during the colonial rule, then hand-woven fabric becoming a political symbol during the independence struggle against the

British oppression, the fate of handloom weavers in India has always been intertwined with India's cultural, economic, and political history. Surprisingly, Indian handloom weavers in the midst of all of these have managed to survive, passing down skills from generation to generation. It's no surprise that India is currently one of the largest producers of the world's hand-woven fabrics.

Through this chapter, I trace the development of Indian handloom which is entangled with India's cultural, economic, and political history through three subsections. Starting from the inception of Indian handlooms during the ancient period, the development of handlooms under the Mughal sultanate, and colonial and post-independence periods, I trace the history and development of handlooms in India in the first subsection. Then in the second subsection, I shift my attention to the development of the handloom industry in West Bengal which was a part of the then-Bengal. Finally, I describe the origin and development of the handloom industry in the Begampur region in the third subsection.

HISTORICAL AND CULTURAL GEOGRAPHY OF INDIAN HANDLOOMS

If we look into the history of technological development among humans, the earliest definite evidence of both weaving and basketry comes from the Neolithic culture around 5000 BC. However, pieces of evidence regarding how ancestors of modern humans lived during the early and middle part of the prehistoric period indicate toward the fact that practices of cloth weaving might have emerged from more primitive techniques of sewing fine leather thongs or strands of sinew during the upper Palaeolithic stage (Crowfoot 1958, 413).

Indian Handlooms during the Ancient Period

The handloom textiles of India are probably the oldest industry accounted by historical evidence. Archaeological evidence also indicates the fact that the Egyptians used to use Indian *Muslin* for dressing their mummies even before 5000 BC. The earliest fragment of cotton cloth with a *Hansa* (swan) design was dug from a site near Cairo in Egypt (Mishra and Das Mohapatra 2021; Kumar et al. 2021). However, the first evidence of handloom weaving in India dates back to the time of the Indus Valley Civilization, which was active from 3300 to 1300 BCE (Gupta 2021). Several archaeological evidence were found at various sites of the Saraswati—Indus Valley Civilization, namely Harappa, Mohenjo Daro, Chanhudaro, Lothal, Urkatoda, and Kalibangan. For example, the first Indian woven and dyed cotton fabrics have been excavated in the ruins of Mohenjo Daro. The famous terracotta figurines from Mehrgarh and the sculpture of "Priest King" from Mohenjo Daro wearing a turban and a robe with or without embroidery respectively indicate a well-developed textile industry even during that period. Earliest specimens of spindle and spindle whorls of stone, clay, metal, terracotta, needles, and dye vats together with woven and madder-dyed (herb dye) cotton fragments wrapped around a silver pot found at different sites indicate that the inhabitants of the Saraswati Indus valley were well versed with the art of spinning, weaving, dyeing, and sewing. Probably, cotton was the most commonly used fiber during this period. Infrequent uses of other fibers, such as wool, jute, hemp, and silk, have also been noted. Wild indigenous silk moth species found at Harappa and Chanhudaro and "silk thread inside copper beads" found from Harappa indicate the use and production of silk (Mark Kenoyer 2004).

In fact, reference to the handloom weaving style in India can also be found during the period of Vedas. Frequent use of clothing metaphors and several terms related to weavers in Rigveda indicate that spinning and weaving were highly advanced and honored occupations in Vedic society. In Rigveda, a weaver was described as "Vasovaya," the male weaver as "Vaya" and the female weaver as "Vayitri." Moreover, texts of the Vedic period provide reference to embroidered garments also in the form of *pesas*. Later Samhitas and the Brahmanas mention a woolen thread called "Varna Sutra" made of goat's hair and sheep's wool.

Mention about the popularity of Indian printed fabric among the women of the eastern Mediterranean can be found in Greek historian Herodotus's account. Megasthenes, a Greek ambassador to the court of Chandragupta Maurya in his book *Indica* mentioned about the Indian robes, *muslins*, and brocades. Needless to say, clothing objects became a source of revenue for the kings. References of which can be found in Kautilya's *Arthashastra* (fourth century BCE). Furthermore, the detailed descriptions of different stages, that is, threads (*sutras*), coats (*varma*) and cloth (*vastras*), through which the skilled artisans performed textile production and the material distribution system among spinners, weavers and people associated with the act of textile-making in *Arthashastra* also indicate the fact the production activities during this period were reasonably well-organized.

Besides, mentions of different types of textiles such as linen (*khoman*), cotton (*kappasikam*), silk (*kosseyam*), weavers (*tantuvaya*), the place of weaving (*tantavitatatthanam*), weaving appliances (*tantabhanda*), and the loom (*tantaka*) and cotton thread (*kappasikasuttam*) and cotton cloth (*kappasikadusam*) can be found in several Buddhist and Jain texts, respectively. Many cities gained glory due to the production of exquisite textiles during this period. Some Buddhist and Sanskrit texts mention Kasi (Varanasi) as one such place that flourished as a regional capital for the textile industry from the time of Mahabharat till the regime of Nandas, the Mauryas, and the Sungas. Kasi was known for the "fabric of dreams," kinknab, a *Banarasi* brocade designed by interweaving silver and gold threads with silk or cotton/silk blended yarns. The brocaded silks with cotton or wool blended with silk were known as Himrus, also the Shikarghar was the finest and most popular motif of Indian kinknab.

Due to the cross-fertilization of ideas, culture, style, and technologies, the Indian handloom industry reached historical glory by the early Mauryan period (322–183 BC). Long-distance trade relationships were established with Egypt, China, Iran, and the Mediterranean during this period. Mention of ancient trade routes and trade of *Muslin* from India can also be found in the first-century Greek text *The Periplus of the Erythrean Sea*. Meanwhile, the silk industry in southern India flourished under the patronage of "Pallava" and "Chola" rulers. Kanchipuram was an outstanding center of cotton and silk weaving under the Pallavas. Later, more textile centers like Tribhuvanam, Arni, Tirupparkkadal, Virinchipuram, Woraiyur, Tirupati, Kalahasti, Gugai, Madurai, Salem, Sulur, Venkatagiri, Dharmavaram, Kumbakonam, Thanjavur, and Vridhachalam flourished under the Chola Empire.

During this period, the grand Indian trade route consisted of *Uttarapath* and *Dakshinapath*, that is, northern and southern land routes. The textile industry in northern India benefited and flourished due to gains from the control of silk routes during the Kushan rule. Meanwhile, the Satavahanas Empire controlled the trade of cotton textiles produced in the Deccan belt across the Indian Ocean from the first century BCE to the third century CE. Indian cotton fragments found at the Red Sea ports of Berenike in Egypt confirm ancient trade relationships.

Handloom weaving in India started to witness a marked change during the Gupta period (fourth to sixth century CE), especially concerning the manufacturing of handloom items, which up until that period were considered utility products and an essential part of the local economy only. Exquisite items were produced only on special occasions at the request of the local elites. However, from the Gupta period onward, looking at the changing market requirement, textile manufacturing was being done at two separate levels, that is, for domestic consumption and trading. Fine-quality fabrics were manufactured for the elite class, and coarse fabrics were made for the poor. Reference to fine fabrics made from silk, cotton, hemp fiber, and goat hair during this period can be found in Hieun Tsang's (a Chinese monk traveler) account. Besides, references to the tie-and-dye process and dye fabric can also be found in Banabhatta's Harshacharita (seventh century CE).

Indian Handlooms under the Mughal Sultanate

With the establishment of Mughal rule, Indian handlooms started to witness many important changes. First, many researchers think the Persian influence in the technique, motif, and technology used in making textiles and fabrics to be the major cause behind the improvement in textile production during this period. Second, the introduction of sericulture on a large scale helped Indian artisans to become less dependent on other countries for the import of raw silk. Third, being avid admirers of Indian art and culture, Mughal rulers established state workshops and appointed officers to supervise the activities of cloth production (Das 2001). It was the beginning of an important change in the history of Indian handlooms, especially regarding the "system of finance," "organization of production," and "marketing."

During this period, textiles were produced in two kinds of *karkhanas* or workshops, viz. (i) independent *karkhanas* run by artisans and (ii) imperial *karkhanas* patronized by the imperial court. Delhi, Lahore, Agra, Patna, Banaras, Ahmedabad, Burchapur, and Dacca were the major centers of textile production. Reference to this can be found in the writings of a French Traveler, Francois Bernier. Under the Mughals, the *Muslin* produced at Dacca (present-day Dhaka, in Bangladesh) reached its pinnacle. During the period, Kashmir and Bengal grew as two important centers of sericulture and silk weaving. Besides, Ahmedabad, Surat, Sindh, Delhi, Agra, Assam, and Malda were other important silk textile centers during the Mughal period. Patan in Gujarat emerged as the main center of patola silk made using the Ikat technique.

Opening up of sea trade routes and the consequent expansion of the export trade during the seventeenth and eighteenth centuries (Niranjana and Vijayan 2001, 3) led Mughal rulers to see the prospect of Indian cloth as an object of foreign trade and the unmatched artistry and finance of Indian handloom weavers. Due to this, they encouraged artisans to take up silk weaving, especially the production of *Muslin* (one of the finest varieties of silk cloth produced in the world) silk items, which provided India with a separate identity in the world of cloth production. This phenomenon can be correlated with the economic boom that the Indian handloom industry witnessed under the Mughal patronage. The silk industry of Bengal owned a fair share of the foreign market. Silk items from Bengal were exported to Afghanistan, Arab, Greece, Iran, and Turkey. The flourishing trend of exporting the Bengal silk saree continued till 1830 (Kumar et al. 2021).

Handloom weaving, which up until that period mostly thrived as a subsidiary occupation, had then begun to be seen as an alternative to agriculture. And those artisans who had an adequate amount of skills started seeing their future in state workshops under the Mughal patronage. It spurred a mass migration of skilled artisans toward the major state workshop established by the Mughal rulers (see Hossain 1988). Those who didn't get the chance in the state workshops continued living in the adjacent cities, producing items similar to those produced by the native courts and state workshops. Different handloom traditions then gradually started to evolve, and specific regional features gradually became distinctively identifiable styles and techniques. Subsequently, this exclusivity in the styles, techniques, and aesthetic elements found within the woven items coming from a particular geographical region gradually consolidated into the formation of distinct handloom weaving traditions across the country.

Indian Handlooms during the Colonial Period

By the late seventeenth century, enticed by business opportunities presented by Indian clothes in foreign markets, the British, Dutch, Portuguese, and French merchants started setting up factories or "Kuthi" and employing local silk weavers. The factories and centers of the British East India Company were established at Coromandel, Surat, and later in Bengal (Kumar et al. 2021). Gradually these European traders with the permission of Mughal rulers introduced the system of making advance payments to the resourceless Indian artisans which ensured the sale of all the items to merchants paying in advance. Not only it shifted the control of the cloth business from the hands of the Mughals to these foreign traders, but this was the beginning of bondage that altered the fate of these skilled artisans forever. Remnants of this can still be found in present-day informal contracts between a *mahajan* (individual entrepreneur) and a resourceless artisan weaver (employee). Indian cotton textile was highly popular in Britain. Hence, the British East India Trading Company (EIC) imported them in the form of calico, a dyed or printed textile.

However, the heavy import of Indian textiles to Britain forced the British administration to take drastic steps. In 1700 AD, King William III of England imposed a fine of 200 pounds on the wearing of Indian silk and calico to discourage the import of Indian handloom fabrics. The Calico Acts (1700, 1721) were introduced that banned the import of most cotton textiles into Britain to revive the British wool and silk industry. Furthermore, restrictions were imposed on the use and sale of most cotton items.

With the establishment of British rule in India handloom industry witnessed another major turnaround. Looking at the ongoing process of industrialization in Europe, more specifically the emerging cotton cloth mills in Manchester, England, the British Government altered its export policy by imposing heavy tariffs on the export of Indian cloths to the foreign market. Moreover, the finest variety of raw cotton was exported to Britain at a cheap subsidized rate with which cloth mills in Manchester started producing clothes that were sold at a cheap price. These decisions had severe effects on the fate of Indian handloom weavers. All of a sudden, this high demand and restricted supply of cotton yarn to the Indian artisans increased the cost of cloth production. It resulted in an inexplicable rise in the price of Indian clothes in foreign markets. Further, the emergence of British mill-made clothes as a competitor led to the shrinkage in the clientele for Indian clothes in foreign markets (see Roy 2002). Subsequently, these decisions further aggravated the woes of weavers in the form of joblessness and impoverishment, discouraging the future generation from taking up handloom weaving, which eventually pushed this beautiful craft toward oblivion. Many (e.g., Thorner 1962; Bagchi 1976; Roy 1999) believe that Indian handlooms witnessed a phase of "deindustrialization" during this period. Understandably, Indians began to rebel against this colonial practice. On August 7, 1905, a meeting was convened in Bengal, deciding that foreign cloth must be boycotted. And thus, the Swadeshi Movement was born. This is how Indian handlooms attained political significance by becoming the symbol of political struggle against British oppression.

Till about the first decade of the twentieth century, the handloom industry still retained an edge in the domestic market. However, the growth and consolidation of the mill sector changed the complexion of competition within India's textile-producing sectors. The handloom sector gradually became dependent on yarn produced by mills. Since the period of the First World War, a competitive relationship grew between these two sectors, and the handloom industry started to face increasing competition from clothes produced by mills. In the year 1928, the Royal Commission on Agriculture was the first to recognize this problem. This commission believed that the development of this village industry on cooperative lines was essential for the survival of weavers in the face of increased competition from organized industry (GOI 1986–87, 1).

Throughout the period of 1920s and 1930s, handlooms continued to grow. The growth in the demand for handmade items could be attributed to the nationalist movement for India's independence, which reached its peak at that point in time. The situation again became adverse for the handloom weavers during the Second World War. Due to war conditions, the prices of yarn rose phenomenally and pushed the raw materials out of the reach of common weavers. The ILO estimated (1960, 7–8) that "compared to pre-war levels, the price of yarn had increased from 600 to 700 %, while the price of handloom products had risen only by 200 to 250%" and that has played an important role in the closing down of many looms during that period. It was realized from around this time that the livelihoods of handloom weavers had been adversely affected by the indiscriminate expansion of mills. The free functioning of spinning mills has not been interfered though, only certain concessions were given to the handloom industry, while excise duty was levied on mill cloth.

Indian Handlooms after the Independence

In the post-independent era, Indian handlooms gained the status of a priority sector. Many important steps were taken in this regard. For example, the Khadi and Other Handloom Industries Development Act was passed in 1952, a national apex body All India Handloom Fabrics Marketing Cooperative Society was established to promote the marketing of handloom fabrics in 1955, and the Handloom and Handicrafts Export Council was set up in 1958 to promote exports of handloom items (Kumar et al. 2021). But powerlooms and mill sectors have emerged as the major competitors of handloom at the same point in time. With their technology, which is relatively less dependent on human skills and productively more efficient, mills and powerlooms were way ahead in the race right from the days of their inception.

A combination of factors contributed to the consolidation of these sectors. One of the primaries was the size of the powerloom industry, which consisted of hundreds of small units set up by enterprising individuals, each with no more than five to ten powerlooms. Some of these were owner-operated while others were run by hired laborers. In this way, powerlooms got all the benefits of being a cottage industry initially but were exempted from labor laws because of their small size. Thus, the powerloom sector emerged as an intermediary between the preexisting handloom and mill segments of the textile industry.

Several protectionist measures were taken to protect Indian handlooms from unfair competition. For example, restrictions were imposed on powerlooms and mills that prohibited them from producing certain kinds of items (Kashyap 1990; Nath, Mrinalini and Sandhya 2001). By setting up the Development Commissioner for Handlooms in 1975, the Indian government also took considerable steps regarding skill upgradation, capacity building, and disseminating technological interventions for reducing the drudgery of the handloom weavers, thereby increasing the earnings of the weavers. Moreover, for inclusive and sustainable growth of the handloom sector, the National Handloom Development Corporation Limited was established in February 1983 as a public sector undertaking under the ambit of the Ministry of Textile. In general, most of the policies at different points in time have tried to protect and promote healthy competition among different sectors of India's textile industry including the handlooms. India's textile policies were often motivated by general concerns such as (i) regulation of inter-sectorial competition, (ii) modernization of cloth-making techniques, and (iii) sickness and rehabilitation of mills (Mishra 1993). Despite all these efforts, the handloom sector started to decline due to competition from cheap imports and design imitation on powerlooms (Kumar et al. 2021).

The official figures available on the growth rate (in terms of yearly share of production) of powerloom show that the number of powerlooms grew from 37 percent in 1980 AD to 68 percent in 1995 AD (Srinivasalu 1996). Even such a growth rate sometimes led the Ministry of Labour to admit that, "the growth of power-loom was so rapid that yesterday's traditional handloom weaving centres also grew to become centres of powerloom industry" (GOI 1988, 3). Powerlooms took away most of the yarn production of the country, and it produced and sold similar varieties of cloth at a much cheaper price than handloom cloth. Because of the low-price level and lower production cost, some of the powerloom products manage to catch the attention of common buyers. Hence, they were often featured at the top of the preference list of entrepreneurs. In this way, these "fast developing," technologically modernized cloth-producing sectors in the country along with the business motive of the entrepreneur gradually started to marginalize the chances of the handloom as one of the major cloth-producing sectors.

However, with government interventions and improvements in handloom weaving techniques, Indian handlooms started to gain worldwide attention again in the past two decades. With ease of business, credit facilities, and marketing opportunities, the sector has started to thrive once again. Product diversification according to the changing market demand has become a sheer necessity rather than a matter of innovation. Nonetheless, silk and cotton weaving predominate the Indian weaving tradition, though wool is also used for weaving in many parts of the country. Due to this reason, today, one gets to see so many types of handlooms operating across India, which produce a variety of fabrics made out of silk, cotton, and wool. *Pashmina* from Leh, Ladakh, and Kashmir Valley; the *Kullu and Kinnauri weaves* of Himachal Pradesh; *Phulkari* from Punjab, Haryana, and Delhi; *Panchachuli weaves* of Uttarakhand; *Kota Doria* from Rajasthan; *Benarasi Silk* of Uttar Pradesh; *Bhagalpuri Silk* from Bihar; *Patan Patola* of Gujarat; *Chanderi* of Madhya Pradesh; *Paithani* of Maharashtra; *Champa Silk* from Chhattisgarh; *Sambalpuri Ikat* from Odisha; *Tussar Silk* from Jharkhand; *Jamdani, Baluchari* and *Tangail* of West Bengal; *Mangalgiri* and *Venkatgiri* from Andhra Pradesh; *Pochampally Ikat* from Telangana; *Udupi Cotton* and *Mysore Silk* of Karnataka; *Kunbi weaves* from Goa; *Kuthampully* of Kerala; *Arani* and *Kanjivaram Silk* of Tamil Nadu; *Lepcha Durry* from Sikkim; *Sualkuchi* from Assam; *Apatani* from Arunachal Pradesh; *Naga weaves* of Nagaland; *Moirang Phee* from Manipur; *Pachhra* of Tripura; *Mizu Puan* in Mizoram; and *Eri silk* of Meghalaya are few of the prominent examples (see Chaudhry 2019).

HANDLOOM INDUSTRY OF BENGAL

Handlooms are often referred to as *tant* in West Bengal (which was part of undivided Bengal under British rule). Mentions of fine-quality cotton production in Bengal can be found in the Chinese travelogue of thirteenth century CE. The earliest record of weaving handloom saree in Bengal can be traced back to fifteenth-century Shantipur in Nadia district (Raniwala 2021). However, needless to say, the practices of handloom weaving in Bengal originated in a much earlier period. For understanding the evolution and growth of handloom weaving in Bengal one needs to understand the sociopolitical turmoil witnessed by the people of the then Bengal. Right from being under "Sashanka's rule" to the "Pal regime that lasted from 750–1162 CE" to witnessing the "13th-Century Turkish invasion," followed by the rule of the Sen dynasty, eventually becoming independent again and then finally becoming part of Delhi sultanate during Akbar's reign in 1575 AD, the fate of artisans in Bengal were deeply entangled with politico-economic decisions that different rulers took at different periods.

A few scholars indicate the fact that Bengal became the center of excellent quality cotton fabrics during the Pal regime (Kumar et al. 2021). However, not many places in present-day West Bengal were well-known for exquisite clothing items. During the eleventh and twelfth centuries AD, weavers of Shantipur did not know how to cut fine yarn like the weavers of Dhaka and Mymensingh districts of erstwhile East Bengal. Rather, women of the weaver family of Shantipur region were known for spinning yarn, and men for the weaved dhoti, saree, and towels made from thick yarn. Weavers used to procure required raw cotton from the villages near Shastipur, especially from the villages of Purba Bardhaman district situated on the west bank of river Ganga. Then the situation started to turn around when some skilled weavers from Dhaka district upon receiving the invitation from the then ruler of Bengal Lakshman Sen, King of the Sen Dynasty, came and settled in Shantipur (Das 2001).

Thereafter, mentions of the textile factories in Bengal can be found in Abul Fazl's book *Ain-e-Akbari.* The handloom industry in Bengal continued to flourish with extensive royal patronage and reached its peak under the Mughal Sultanate between the sixteenth and eighteenth centuries. The art of making *Muslin* (an exquisite silk item) and *Jamdani* (an exquisite cotton item) became prominent during this particular phase. Mughal rulers, in general, particularly Emperor Akbar and Begam Nur Jahan, were very fond of liter weaving of handloom *Muslin* produced in Bengal (Bhattacharya 1967). Understandably, many *Muslin* factories were established in different parts of Bengal under the direct supervision of the then ruler of Bengal, Ibrahim Khan. Later, Murshidabad became a new center of weaving under the regime of Nawab Murshid-Quli Khan (1717–1727 CE). *Baluchari* (another exquisite silk item) came into existence under Murshid-Quli Khan, much after the *Muslin. Baluchari* saree was first produced in a very small village named Baluchar (now known as Jiaganj), a distant place situated on the bank of river Bhagirathi in the district of Murshidabad. The popularity of Murshidabad *Baluchari* and *Jamdani* sarees can be assumed from the fact that Tipu Sultan sent people of his kingdom (Karnataka) to Bengal to learn sericulture and facilitated the establishment of silk industry in Mysore (Kumar et al. 2021).

In due course, places like Dhaka and Tangail (both situated in present-day Bangladesh) and Murshidabad and Shantipur (both in West Bengal, India) became important silk cloth-producing hubs of undivided Bengal. Thereafter, factors like geographical proximity, climate, and soil required for cotton cultivation, the changing nature of riverine trade along with the change in the flow of river Bhagirathi (Ganga) played a part in the diversification of cloth production activities and the spread of weaving traits across Bengal. During the eighteenth century, due to the flooding of a tributary of the Ganga (Bhagirathi), the Baluchar village got submerged, and the artisans had to move to safer locations, leaving behind the facilities and infrastructure provided to them by the Nawab. This forced them to migrate and set up their base about 200 kilometers away in Bishnupur under Malla's patronage (Gatha 2014). Meanwhile, weavers of Shantipur continued to flourish and influence with their produce of fine cotton items such as *Jamdani*, *Nilambri*, and *Meghdambru* which had their share of clientele. Gradually, weavers of Nabadwip (in Nadia district), Dhatrigram and Samudragarh (in Burdwan district), and Dhaniakhali, Rajbalhaat, and Begampur (in Hooghly district) started learning the craft from these already flourishing centers of cloth weaving.

The situation and condition of handloom weavers in Bengal started becoming tricky thereafter along with the weakening of the Mughal Empire and the entry of European traders within the arena of Indian cloth business. The local merchants under the control of Sultans and Badshahs of Delhi performed the role of distributing Indian cloth across the world up until that period. They exported fine Indian clothes to places like Kabul, Baluchistan, Iraq, Iran, Arab, Turkey, Sri Lanka, Italy, and other Western European countries through either land or sea routes. There was considerable demand for Indian clothes in the European market up until the sixteenth century AD as textile production in Europe began only after that period. Weavers enjoyed their liberty in the production of cloth up to the time of Nawab Alivardi Khan. Practices of doing exclusive business emerged during the regime of Siraj-Ud-Daula (then Nawab of Bengal). However, weavers had the opportunity to appeal to the Nawab's court for redressal of their grievances (Roy 1996, 68-69). The local weavers continued to produce these exquisite items in the face of the Dutch, Portuguese, and British struggle to cease exclusive export rights to Indian handmade objects. That was a good time for the weavers of Bengal in terms of independence of production and income.

This situation started to degrade as soon as the East India Company, after their victory over Nawab Siraj-Ud-Daula in the battle of Palasi, seized control of all the handloom cloth production and business activities in and around Bengal. They started exercising their exclusive right to export Indian clothes to the Far East and Europe. The poor skillful artisans of Bengal could not resist because they were already under the bondage of these traders and more so they could easily sense their vulnerability as Bengal province then was undergoing the process of political transition.

The condition of these artisans in Bengal continued to degrade further under British rule in India. Prolonged colonial influence and the changing nature of export and industrial policies certainly have changed the course of the handloom industry in West Bengal. A gradual development of opinion against the import of goods from India on the ground of the growing prospect of the cotton textile industry in England especially has accelerated the process of decline (Das 2001; Hossain 1988, 22). Moreover, cheap clothes brought in from Manchester made life difficult for handloom weavers (Banerjee 1972, 285). Between 1855 and 1947, West Bengal witnessed a rapid development of spinning mills. Among the total 112 jute mills in India 101 were established in West Bengal (Banerjee 1972, 297). Needless to say, the handloom industry faced quite tough competition from mills-made products. It affected the poor artisans of Bengal as a huge number of them met their livelihood activities through handloom weaving.

Partition of Bengal during the time of independence in 1947 forced several weaver groups from Bangladesh to migrate to India and rehabilitated in different parts of West Bengal. Phulia, close to Shantipur in Nadia district, became a new home for a few weavers coming from Tangail (in Bangladesh). Again the "Basak" community of Tangail district settled in "Katwa" Dhatrigram, Ketugram, and Samudragarh areas in Burdwan district. These weavers brought their ancestral weaving traditions called "Begum Bahar" (known for using silk warp and cotton weft) with them. Later on, this transformed into the practice of using both cotton warp and weft. Other weaver communities coming from Bangladesh settled in the different parts of Hooghly and Burdwan districts. Gradually, over the years, each region has developed its signature style and became well-known for its varieties of *tant* sarees (Raniwala 2020).

HANDLOOM WEAVING TRADITION IN BEGAMPUR AND ITS EVOLUTION

The handloom industry in the Hooghly district emerged long back, even before the colonial rule. Subsequently, all other industries like Embroidery,

Brass, Bell metal manufacturing, and Brick and Tile making emerged one after another. During the late nineteenth and early twentieth centuries, all four subdivisions had places like Shamaspur, Dhaniakhali, Mahmudpur, and Gurap (under Hooghly subdivision); Rajbalhat, Antpur, Dwarhatta, Begampur, and Kharsarai (in Serampur subdivision), Haripal and Koinkala (in Chandannagar subdivision); and Badangunge, Kalme, Khanakul, Krishnanagar, and Mayapur (in Arambagh subdivision) along with French Chandernagore (present-day Chandannagar) were important handloom weaving centers (O'Malley and Chakravarti 1912, 183). Weavers generally made *dhotis*, *sarees*, *chadars*, and *gamchas*. Fine clothes were made only in Serampore, Haripal, Dhaniakhali, and Kalme of which clothes made in the first and last two towns were commonly known as *Farasdanga.*

The historical record indicates the fact that cotton cloth production in Begampur started around the 1860s. Even though O'Malley and Chakravarti (1912) don't directly mention the weavers of Begampur, but they mention the name of Kharsarai which is adjacent to Begampur. Moreover, it would not be wrong to assume that the weavers of Begampur along with weavers of Kharsarai produced those fine clothes for which Serampore became famous during that period. Much like in other parts of Bengal, geography and climatic shifts played a crucial part in the development of the handloom weaving tradition in the Hooghly district. For example, O'Malley and Chakravarti (1912, 184) mention that owing to the "restriction in the Mulberry-growing areas due to Damodar-flood and degeneracy of silk-worm due to disease" places of silk weaving became confined to few places under Serampore and Arambagh subdivision. Invariably this has led weavers of the surrounding areas (including Begampur) toward exclusive cotton weaving.

Pieces of evidence also indicate the fact that the weavers of Begampur and Kharsarai (under the Serampore subdivision) were greatly influenced by the weavers of *Farasdanga* tradition (under the Chandannagar subdivision) in terms of practices, tools, and techniques used for cloth production and aesthetic elements within the woven items. Reference of which can be found in O'Malley and Chakravarti's (1912, 183) writings "the vitality of industry in this district and especially in Serampore, is attributed to the use of improved handloom, which is simply the English Fly-Shuttle-Frame Looms invented by John Kay and was introduced from Chandernagore more than 50 years ago." Frame looms were quite distinct from country looms (pit looms) in which the shuttle was driven manually between the warp threads. The fly-shuttle-frame looms, on the other hand, contained a handle attached to a string and a lever mechanism to drive the shuttle through the warp threads. This measure was taken to economize the labor.

The handloom weavers of Begampur too were greatly affected by alterations in the export and the industrial policies brought in by the British government. Of these 101 jute mills that were established in the entire Bengal, the first jute spinning mill was established at Rishra, Hooghly, in the year 1855 (O'Malley and Chakravarti 1912). Despite the introduction of the frame loom, weavers of Begampur, because of their lack of knowledge of dyeing of raw cotton threads and most importantly lack of creative elements in products made out of the coarse quality of yarn, remained in the shadow of other developed centers of handloom weaving in Hooghly district. Therefore, the situation the handloom weavers of Begampur faced amid the alteration in export and industrial policies by the British government was dreadful, to say the least. Facing tough competition from mill-made and cheap imported clothes was already a challenge for the weavers of developed handloom traditions that were producing high-quality items containing attractive designs, so one could easily imagine the situation of the weavers who were producing cheap average products and faced the direct competition from mill-made and cheap imported clothes. Due to this, there was a huge decline in the number of practicing handloom weavers. As O'Malley and Chakravarti (1912, 182) report "the number of person engaged in cotton weaving decreased by about 33 percent in 20 years, and those who clung to their old handicraft had for the most part to supplement their earnings from agriculture, services etc."

Meanwhile, weavers of Begampur region continued to pick up important elements of cloth making such as dyeing, starching, drumming, denting, and drafting and aesthetic content from developed handloom weaving centers of district Hooghly and West Bengal during both colonial and postcolonial periods. According to the local legend, the art of dyeing raw cotton yarn was not known to weavers of Begampur region. They used to collect dyed yarn from other developed centers in the district. The practice of dyeing raw cotton yarn started when senior weavers like Keshab Dey and Jagabandhu Sil invited skilled dyers from Kaikala and Haripal (important centers of handloom weaving in Hooghly district). Gradually weavers of Begampur, who up until that period were using treadle weaving techniques and producing cheap clothes from No. 40 and No. 60 cotton yarns, started learning the art of making designs in the body of woven items with the help of *dobby*. Moreover, weavers because of their kin base in important handloom weaving centers started introducing new designs much in the same mold as those found in Dhaniakhali and Rajbalhat. This strategy was often adopted by the weavers of Begampur region to attract the attention of their customers toward their products.

In terms of the nature of the organization, cloth production activities in Begampur over the years have been carried out in informal terms—that is, under the supervision of *mahajan* (individual entrepreneur) or master weaver where poor artisans languish at the bottom of the hierarchy, and these two trading classes often exercised their supremacy and control. To save poor artisans from the clutches of these two trading classes handloom weavers' cooperatives were introduced in Begampur region during the 1970s. Bara-Begampur Samabay Samity was one of the first weavers' cooperatives that was set up in this region. But it could not survive due to acts of forgery, misappropriation of funds, and most importantly heavy pressure from the local *mahajans*. Most of the cooperatives in Begampur region thereafter became dysfunctional much in the same manner.

The scenario began to change as the Weavers' Service Centre (WSC) in Kolkata initiated the Cluster implementation program in Begampur region in the year 2010. Under this program, 260 weavers were trained in designing, dyeing, preparatory processes like drum warping and sizing, and more importantly, in techniques of dobby and jacquard weaving. This was an important step toward product diversification. Because, up until then, the art of making clothes through jacquard looms was unknown to the weavers of this region. Moreover, soft skills were imparted among the weavers to enhance their confidence. Further, a state-government-financed development program was also carried out in the year 2012. With modifications such as the use of improved steel reed, pick, and finer cotton yarn for better texture, dobby with more levers, jacquards of 100 hooks for new designs in attractive color combinations, and engaging frame looms for sarees and narrow width looms for stoles, this program too tried to take necessary steps toward required technological upgradation. Further, improved yarn dyeing and colorfastness were also initiated as part of this program. Kharsarai Madhyampara Samabai Samity was established in the year 2013, which took the baton of training the local weavers toward skill upgradation. All of these brought in visible improvements in the handloom industry in Begampur region.

CHAPTER SUMMARY

This chapter has delved into the social, political, and economic contexts that have shaped the functioning of the handloom industry in this region. While trying to underscore the intrinsic link between handloom weaving and the Indian economy, this chapter meticulously traced the historical trajectory of Indian handlooms, especially in the Bengal and Begampur regions, revealing the evolution and development of weaving practices over time. This historical backdrop provides crucial insights into the handloom industry's resilience and its pivotal role in shaping the local identity and economy.

The chapter shows that Begampur's history is a tapestry of influences, marked by the footprints of Mughal emperors, colonial rulers, and the resilience of local artisans. It is a history woven with threads of culture, tradition, and craftsmanship. Even though there is no clear historical reference to the beginning of handloom weaving in Begampur, the influence of the Mughal rulers on the handloom industry of this region is unquestionable. The handloom industry in Begampur region began to flourish along with the development of other renowned handloom weaving centers in the country and the state, when due to the discerning tastes of Mughal royalty textile items bearing the mark of exquisite artistry became highly sought after and prized. Then, as time flowed onward, weaving practices in Begampur evolved, adapting to changing circumstances and technological advancements. The arrival of the British colonial rulers ushered in a new phase in the history of handlooms. Initially, the British demand for Indian textiles led to the proliferation of weaving communities, including those in Begampur. The handloom industry became a vital source of economic sustenance for the town and its people. However later, owing to growing textile industries in Britain, the British Government altered its export policy and imposed heavy tariffs on the export of Indian cloths to the foreign market. Moreover, the finest variety of raw cotton is exported to Britain at a cheap subsidized rate with which cloth mills in Manchester started producing clothes that are sold at a cheap price. This has severely affected the fate of Indian handlooms.

Needless to say, the process of industrialization has negatively affected the handloom industry in Begampur region, as West Bengal (i.e., a part of undivided Bengal during the colonial period) witnessed a rapid development of spinning mills between 1855 and 1947. The magnitude of impact on the handloom industry can be assumed from the estimate that among the total 112 jute mills in India 101 were established in West Bengal (Banerjee 1972, 297). Furthermore, the Indian handloom industry continued to witness steep competition from mills and powerlooms during the post-independence period as well. Despite many valiant protectionist measures taken by the Indian government, powerlooms especially, because of their small size, were able to escape the imposed restrictions. Thus, powerlooms continued to enjoy the dual benefits of governmental financial assistance and tax omission due to their small-scale production. The adoption of neoliberal economic policy during the early 1990s put handloom weavers under more difficulties as the Indian government started becoming lenient toward other important components of India's textile sector. Even though it helped in promoting healthy competition with different sections of India's textile sectors, it also pushed handloom weavers toward the vulnerabilities associated with the market economy and the ill effects of the process of commercialization and globalization. Hence, product diversification and technological upgradation became one of the most common survival strategies for handloom weavers across the country.

Chapter 3

The Social and Religious Life of Handloom Weavers in Begampur Region

Due to its relative distance from Kolkata, Begampur has remained a serene rural town nestled away from the urban bustle. It has been home to generations of handloom weavers who have crafted textiles with unmatched skill and dedication. Handloom weaving is not merely a vocation in Begampur. It is also a way of life. The weavers here don't just create fabrics; they craft narratives that are etched with the threads of culture, heritage, and identity.

With the rhythmic clatter of looms, the interplay of colorful threads, and the intricate patterns emerging from skilled hands, Begampur as a place also provides a captivating tapestry that weaves together the social and the religious lives of handloom weavers of this region. Beyond the looms and the threads, the weavers' lives of this region are a fascinating mosaic of social interactions and religious practices that have evolved over centuries. The cultural heritage of Begampur presents a blend of various influences, including Hindu, Muslim, and British. As a result, the religious sentiment, too, finds its profound expression in the lives of these weavers. Their faith transcends the boundaries of religious diversity and weaves a tapestry of spirituality that is as vibrant as the threads they work with. The region celebrates numerous festivals, including Durga Puja, Eid, and Christmas, reflecting its diverse population. The cuisine of Begampur is also a fusion of flavors, with Mughlai and Bengali dishes coexisting harmoniously.

Therefore, in this chapter, I embark on a journey to explore the intricate threads of the social and religious life that define the existence of these master craftsmen of Begampur region in West Bengal. In this exploration, I first delve into one of the core aspects of the social life of the handloom weavers in Begampur region which includes a description of their ethnic origin and prolonged religious cohabitation. After that, I meticulously explore some of the primary social institutions such as family, marriage, and kinship in terms of the roles and functions of these primary institutions in the sustenance of the social and economic existence of these handloom weavers in Begampur region. Other than studying the types, roles, and functions of these primary institutions I also try to explain the interrelationships, such as how the roles, statuses, and familial structures interlace to form the foundation of their unique community life. Then I will try to provide a detailed description of the life-cycle rituals of the handloom weavers of Begampur region, especially concerning "birth," "marriage," and "death" rituals as they reflect some of their unique identity, beliefs, and practices as a group. Meanwhile, I shall venture into the sacred realm of the major religious ceremonies and festivals observed by the handloom weavers of Begampur region as well, seeking to understand how these beliefs shape their daily lives, their artistry, and their collective identity.

ETHNIC ORIGIN AND RELIGIOUS COHABITATION

Tanti or *Tantubay* in general are believed to be a functional occupational group (Risley 1981, 295) found across different states in India. The designation of the term *Tanti* was based more on their occupation rather than on any particular beliefs or group identity, due to which the concentration of this community is not uniform across all the states. The greatest concentration is believed to be in the states of Gujarat, Maharashtra, Jharkhand, Bihar, Uttar Pradesh, West Bengal, Assam, and Odisha. Therefore, it is almost impossible to trace any uniform ethnic origin of this particular community.

Nonetheless, the majority of *Tantis* in West Bengal follow Hinduism as most of them are born and brought up amid Hindu religious beliefs and practices. Hindu religious scriptures offer three probable theories regarding the origin of *Tanti* as a caste group. The first theory projects *Tantis* to be the descendants of Shiva Das or Ghama Das and his wife Kusbati. Shiva Das was believed to have been born from the sweat (*gham*) that fell from Lord Shiva while he was dancing. Meanwhile, his wife Kusbati was created by the Lord Shiva from the blade of *Kusa* grass. Shiva Das and his wife had four sons, namely Balaram, Uddhab, Purandar, and Madhukar who were the ancestors of four sub-castes bearing the same names. The second theory believed the *Tanti* to be the offspring of Manibandha (the father) and Manikar (the mother). Meanwhile, the third theory subscribes to the view that *Tanti* along with all the artisanal castes were believed to have begotten with the union of Sudra woman and celestial artificer Viswakarma (Risley 1981, 311). However, due to the prolonged cohabitation of Hindu and Muslim religious communities in Bengal, the occurrence of Muslim *Tanti* in West Bengal is not that uncommon either. Jola, Momin, and Ansaris are believed to be the most common sects of Muslim weavers.

Again, *Tanti* as a caste group in Bengal historically had many internal divisions or subgroups such as Ashwini, Bolorami, Purandari, Madhukari, Kanajia, Tiruthia, Kundu, Gala, and Matia. However, there was no particular distribution pattern of these subgroups across Bengal, except for the fact that Aswini *Tanti* who claim to be the original stock and originator of five subordinate endogamous groups deriving their names from their localities, were most commonly found in the western part of Bengal. The women of this group do not wear nose rings, and this is regarded as a mark of social distinction. Similarly, Bara-Bhagiya or Jhampaniya and Chhota-Bhagiya were most frequently found *Tanti* subcaste in the eastern part of Bengal. Of these two subcastes, Bara-Bhagiya derives their name from *jhampan* or sedan chair in which the bridegroom sits when going to fetch the bride. This group in general assumed the title of Basak which otherwise was taken up by either rich people or cloth merchants. The relatively less frequent Chhota-Bhagiya on the other hand contained *Kayasthas*, who were expelled from their caste for becoming weavers (Risley 1891, 296). Titles such as Jachandar (appraiser), Mukhim (supervisor), Dalal (broker), and Sardar (head of group) which were assumed while working for the East India Company are still quite common among weaver caste groups.

Obviously, weavers in Begampur, because of their location in West Bengal (i.e., western part of the then undivided Bengal), trace their origin from Aswini *Tanti*. Generally, the *Tantis* of Begampur use titles such as Bhar, Laha, Guin, Das, and Kundu. Moreover, Begampur presents quite a similar picture in terms of religious cohabitation (see figure 3.1). The census data of

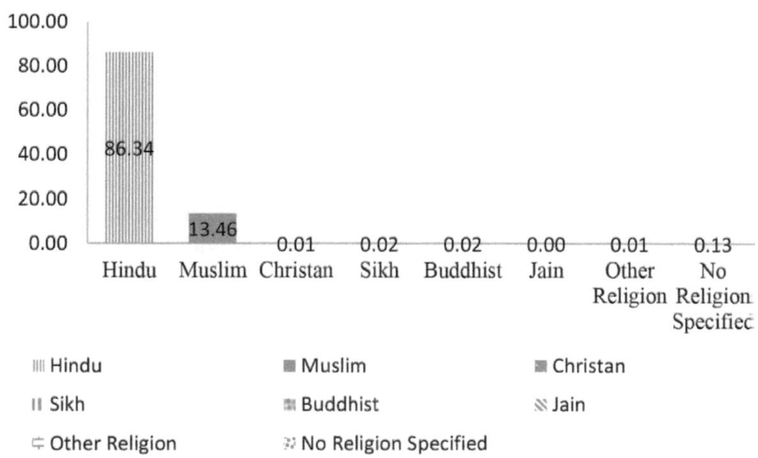

Figure 3.1 Distribution of Total Population in Begampur Region in Terms of Religion.
Source: Census of India, 2011

2011 shows that 86.34 percent of the total population in Begampur region has reported themselves to be Hindus, meanwhile 13.46 percent claim themselves as Muslims. Interestingly, 0.13 percent of the total population also reported of their non-alliance with any sort of religious belief. The proportion of Sikh, Buddhist, and Christians in the total population is quite negligible, that is, 0.02, 0.02, and 0.01 percent, respectively. Data also shows that there is no Jain population in Begampur region.

MARRIAGE

Historically, *Tantis* were known for marrying their daughter before the attainment of puberty (Risley 1891, 297). However, there were exceptions as well, especially in the cases of poor artisan families who couldn't afford the cost of marriage. Compared to the entire population in general, the handloom weavers of Begampur region usually marry at an early age. But they certainly don't follow the customary rule of marrying the daughter before the attainment of puberty. Nor do the male members marry before the attainment of adulthood. However, there is a prominent disparity in terms of their age at marriage in the case of weavers caste female members compared to their male counterparts. Due to either poor economic conditions or most importantly to avoid legal complications, the female members usually marry within the age group "15–19." In comparison, the male members marry between twenty and twenty-four years of age. The weaver caste population of Begampur region shows that there is a much higher number of married people (59.95%) in comparison to the number of unmarried (34.05%) (see figure 3.2). Again, 60.97 percent of those married individuals are men and 58.96 percent are women, and 38.04 percent and 30.18 percent of the total unmarried population are men and women, respectively (Banerjee 2014, 32). The unmarried population usually contains a large chunk of juveniles who haven't attained adulthood or those male individuals who don't have the economic means to withstand the economic needs of starting a family.

Much like any other caste-based occupational group handloom weavers of Begampur region generally followed the rule of group endogamy[1] and clan exogamy.[2] Historically, both the endogamous and exogamous rules of marriage, in general, were followed precisely to maintain social and cultural cohesion and avoid sexual anarchy. Inter-caste, inter-creed, or inter-community marriages were avoided as they present possibilities of jeopardizing any community's social and cultural homogeneity. However, the reason behind the emergence of such practices in Begampur region is much more economic than cultural. The weaver caste individuals follow the rule of group endogamy because it allows them to have partners who are quite accustomed to their trade and the skill sets of each and every responsibility, they are likely

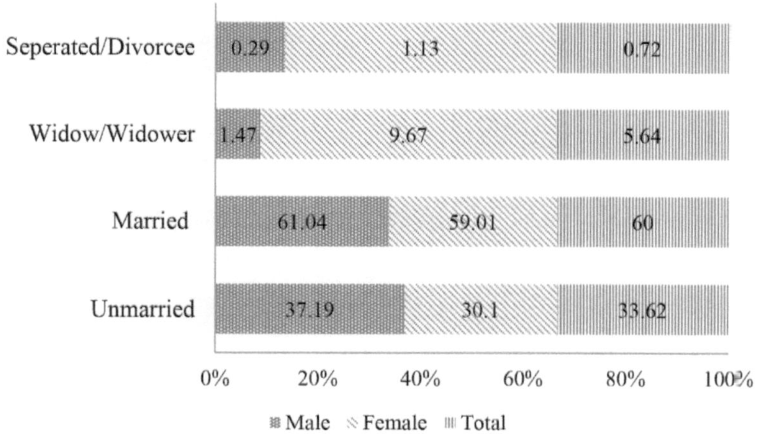

Figure 3.2 Distribution of Studied Population in terms of Marital Status. *Source*: Author's Photo

to share as a spouse in the future. Meanwhile, the rule of clan exogamy is followed as it allows them to expand their network of kindred. Eventually, this enhances their social capital and subsequently helps these handloom weavers in pursuing their economic interests. Nonetheless, that doesn't mean that no cases of inter-group marriage have been reported in Begampur. In recent years, along with occupational shift among the handloom weavers of the Begampur region, instances of inter-group or inter-caste marriages have grown considerably. Perhaps released from the social obligation of finding a suitable match from their own sects, the younger generation has started marrying outside their own caste, group, or community.

Historically, weaver caste families taking bride prices have been reported (Risley 1891), which can be found in many matrilineal societies. But Begampur presents a completely different scenario in this regard. Instead of taking bride price, weavers caste parents of Begampur region nowadays offer dowry to the family members of the groom. Perhaps this inclination toward providing dowry has emerged due to a number of factors such as—(i) social and ritual influence of other inhabiting caste groups, (ii) shift toward patrilineality, and (iii) more so as a social means of deeming more respectable status within their own society.

Meanwhile, marital distance and the frequency of occurrences in Begampur present quite an interesting scenario (see figure 3.3). This flow diagram has been prepared from genealogical analysis which I have collected during the course of the prolonged fieldwork. It reveals that handloom weavers of the Begampur region have preferred having their spouses from within their own village. Marked by the relatively darker shade of blue circle right at the center

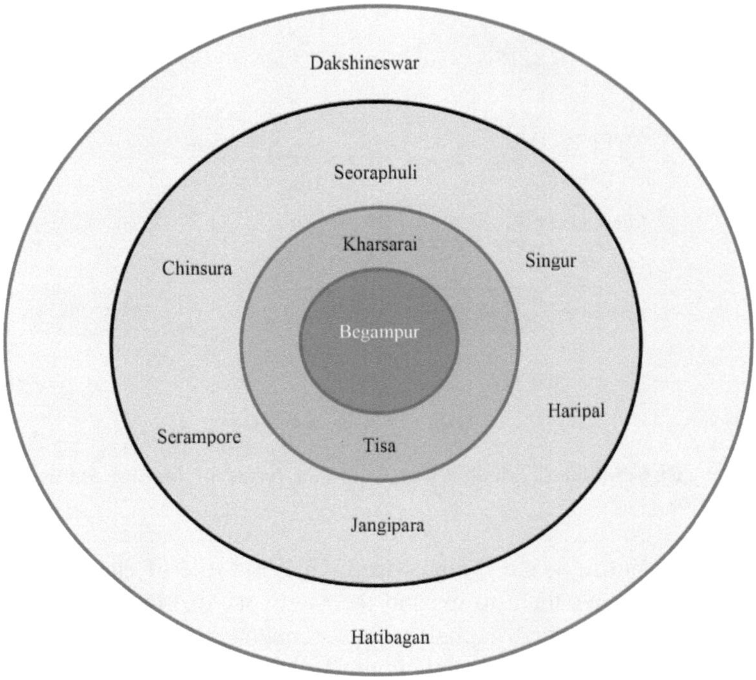

Figure 3.3 Marital Distance and Their Frequency of Occurrences. *Source*: Author's Photo

it denotes that the frequency of such cases has been highest across generations. However, it must be mentioned that the case of choosing their partners from their own village is much higher in the ascending generations compared to the descending ones. This frequency in the descending generation has decreased comparatively. Besides, there are instances of weaver caste people choosing spouses from surrounding villages like Kharsarai and Tisa, situated just on the outskirts of Begampur. Marked by a relatively lighter shade of blue circle in the diagram this was quite popular practice among the members of ascending generations. Perhaps the second most preferred choice. However, this certainly doesn't mean that the weavers of this region have taken an apprehensive approach in terms of choosing their partners from relatively distant places and in the process establishing kinship ties that had the possibility of helping them in the future. Marked by a far lighter shade of blue circle in the diagram, this perhaps is the third most preferred choice. This is relatively more common among relatively younger members compared to their predecessors. There are instances where weaver caste people establish marital relationships with people living in relatively distant places such as Serampore, Seoraphuli, Chinsura, Singur, Haripal, and Jangipara. Finally, the instances of people choosing partners from far distant places are quite few and far between, because it has been marked by the lightest shade of blue circle right at the periphery of the diagram.

Furthermore, much like the rest of the world, monogamy is the most preferred form of marriage among the handloom weavers of Begampur region. Nonetheless, it must be mentioned that polygamy was historically permissible among the weaver caste in cases of proven barrenness of wives (Risley 1891, 298). However, no such instances were found in Begampur. Perhaps increased legal complications and fear of providing alimony have curved down the tendencies of polygamous marriages. My own observation regarding the weaver caste population of Begampur shows that 59.95 percent of the married population prefers monogamy. Their reasons are quite simple. Different tasks of handloom require a constant level of concentration throughout the day. Therefore, the maintenance of peaceful and a congenial domestic environment is of utmost importance to them for the successful execution of these tasks. Moreover, another reason behind this preference is that handloom weavers of the Begampur region observe Hinduism, and the Hindu Marriage Act doesn't allow them to have multiple partners at the same point in time. This act allows a married person to marry another individual in case of death or divorce from their previous partner only. Both the mentioned cases are quite rarely found among the handloom weavers of Begampur. Only 5.99 percent of the weaver caste population reported being either widows or widowers, of which 0.97 percent are men and 10.84 percent are women. And the rate of divorce is almost negligible among the weaver caste population of this region.

FAMILY

Needless to say, the weaver caste society of Begampur region is patrilineal in nature which follows the patrilineal rule of descent.[3] Historically, the traits and characteristics of typical weaver caste families of this region were quite similar to those of rural agricultural households, in which male members held the key economic roles leaving unpaid activities for their women and children. Handloom weavers used to live and meet their livelihood in patrilineal joint families,[4] which much like in agriculture demanded different household members to collaborate for a common cause contributing to the pooling of resources to meet the basic needs such as housing, food, and education for all the members. However, due to the growing mechanization within the handloom weaving industry of the Begampur region and the emergence of other lucrative livelihood sources, this region has witnessed a massive turnaround. Supporting the needs of a huge pool of family members from handlooms became impossible due to meager opportunities for individual growth, and stagnancy in the wage and earnings. As a result, patrilineal joint families of this region started breaking down along with the occupational shift of adult male members. Currently, patrilocal nuclear families[5] are the most prevalent form of family that can be found among the weaver caste community of Begampur region. Theoretically, this is not conducive to carrying out a series of activities in handloom cloth production. But these patrilocal nuclear families possess a typical character that is perhaps unique to Begampur only. Despite becoming separate along with the separation of the hearth, the adult male members of the nuclear families along with their wives and children continue to live within the same household, where their wives and children take active part in different activities of handloom cloth production.

The family units of the handloom weavers in the Begampur region are not much different in terms of their role, function, and importance. Weaver families of this region much like any other found across the globe (Dykeman 2019) act as the first and most influential agents of socialization. At least during the initial stages, the weaver caste toddlers get to learn their roles as responsible citizens and most importantly as members of an artisan community from their family members. During this particular stage, the adult family members teach their children basic values, norms, and behaviors necessary for functioning in society. Besides, introduction to a broader social network, which connects them with members of extended family, friends, and the community, takes place through family members. Invariably this leads to accumulation of social capital in the form of familiarity and interaction fostered through social skills, cooperation, and a sense of belonging to a larger social fabric. Needless to say, the weaver caste family is also responsible for providing care and nurturing to children, the elderly, and vulnerable family members, which are prerequisites of physical and emotional well-being, fostering healthy development. Hence, they offer comfort, love, and understanding during times of joy, sadness, and crisis. It helps them navigate through life's challenges, maintain mental health, and build strong relationships outside the family (Fishel 2018).

Weaver caste families also instill social norms and values, promoting moral and ethical behavior within the household. Eventually, this helps in maintaining order, discipline, and a sense of responsibility, contributing to a harmonious and law-abiding society by teaching individuals to respect rules and norms. But, most importantly, weaver caste families of Begampur region play a very crucial role in transmitting cultural values, traditions, and practices (Mandara et al. 2009). Weaving skills are often passed down from one generation to the next, ensuring the preservation of traditions and techniques. Families serve as both a source of emotional support and a training ground for the next generation of weavers. The skills and knowledge of handloom weaving are learned within the family environment, which ultimately helps in the preservation of their identity and heritage, ensuring continuity and cohesion. Last but not least, weaver caste families often serve as the primary economic unit in the pooling of resources to meet basic needs such as housing, food, and education. Family members of weaver caste do collaborate and tend to engage almost all the household members in various pre- and post-loom activities to provide financial stability and ensure that essential resources are available. The role of every household member in the weaving process is distinct.

KINSHIP

Almost all the inhabitants in Begampur use Bengali as their native language. Understandably weavers of Begampur region in their daily lives depict some of the core characteristics of Bengali customs and culture, where they show affection and warmth toward their siblings, family members, kinsmen, and neighbors, respect the elderly, and often live within a close-knit homestead-based joint family environment centering on shared common resources. The Bengali kinship system, unlike the Eskimo[6] or Hawaiian[7] system, is much more complex and well-known for providing equal emphasis to both patrilineal and matrilineal kinsmen at the same point in time.

In terms of kinship behavior, these Bengali-speaking handloom weavers of Begampur region show a prevalence of avoidance,[8] joking-relationship,[9] teknonymy,[10] and avanculate.[11] Traditionally, the weaver caste married male members avoided their elder sister-in-law and mother-in-laws, and the weaver caste married female members avoided their father-in-laws and husband's elder brother. The female members especially tend to avoid taking the name of their father-in-law, husband, and husband's elder brother. These norms were followed as a sign of reverence for the patriarchal system. However, such practices are fading away fast with the changing dynamics of education and occupation in this region. However, the practice of maintaining a fun-filled relationship with the wife's/husband's younger brothers/sisters still holds its forte that depicts the same warmth and affection. Despite being more inclined toward the patriarchy, the society of handloom weavers still shows the remnants of its past where it used to be matrilineal in nature in the much earlier period. The practice of avanculate where the maternal uncle performs the ceremony of first feeding of cereals is one of the prominent examples.

Interestingly Bengali-speaking handloom weavers of Begampur region often make a distinction between consanguineal[12] (*atmiya*) and affinal[13] (*kutum*) kinsmen. The characteristics of the Bengali kinship system include features such as (i) the use of kinship names for the elderly instead of using the actual name as a sign of respect and (ii) the use of separate denotative[14] kinship names for almost all the kinsmen belonging to ascending generation except in the cases of father's elder and younger brother and sister and mother's elder and younger sister and brothers where classificatory kinship name is used. Generally, each male and the female members of both father's and mother's generation are distinguished from one another based on age and gender (see table 3.1). Moreover, one gets to see the lumping together of siblings along with cross-cousin and parallel cousins in the ego's generation and the use of classificatory[15] kinship names for them. Members of this generation are distinguished based on age and gender only. Again, the use of denotative kinship terms in

Table 3.1 Generation-Wise List of Kinship Terms in Begampur

Generation	*Kinship Category*	*Kinship Name*	*Type of the Terms*
2nd Ascending Generation	Father's Father	Thakurda	Denotative
	Father's Mother	*Thakurma*	Denotative
	Mother's Father	*Dadamosai/Dadu*	Denotative
	Mother's Mother	*Didima*	Denotative
1st Ascending Generation	Father	*Baba*	Denotative
	Mother	*Ma*	Denotative
	Father's Elder Brother	*Jetha/Jethu*	Denotative
	Father's Elder Brother's Wife	*Jethima*	Denotative
	Father's Younger Brother	*Kaka/Kaku*	Denotative
	Father's Younger Brother's Wife	*Kakima*	Denotative
	Father's Sister	*Pisi*	Classificatory
	Father's Sister's Husband	*Pisemosai*	Classificatory
	Mother's Brother	*Mama*	Classificatory
	Mother's Brother's Wife	*Mamima*	Classificatory
	Mother's Sister	*Masi*	Classificatory
	Mother's Sister's Husband	*Meso*	Classificatory
'0'/Ego's Generation	Elder Brother	*Dada*	Classificatory
	Younger Brother	*Bhai*	Classificatory
	Elder Sister	*Didi*	Classificatory
	Younger Sister	*Bon*	Classificatory
1st Descending Generation	Son	*Chele*	Denotative
	Daughter	*Meye*	Denotative
	Bother's Son	*Bhaipo*	Classificatory
	Brother's Daughter	*Bhaijhi*	Classificatory
	Sister's Son	*Bonpo*	Classificatory
	Sister's Daughter	*Bonjhi*	Classificatory
2nd Descending Generation	Grandson	*Nati*	Classificatory
	Grand-daughter	*Natni*	Classificatory

Source: Author.

the first descending generation is restricted to kinship categories such as son and daughter only. Even though there are specific kinship terms in the cases of the rest of the kinship categories of this particular generation, their usage is more or less classificatory in nature. The second descending generation shows the prevalence of the use of classificatory kinship terms for kinship categories such as grand-son and grand-daughter which are simultaneously used for an individual's son's and daughter's son/daughter.

Therefore, characteristically the kinship system in Begampur is much closer to the Sudanese[16] system in terms of its emphasis on each separate category of kinsmen. However, these two systems are not exactly identical in terms of their characteristics. In the kinship system prevalent in Begampur, except for the siblings, the brothers and sisters are not distinguished from each other as found in the Sudanese system. Rather from the analysis of kinship behavior and terms it would not be wrong to assume that the kinship system of this region (at least in its present form) is slightly inclined toward a patriarchal system. Moreover, along with a change in family structure, the importance of certain kinsmen certainly has reduced a way bit. This certainly may also have a certain economic correlation.

LIFECYCLE RITUALS

Birth

In the yesteryears, the weaver caste pregnant women used to deliver their children at their matrilineal homes under *Dhaima*'s supervision. Traditionally, in those days, the mother and the newborn baby used to stay with their matrilineal family after the child's birth. Sometimes the length of this stay used to be as long as six months. However, nowadays instances of childbirth at home have become almost negligible. Depending upon the availability of economic resources of the prospective father and their family members most of the delivery takes place in nearby government hospitals or private nursing homes. Again, depending upon the complexity involved with pregnancy, childbirth either takes place in the form of cesarean delivery under the supervision of a practicing medical doctor or in the form of normal delivery under the supervision of a certified nurse. The general norm of mother and newborn staying with the maternal family is also diminishing fast.

Nowadays, in the cases of childbirth, weaver caste family members observe a pollution period of twenty-one days. During this entire period, the mother and the newborn are often kept in a separate room which is called *antur-ghar*. Usually, neither the mother nor the newborn comes out of this room during this entire period. Entry to this room is often restricted. Only family members are allowed to enter this room who generally go in with a supply of food and clean clothes. Outsiders are often prohibited. This serves as both a safety measure for mother and newborn and as a form of social taboo as well. The rigidity regarding such taboo nonetheless is also fading gradually as many kin members do visit the household just to see the newborn. In such cases, kin members are often requested to follow standard safety measures of making themselves clean or wearing hygienic clothes, etc.

During this twenty-one-day pollution period, the family members of newborns are not prohibited from taking any particular kind of food item. They can even consume nonvegetarian foods. But the general norm is to cook and consume a simple menu consisting of rice/roti, dal, and curry. However, the mothers of the newborn are often asked to restrain themselves from consuming wet food, citrus fruits, and sweets. Instead, the mother is often provided dry and nutritious food items such as flaked rice, puffed rice, dal, and curry. This is often followed as a precautionary measure so that the mother of the newborn can physically recover fast from the hassles of child delivery.

However, the twenty-one-day-pollution period following a child's birth comes with certain other social restrictions and prohibitions. For example, the patrilineal family members of the newborn especially are often prohibited from participating in any kind of ritual and worship during these entire twenty-one days. Moreover, restrictions are imposed on family members from using comb, oil, and shampoo. Trimming of hair, shaving of beard or mustache, and clipping of nails are also prohibited.

On the twenty-second day, the mother and newborn come out of *antur-ghar* in the presence of a priest (*Brahmin*) and barber (*Napit*). A purificatory ritual marking the end of this pollution period is performed subsequently. This ritual takes place at the *Monasha-than* of household where both the mother and newborn take baths with clean water and wear new clothes. The old used clothes are often abandoned away from their settlement. After which the priest chants the hymns and the barber clips the nail.

Traditionally, the naming of a child used to be a big thing in a weaver caste household which used to be performed right at the end of the pollution period. Often the elderly members of the household used to play a key role in this regard. However, with the advent of the birth-registry system, no such instances are found among the weaver caste population in the Begampur region. Nowadays names of the children are decided in haste, that is, within three to four days of childbirth as part of the documentary procedure to be submitted to the requisite authorities for the generation of birth certificates. Usually, the father and mother finalize the official name meanwhile the child continues to get several other names from other family members in due course.

The ceremony of the first feeding of cereals or *anyaprashan* is performed in the sixth month in the case of a newborn baby boy and in the seventh month in the case of a newborn baby girl. This ceremony is often arranged by the patrilineal family members of the newborn. A ritualistic ceremony is arranged as a symbolic gesture of offering the cereals for the first time. The priest comes and looks after the proceedings of this entire ceremony. But most importantly the maternal uncle of the newborn plays a crucial role as he feeds the newborn with his own hand. In the absence of the maternal uncle, the grandparent performs the role. A feast is arranged on the day; depending upon the economic resources, neighbors and close kin members are invited who shower their blessing upon the newborn. In some cases, the maternal uncle or the grandparent of the newborn arrange such a separate small ceremony in their own house as well.

Marriage

Traditionally, "marriage by negotiation" was and still is the most prevalent method of acquiring mates among the weaver caste population in Begampur region. However, growing instances of "love marriages" have also been reported. Group endogamy and clan exogamy have been a norm that has been followed for a long period of time. And, the weaver caste population of this region was no exception to this rule. However, due to the non-availability of suitable partners in and around Begampur, the rule of clan exogamy hasn't been followed with such rigidity. Instead, cases of people marrying within their own clan members have been found.

Traditionally, negotiation is the first step of marriage where often professional negotiators play a crucial role of being a mediator between the two families. The negotiator first provides the information of the prospective bride and groom to their respective families. After which the elderly family members of the prospective groom approach the family members of the prospective bride.

First, the elderly family members including the parents and grandparents of the prospective groom visit the house of the prospective bride. A small token of snacks tea and sweets are given to these members. While trying to gauge the compatibility of the prospective bride and the groom the members of the two families sit together and mingle with one another. When the prospective bride arrives at this gathering, she is often asked questions about her willingness, and knowledge about managing a family, cooking, and other household chores. Upon receiving a positive response from the elderly family members of the prospective groom, the elderly family members of the prospective bride give a return visit. Here also the elderly members including the parents of the prospective groom and other close relatives are welcomed similarly. They are offered snacks, tea, and sweets. Here also much similar to the case of the prospective bride, the prospective groom is often asked questions about his occupation, hobbies, habits, and extracurriculars amid a similar family gathering. With satisfaction from both parties in the first phase, this string of visits is extended further to the second stage.

In the second stage, the elderly family members of the prospective groom along with the prospective groom himself visit the house of the prospective groom. Here, the members of the two families sit together to fix the date and time of marriage. During such meetings, many mundane but important elements like gifts and offerings to be received from both the end and the number of people attending the ceremonial meal in the two respective households are decided. Apart from these a small homely blessing ceremony of the prospective bride is arranged where the elderly family members of the prospective groom offer their blessing as a token of fixation of marriage (*paka-dekha*). The elderly family members of the prospective bride similarly shower their blessing upon the prospective groom while they visit the house of the prospective groom. However, with the growing tendencies of love marriages and court marriages, these rituals are gradually diminishing. Nowadays even in the case of marriage by negotiation or arranged marriages, the custom of offering a blessing as part of the fixation of marriage is not being followed. Instead, the blessing ceremony is often arranged on the day of marriage.

The respective friends, relatives, and close kin members of the prospective bride and the groom subsequently arrange a last bachelor meal (*aaiburobhat*) one after another. The prospective bride and the groom continue to attend such ceremonial meals and receive gifts until a day before the marriage when the ritualistic ceremony of marriage starts with the arrangement of such ceremonial last bachelor meal (*aaiburobhat*) in the two respective houses, that is, in the households of the prospective bride and groom. A ceremonial feast is arranged on the occasions when friends, close relatives, and neighbours are invited who sit and eat together with the prospective bride and groom.

The ceremony of "smearing of turmeric on the body" (*gayehalud*) takes place in both households on the day of marriage. First, a group of married women brings water from the nearby pond. Then the groom stands over a *janta* and the group of married women goes around him with water filled in the metal pot while the priest chants the hymn. After which a paste of oil and turmeric is smeared over the face and the body of the groom and bathed with water brought in the metal pot. The same paste of oil and turmeric is then carried to the house of the bride along with fish and sweets which are considered holy according to the Bengali belief system. Then the paste is applied over the face and body of the bride much similar to the case of the groom. After which she is bathed with water.

Depending upon the *lagna* (interval between which marriage is ought to take place) and distance between the two households the groom, the priest, and barber along with a few of his close friends start the journey toward the bride's house. A marriage procession including the family members, relatives, and neighbors follows the groom. Most of the weavers caste marriages take place either in the evening or late in the night. When the groom's carriage reaches the bride's house the mother of the bride along with other elderly female members welcomes the bride with a ceremony called *boron* by providing him with an *aarti*, a drink, and sweets. The groom is then taken inside the household where he is asked to sit in a place specially made for the groom. Meanwhile, the priest and the barber (*Napit*) along with their counterparts in the bride's household look after the preparation of marriage. This provides an opportunity for those who haven't showered their blessing upon the groom already.

After all of these, the groom is taken to the place of marriage (*chadnatala*). After a while, the bride also comes and joins the ritual. Initially, the barber plays the key role right at the beginning. The symbolic ritual of *subhodristi* (holy first site) takes place under his supervision. During this ritual, the bride sits over a wooden plank covering her face with a pair of betel leaves. The sitting bride is then carried to the place of marriage (*chadnatala*) by the bothers and bother-in-laws. The bride sitting over a wooden plank is then taken around the groom seven times. After which they exchange sites with one another. This ritual is often followed by the ritual of exchanging garlands (*malabodol*) between the bride and groom. The relatives and the kinsmen holding the sitting bride intentionally raise the wooden plank higher to make the task of exchanging the garlands for the groom as much more difficult as possible. Similarly, the friends and relatives lift the otherwise standing groom in their arms to make the task of exchanging garland difficult for the bride. During the entire episode often a friendly banter is exchanged between the members of two households. This entire episode is often projected as a symbolic representation of whether the bride or the groom would eventually get the upper hand during the course of married life. But the whole thing is done in a lighthearted manner.

With the completion of such rituals, the priest takes over the responsibility for the rest of the rituals involving marriage. First, the bride and groom are asked to sit in front of a *hom-kunda* (a place of holy fire) where the bride sits on the left and the groom sits on the right side-by-side. The priest and the father of the bride also sit along with the bride and groom, at the two ends. The priest ties a knot (*gantchora*) with the cloth of both the bride and the groom. While chanting hymns the priest usually asks the father of the bride to perform the ritual of handing over of the bride (*sampradana*). In case of the absence of the father of the bride, *sampradan* is often performed by any of the elderly patrilineal kin members like a grandparent or uncle. During the *panigrahan* (receiving of the bride's hand in marriage) the right hand of the bride is placed over the right hand of the groom and then betel leaf, flowers, and garland are placed over both the hands. The priest again chants a series of hymns. Thereafter, the priest performs a *yajna*[17] where the bride and the groom take a vow to follow the norms of being married to one another as per the instruction of the priest. During the course, the groom adorns the hands of the bride with *sankha* (conch-shell bangle), pola (bangle of red-coral), and *noya* (iron bangle). Then the priest asks the bride and groom to stand and go around the holy fire seven times (*sat-pak*) as part of making their vow everlasting, that is, believed to be for at least seven afterlives. This ceremony is followed by a ritual called *sindur-dan* where the groom applies vermillion over the hair comb of the bride with the help of *kunke* (rice measuring utensil). This marks the completion of the marriage.

Then friends and relatives take part in the grand meal arranged by the family members of the bride. The bride and the groom who otherwise are on a fast for the entire day now take food after their marriage. Most of the groom's relatives and kin members who went to attend the marriage ceremony return to their respective houses on that very night after the meal. The bride and groom are then taken to a separate room called *basar-ghar*. Along with the bride and groom, several groom's friends and young relatives of the bride sit together for the entire night. They chat, sing, and spend the entire night without falling asleep.

A blessing ceremony for the departing bride and groom is arranged on the next morning. Here most of the elderly family members bless the bride and groom together and wish them happiness and prosperity for their upcoming married life. With the completion of this ritual, the groom's party (*bor-jatri*) resumes their journey back to the groom's house along with the bride and groom. Upon reaching the groom's house the bride and groom are first welcomed (*boron-kora*) with an *aarati*. A similar blessing ceremony for the newly married bride and groom is arranged in the groom's house as well. Here the kin members, relatives, and neighbors bless and wish them well for their upcoming married life. The newlywed bride especially receives a lot of gifts during this blessing ceremony. Then the bride and the groom are taken to two separate rooms where both take a bath and change their clothes put on during marriage. A ritual called *kalratri* is followed for the rest of the day and at night where the bride and groom are not allowed to see or talk to each other.

The rituals of *bhat-kapor* and *boubhat* are arranged on the next day afternoon. During the *bhat-kapor* ritual, the groom hands over a saree and food item kept in a brass plate to the newlywed bride and takes a vow that he takes the responsibility of providing for the rest of their life. During *boubhat* the newlywed bride cooks *payas* (traditional rice pudding) in brass utensils brought in from his ancestral home and serves it to kinsmen and relatives. This ritual is considered symbolically very important as it epitomizes elements of social sanction by these groups. A grand celebratory feast is arranged on the night when the bride's party (*kone-jatri*) provides a return visit along with their close relative and kinsmen. Food and drinks are offered to these guests. At the end of this meal bride's relatives and kinsmen return to their home. Then the bride and the groom spend the first night together over a *phulosojja* (bed decorated by petals of flowers). On the eighth day after the wedding, both the couples go to the bride's house and stay there for a day. During this time, the knot which was tied on the wedding day is undone which marks the official ending of the wedding ceremony.

Death

The close relatives and kinsmen are informed first in case of death among the weaver caste population. The family members of the deceased break this information. The body of the deceased is kept over a handmade bamboo frame near the courtyard just beside the *Monasha-than*. Generally, the eye of the deceased is covered with Tulsi leaves and then *chandan* is applied to the forehead. If the deceased person is a married male, then the *sankha* (conch-shell bangle), *pola* (bangle of red-coral), and *noya* (iron bangle) on both the hands of his wife are broken. In case the deceased person is a married female then *sankha* (conch-shell bangle), *pola* (bangle of red-coral), and *noya* (iron bangle) on hands are taken off, but vermillion (*sindur*) and lac-dye (*aalta*) are applied on the head comb and feet, respectively. The entire body is then covered with white loin cloth.

The body of the deceased is then lifted on the shoulders by close consanguineal kin members (i.e., usually the son, cases of other close relatives have also been reported in the case of absent son) and carried to the nearby crematorium. Nowadays the bodies of the deceased are also taken to distant crematoriums as well as in places such as Srerampore and Bhadrakali. Often small vehicle suitable for carrying the body of the deceased along with a few other men is arranged for the purpose. A small procession including close male relatives and neighbors follows the group carrying the deceased. On their way to the crematorium, these relatives and family members often throw *khoi* (puffed rice), *batashas* (aerated sugar candies), and coins on the street.

Upon reaching the crematorium, first, the loin cloth placed over the body of the deceased is taken off and *ghee* (butter) is applied over the entire body. And then usually the eldest son performs the ritual of *mukhaagni* (providing fire to the deceased). Again, if the deceased doesn't have a son, then the daughter or the grandson can also perform this ritual as well. The body is then placed over a *chita* (funeral pyre). The *Dom*[18] then sets fire and completes the process of cremation.

The Dom then hands over the cremated ash remains to son/s or close relatives of the deceased. The cremated ash remains are then smeared with the soil of river Ganga and then immersed into river Ganga. All the people then take a bath in the river. The son/s or the person performing the ritual of *mukhagni* abandons their clothes put on during this entire episode and wears new loin cloth only. This is known as *kacha-golai-kora.*

Traditionally, the weaver caste people in the Begampur region used to observe a pollution period of thirty days in the event of death. But, nowadays, looking at the hazards of striking a balance between social life and following taboos and restrictions associated with death pollution, this has been curtailed down to twelve to fifteen days. During the course of this entire pollution period, several restrictions are imposed on the blood relatives of the deceased including the sons. These restrictions include a prohibition on consuming nonvegetarian food items, using oil, shampoo, and soap, combing hair, clipping nails, shaving, and trimming. Often a simple vegetarian meal is cooked for the rest of the family members' meanwhile, the son/s observe far greater restrictions. They are prohibited from taking this simple meal as well. For breakfast and dinner, they are permitted to take fruits, milk, and puffed rice only and even had to cook their separate lunch (*hobbishi*) in an earthen pot (*sora*) with the help of jute woods.

On the eleventh day, the priest takes the sons to a nearby bathing *ghaat* and performs a ritual called *ekadosha.* On the fifteenth day, both the priest and the barber come and begin the purification ceremony involving all the family members. During this ceremony, all the family members clip their nails, a few trim their hair after which they take a bath in the bathing *ghaat.* The sons shave their head hair, mustache, and beard. All the family members abandon their old clothes and wear clothes brought in by their affinal kinsmen. On the next day morning, the ceremony of *shradhya-shanti* is arranged. The sons who are on a fast along with two priests take part in the ceremony of *pinda-daan* (giving charity to the body of the deceased). With the completion of these rituals, a small customary meal arrangement is arranged for the feeding of the *Brahmins* including those officiating priests. On the night another ceremonial meal (*niyom-bhongo*) is arranged as an epitome of the resumption of normal social life to which friends, relatives, and neighbors are invited. Nonvegetarian food is served and consumed on the day.

RELIGIOUS CEREMONIES AND FESTIVALS

The weaver caste population in Begampur region generally observes most of the common Bengali religious ceremonies and festivals (see table 3.2). First and foremost, *Poila-Boisakh* or *Noboborsho* is one of the first festivals according to the Bengali calendar. This festival is celebrated in the month of *Boisakh* (April–May) on the occasion of Bengali New Year. It is often considered a joyous and auspicious occasion for the Bengalis in general and businessmen in particular. During this auspicious occasion, businessmen arrange Puja in their shops and invite customers, people visit the temple and seek blessing, friends and relatives visit each other's houses, buy and wear traditional attire, participate in processions, and enjoy various cultural programs and traditional Bengali food. Apart from having a profound religious significance and being one of the most important events in the Bengali calendar, this festival also plays a vital role in preserving and promoting the unique cultural heritage of the Bengali people. It brings the community together, fosters a sense of unity, and allows individuals to express their devotion and creativity in colorful and meaningful ways. The weaver caste people show no exception in this regard. Instead, because of their long association with the cloth-making business they see this auspicious occasion as an opportunity of expanding business.

Similarly, weaver caste mother-in-laws in Begampur region observe *Jamai-Shosti* in the month of *Joistha* (May–June) just like in rest of the West Bengal. Weaver caste mother-in-laws keep fast for the well-being of their son-in-law and invite them for a celebratory lunch. Both mother-in-law and son-in-law exchange gifts with one another.chapter

Rath Yatra, which is also known as the Chariot Festival is observed in the month of *Aasadh* (June–July). This festival is also considered to be one of the major ones among Hindus devoted to Lord Jagannath, an avatar of Lord Vishnu and his two siblings. It is a significant religious event in the state of West Bengal, particularly in Puri and Kolkata and their surroundings. It involves the grand procession of Lord Jagannath, Balabhadra, and Subhadra on elaborately decorated chariots. Devotees throng the streets to pull the chariots, seeking blessings and participating in this spectacular event. Devotees believe that pulling off the chariot brings peace, prosperity, and happiness. Even though this festival is not as prominent as can be found in places like Puri (in Odisha), Mahesh (in Serampore, Hooghly), Kolkata, and its surroundings, the weaver caste population do have their separate chariot in Begampur region. All the rituals and rites are observed in the same manner.

A few of the weavers do take part in *Jol-Yatra* which otherwise is a prevalent event among the Saivites. Because of their settlement near the temple of Lord Shiva at Tarkeswar, many devotees fetch holy water from Ganga near

Table 3.2 List of Religious Ceremonies and Festivals

Month	*Name of the Festival*	*Purpose*	*Participants*	*Proceedings*
Boisakh (April–May)	*Poila-Boisakh/ Noboborsho*	This festival is celebrated on the occasion of the very first day of Bengali calendar. Considered joyous and auspicious occasion for the Bengalis, businessmen in particular	All Bengali-speaking natives	(i) On this auspicious occasion people visit temple and seek blessing (ii) Friends and relatives visit each other's house (iii) Businessmen arrange *Puja* in their shops and invite customers (iv) People buy and wear new clothes
Joistha (May–June)	*Jaamai-Soshthi*	This festival is celebrated for the well-being of the son-in-laws	All married male and their mother-in-laws	(i) The mother-in-laws keep fast for the well-being of their son-in-law (ii) Son-in-laws are invited for celebratory lunch (iii) Both mother-in-law and son-in-law exchange gifts
Aashadh (June–July)	*Ratha-Yatra*	Also known as the Chariot Festival, this is considered to be one of the major one among Hindus devoted to Lord Jagannath, an avatar of Lord Vishnu and his two siblings. Devotees believe that pulling of chariot brings peace, prosperity, and happiness	Devotees of Lord Jagannath and his two siblings	(i) Devotees pull the rope of the chariot and chant *Jai-Jagannath*
Shrabon (July–August)	*Jol-Yatra*	Performed for the general well-being and blessing of Lord Shiva	Devotees of Lord Shiva	(i) Barefooted devotees take the holy water from river Ganga and carry it to the temple of Lord Shiva in Tarakeswar as their piece of offering (ii) The entire journey is done on foot by walking

Bhadro (August–September)	*Monosha Puja*	Performed for protection from snake bites	All the villagers	(i) The priest comes and performs a puja and a ceremonial offering at the *Monosha-than* of every household (ii) Often fruits, flowers, and incense sticks are offered (
	Janmastami	Observed as the birthday celebration of Lord Krishna	All the villagers	i) Devotees fast, sing devotional songs (ii) Vegetarian food is cooked and consumed during the observance
Aashwin (September–October)	*Durga-Puja*	The biggest Bengali festival. This 5-day-long festival is performed as an epitome of celebration of the victory of goddess Durga over demon *Mahisasura*, who along with her children comes down from Kailash to her maternal house and brings prosperity.	All the villagers	(i) Goddess Durga is collectively worshipped for 5 days in a number of Pandals (ii) Often the priest officiates the proceedings of puja rituals (iii) Often an animal sacrifice is made on the 3rd day (i.e., *Astami*) (iii) People buy and wear new clothes and visit the houses of relatives and friends (
	Laxmi Puja	Performed for the prosperity and well-being of the householders	In most of the households	i) The priest comes and performs a puja and a ceremonial offering at the *Thakurghar* of every household (ii) Often fruits, flower, and incense sticks are offered and *Laxmi-Panchali* is read on the occasion

(Continued)

Table 3.2 (Continued)

Month	*Name of the Festival*	*Purpose*	*Participants*	*Proceedings*
Kaartik (October–November)	*Kali-Puja*	Performed on an *Aamabashya* for the well-being and prosperity of the villagers	All the villagers	(i) Goddess Kali is collectively worshipped in a number of Pandals (ii) The priest looks after the ritual and offering (iii) Houses are decorated and lit with oil lamps, candles, or "diyas" (iv) All the family members gather around in the evening to burst crackers together (i) Elder sisters having younger male siblings arrange for a blessing ceremony and foods (
	Bhai-Phonta	Performed for the well-being and long-life of the brothers	All the sisters	ii) Meanwhile brothers provide gifts to their sisters
Agrohayan (November–December)	*Jagatdhatri Puja*	Performed for the well-being of householders	A few householders	(i) Goddess Jagatdhatri is worshipped in a few separate households (ii) The priest looks after the proceedings (iii) Often fruits, flowers, and incense sticks are offered
Poush (December–January)	*Tant-Viswakarma Puja*	Performed for the well-being and prosperity of the weavers	Every weaver household and all the villagers of Begampur	(i) The priest comes and worships the loom itself (ii) Often fruits, flowers, incense sticks *moya*, and *tiler-khaja* are offered at the place of worship

Maagh (January–February)	*Moha-Shivaratri*	The festival commemorates the wedding of Lord Shiva and Devi Parvati. Observed for the well-being of the husbands. Sometimes the unmarried female also participates with the wish of getting a good husband	Married and unmarried female	(i) The married females keep fasts until they offer holy water and other offerings to lord Shiva in a nearby temple
Phalgun (February–March)	*Dol-Purnima*	Observed as an epitome of eternal and divine love between Radha and Lord Krishna.	All the villagers	(i) All the villagers sing and chant *Hore-Krishna* and apply color to one another (
	Saraswati Puja	This puja is performed to seek the blessing of Devi Saraswati, who is a goddess of knowledge	Students, teachers, and people associated with the attainment of any form of knowledge	i) The priest looks after the ritual proceedings and offers fruits, flowers, and incense sticks (ii) Students and teachers offer *Anjali* and seek blessings
Chaitra (March–April)	*Gajan*	Performed in order to supposedly gain prosperity and success from the Hindu Gods, Shiva and Durga	Sanyashis and the rest of the villagers	(i) The Sanyashis keep fast starting from the last week of the last Bengali month Chaitra up to the last day called *Sankranti* (ii) A number of open-air drama are arranged (iii) Lord Shiva and goddess Durga are offered fruits, flowers, and incense sticks

Seaoraphuli Ghat and then walk on foot up to Tarkeswar temple. During this journey in the month of *Shrabon* (July–August), they don't stop or rest. Upon reaching their destination these devotees spill the holy water over the Shivalinga as a mark of their devotion toward Lord Shiva.

Much like what is found in different parts of West Bengal, worship of goddess Monosha or *Monosha-Puja* takes place in every weaver household of Begampur region in the month of *Bhadro* (August–September). Often a priest is called for the occasion who chants hymns and offers flowers, fruits, and incense sticks at the *Monosha-than* of every weaver household. This puja is performed out of the belief that goddess Monosha will protect them from the events of snake bites. Weavers observe the Janmashtami festival during this same month, which marks the birth of Lord Krishna. Unlike what is common to this festival across different Indian states where devotees engage in *Dahi-Handi* competitions, where pots of curd and butter are suspended high, and young men form human pyramids to break them in a manner reminiscent of Krishna's childhood pranks, the weaver caste devotees simply keep fast, sing, and dance. Moreover, they cook and consume vegetarian food as part of this observance.

Durga Puja is arguably the most celebrated festival in West Bengal and other Bengali communities around the world. This festival is observed in the month of *Aashwin* (September–October). Through this five-day-long grand celebration, the victory of the goddess Durga over the demon Mahishasura is celebrated. It is believed that during these days goddess Durga along with her children comes down from Kailash to her maternal house and brings prosperity. Elaborate clay idols of Durga and her family are crafted and worshipped with great enthusiasm by many Pandals. Often the priest officiates the proceedings of puja rituals, an animal sacrifice is made on the third day (i.e., *Astami*), people buy and wear new clothes, and visit the houses of relatives and friends. The streets come alive with colorful decorations, cultural programs, and traditional dance forms like *Dhunuchi Naach*. The festival also includes Sindoor Khela, where married women apply vermilion to the goddess and each other, symbolizing marital bliss. Begampur, as a place, is not an exception to the overall scenario. Weavers because of their Bengali ethnic background do take part in this festival. This auspicious occasion serves as a business outlet where the weavers get to see the maximum volume of sales. Apart from goddess Durga, many weaver households worship goddess Laxmi as well in the same month just after Durga puja. Usually, here also often a priest is called who chants hymns and offers incense sticks, raisins, fruits, flowers, etc. At times Laxmi-Panchali is also read on the occasion. This puja again is done for the general prosperity and well-being of the householders.

There are two main festivals in the month of *Kartik* (October–November), that is, Kali puja and *Bhai-Phonta*. Despite Diwali (also known as Deepavali) originally not being a part of the Bengali religious pantheon, particularly the weaver caste population of Begampur region and the Bengali population in general, celebrate both *Kali puja* and *Deepavali* with great zeal and enthusiasm. Devotees offer prayers and sacrifices to the goddess Kali, often accompanied by traditional Bengali sweets and fireworks. The festival emphasizes the triumph of good over evil. Similarly, they light oil lamps (*diyas*), burst firecrackers, and decorate their homes to commemorate the return of Lord Rama to Ayodhya. The goddess Lakshmi, the deity of wealth and prosperity, is also worshipped during this festival. In the same month festival of *Bhai-Phonta* is observed, which has its different share of name in different parts of India. The same festival is known as *Bhai-Dooj* in the northern part and *Yama-Dwitiya* in the southern part of India. During this festival, the elder sisters bless their younger siblings and chant "*Jomer-Duyare Porlo-Kanta . . . Ami Di Amar bhai Ke Phonta . . . Yumuna Dei Jom Ke Phonta.*" In case the sister is younger than her male sibling same ritual is followed except for the ceremony of blessing. In the end, they exchange gifts with one another. The bonding of love shared between brothers and sisters has even influenced a few neighboring Muslim families to take up this practice. A few cases have been reported in this regard.

Although quite infrequent, a few resourceful weavers exclusively arrange *Jagatdhatri puja* in their own households. This puja is observed during the month of *Agrohayan* (November–December). The priest looks after the ritual proceedings and offers incense sticks, fruits, and flowers to the deity. This puja is performed for the well-being of the family members.

Tant-Viswakarma-Puja is perhaps the biggest festival for every weaver caste household in Begampur. This festival is observed in the month of *Poush* (December–January) where often the priest goes to each weaver household and worships the loom with flowers, incense sticks *moya*, and *tiler-khaja*. This puja is often performed for the well-being and prosperity of the weavers. Furthermore, this ceremony apart from being important in terms of ritualistic belief also comes very close to the festival of Durga puja in terms of grandeur. Currently, the clay idol of lord Viswakarma is worshipped in as many as thirty separate pandals in and around Begampur. The entire region lit up with miniature lights and decorations. Even one gets to see the voluntary involvement of the neighboring Muslim population.

As part of Hindu religious belief, the weaver caste population in the Begampur region takes part in the festival of *Moha-Shivaratri* in the month of Magh (January–February). The festival commemorates the wedding of Lord Shiva and Devi Parvati. Usually, the married females keep fasts until they offer holy water and other offerings to Lord Shiva in a nearby temple. It is observed for the well-being of the husbands. Sometimes the unmarried female also participates with the wish of getting a good husband.

Weavers also observe *Dol-Purnima* or Holi in the month of *Phalgun* (February–March). Holi which is the festival of colors is observed as an epitome of eternal and divine love between Radha and Lord Krishna. People play with colored powders and water and celebrate this with great enthusiasm. They dance to traditional songs and savor special sweets like malpua and gujiya. It also symbolizes the triumph of good over evil and the arrival of spring. The young weaver caste population, especially the students, worship Devi Saraswati during the same month. Often priests are called who look after the ritual proceedings. The worship is a significant event in educational institutions because Devi Saraswati is the goddess of knowledge. Students and teachers often offer *Anjali* and seek the blessings of the goddess for success in their studies and creative endeavors. Idols of Saraswati are adorned with books, musical instruments, and art materials.

Finally, weavers of the Begampur region also observe the festival of *Gajan* during the end of *Chaitra* (March–April), that is, precisely during the last week of the last month in the Bengali calendar. Lord Shiva and Goddess Durga are worshipped during this festival for general well-being and prosperity. The Sanyashis keep fast in their honor. Often open-air drama and acts are arranged.

CHAPTER SUMMARY

This chapter has shed light on the social and religious life of handloom weavers living in Begampur region. In so doing, this chapter shows that most of Bengali-speaking Hindu handloom weavers of this region trace their origin from Aswini *Tanti*, a sect within the weaver community whose existence was predominant in the western part of the then undivided Bengal (i.e., before the partition and attainment of independence). However, few Muslim families in this region are associated with different tasks of handloom weaving. None of these Muslims trace their origin to *Jolah*s, *Momin*s, or *Ansari*s. In most of these cases, one gets to see the predominance of Muslim women who either perform the preparatory tasks or embroidery works. This chapter also highlights the fact that due to prolonged religious cohabitation, the Hindu majority and few Muslim families presently maintain a peaceful economic and religious coexistence in Begampur region. Sometimes people of these two different sects have been seen attending different religious ceremonies and festivals of each other.

The chapter further shows that the Bengali-speaking Hindu weaver caste families of Begampur region used to marry their daughters at an early age compared to their sons. Arranged marriages were preferred over other ways of acquiring mates. Furthermore, "clan exogamy" and "group endogamy" used to be one of the most preferred rules of marriage. Literary evidence (see Risley 1892) also indicates the fact that practices of bride price were also present among the handloom weavers of West Bengal. However, the scenario has started to change along with the growth of education and awareness. Due to the changing economic and social requirements, the handloom weavers of this region invariably had to bring in many social adjustments such as loosening restrictions on the rule of clan exogamy and group endogamy and providing enough liberty in choosing the ways to acquire mates, which are now blooming as the new norms. Poverty also played its part in this regard, due to which most of the artisan families avoided marrying their daughters at an early age. The practice of taking bride price has almost vanished as it is looked down upon by the society at large. Invariably, owing to ongoing changes in the economy and education there has been a change in family structure and kinship pattern as well. Currently, most of the handloom weavers of this region are unable to maintain their traditional norm of living under joint families, taking food cooked from the same hearth, while taking part in a common hereditary guild due to prolonged impoverishment. Often the meager amounts of their monthly income do not provide any realistic opportunities to maintain a higher number of family members within one household. Due to this reason, many joint families in Begampur region have split into several nuclear families who continue to live under the same homestead. This certainly has resulted in the loosening of kinship ties to a great extent. However, findings also show that kinship ties haven't been entirely eradicated. The weaver families of Begampur region still rely upon kinship networks for the allocation of different tasks of cotton cloth production, especially while finding prospective brides and grooms for their family members.

A lot of changes have occurred concerning the life-cycle ritual of the handloom weavers of Begampur region as well. For example, to ensure the safety and well-being of both the mother and the child, the customary practice of childbirth in which the delivery used to take place in the matrilineal homes of pregnant women has changed to the growing instances of institutional deliveries. Nowadays, depending upon the economic resources, most of the childbirth in this region takes place in either government institutions or private nursing homes, where medical doctors or nurses supervise in place of *Dhaimas* of the earlier instance. The naming of the child is another instance that now has become completely formalized. Earlier the name for a child used to be decided right at the end of the pollution period. The elderly members of weaver households used to play a key role in this regard. However, things began to change along with the advent of the birth registry system. Owing to the obligation of submitting documents to the requisite authorities for the generation of birth certificates the name of a child nowadays is often decided in haste, that is, within three to four days of childbirth. Even marriage rituals, other than some of the previously mentioned ones, show a few other changes. The custom of offering a blessing during negotiation as a symbol epitomizing the fixation of marriage is not being followed. Instead, nowadays the blessing ceremony is often arranged on the day of marriage. Perhaps people's growing inclination toward some other ways of acquiring mates has led to the adoption of such measures. The practice surrounding the cremation of the deceased also has encountered quite a change. Instead of nearby crematoriums bodies of the deceased nowadays are taken to distant crematoriums in places such as Srerampore and Bhadrakali due to growing awareness regarding environmental pollution. As a result, practices of burning the bodies over funeral pyres have decreased considerably. Instead, instances of using electrical crematoriums have grown. Furthermore, in order to strike a balance between social life and following some of the hazardous taboos and restrictions the observance of thirty-day-long death pollution has now been curtailed down to fifteen days.

The religious ceremonies and festivals of the handloom weavers of Begampur region are not much different from other Bengali-speaking Hindu caste groups found in this region. The weaver caste people of this region often follow the Bengali Hindu calendar. Hence, year-wise observance of some rituals and religious festivals like *Poila-Boisakh*, *Jaamai-Soshthi*, *Ratha-Yatra*, *Jol-Yatra*, *Monosha Puja*, *Janmastami*, *Durga-Puja*, *Laxmi Puja*, *Kalipuja*, *Bhai-Phonta*, *Jagatdhatri Puja*, *Moha-Shivaratri*, *Dol Purnima*, *Saraswati Puja*, and *Gajan* are quite common. But there is an exception as well. The handloom weavers of this region arrange their own *Tant-Viswakarma Puja* in the month of *Poush* (December–January). The ritual and idol used for this *Viswakarma Puja* are quite different from the one performed before the *Durga Puja*. Often the celestial god *Viswakarma* sits over a horse in place of an elephant that is found usually. The arrangement is so grand and lavish that even the Muslims residing in Begampur and nearby villages visit and attend this religious ceremony.

NOTES

1. Endogamy is one of the rules of marriage that restrict an individual from marrying outside his group, creed, and caste.

2. The rule of exogamy encourages individuals to marry outside their own family and bloodline.

3. Patrilineal rule of descent refers to the practice of tracing ancestry and line of inheritance through the male line, that is, from father to his son to his grandson.

4. Joint families usually contain multiple generations, consisting of more than two adult married members of opposite sexes belonging to two different generations and their own or adopted unmarried children.

5. Nuclear families are those basic units that arise from the social institution of marriage. It generally contains two generations consisting of two married adult members of opposite sexes and their own or adopted unmarried children. Patrilocal families are commonly found in patrilineal societies where a married couple starts living in their patrilineal household (i.e., the household of the groom's parents).

6. The Eskimo kinship system is quite common among societies in Western Europe. Characterized by its preference to immediate members of a nuclear family who are often distinguished by the terms of references, the Eskimo kinship system in general lumps together the entire generation of cousins irrespective of their gender and uses one single classificatory kinship term for them (see Ember, Ember, and Peregrine 2007, 397).

7. The Hawaiian kinship system deemphasizes the members of the nuclear family. Instead, under this system, members of the same generation of an extended family are distinguished only by gender. For example, an individual's father and all the male members of the same generation would have the same kin name, meanwhile that individual's mother and all the female members would have a common kin name. This kind of kinship system is frequently found among Polynesian Islanders where one gets to see the prevalence of ambilineal descent (Ember, Ember, and Peregrine 2007, 397).

8. Avoidance is a sort of kinship behavior where certain kin members such as daughter-in-law and father-in-law or son-in-law and his mother-in-law need to socially avoid one another. Instances of this kind of kinship behavior have been found in many patrilineal societies of Southeast Asian countries including India (see Majumdar and Madan 1999, 87–92).

9. Joking-relationship is just the opposite of avoidance where two kin members such as a younger brother-in-law and his sister-in-law or grand-father and his grand-daughter are permitted to joke, sometimes use obscene language to tease one another. This kind of kinship behavior has also been found in many patrilineal and some tribal societies of Southeast Asian countries including India.

10. Teknonymy is a sort of kinship behavior where women/men are socially forbidden to take the name of the father/mother of their child. Instead, the respective father/mother is often referred to as the father/mother of their children and is often called by the name of the child. This type of kinship behavior is quite common in tribal societies across different continents. It has also been found among many Indian tribes and traditional medieval Bengali societies.

11. Avanculate is a sort of kinship behavior in which the maternal uncle plays quite an important role in the life of an individual. This kind of kinship behavior is still quite prevalent among different tribal and traditional Bengali societies.

12. The term consanguineal kin refers to those kin members formed through blood relationships. That means an individual's consanguineal kin includes his/her own father, brother, sister, patrilineal cousins, paternal uncles and their wives, aunts and their husbands, etc.

13. The term affinal kin refers to kin members formed through marital relationships. That means an individual's affinal kin includes his/her maternal uncles and their wives, aunts and their husbands, matrilineal sisters, brothers, cousins, etc.

14. The denotative kinship terms are a particular type of kinship term according to their range of application. This particular type of kinship term is often used for denoting only specific kinship categories such as father and mother (see Murdock 1949).

15. The classificatory kinship term is another category of kinship term those are used while referring to an entire generation of kin members, such as brother and sister, who can be an individual's own brother or sister or they can be cousin brothers and sisters. In both cases, the same term is used (see Murdock 1949).

16. The Sudanese kinship system is perhaps the most complex kinship system found across the world. Under this system, hardly any kinsmen are lumped together. Instead, each category of relative is given a specific denotative kinship term to distinguish them based on class occupation and political power. This kind of kinship system is found in many patrilineal and Muslim societies such as Turkey and Sudan (see Ember, Ember, and Peregrine 2007, 397).

17. Yajna (Sanskrit: "sacrifice") also spelled yajña, in Hinduism, is an offering to the gods based on rites prescribed in the earliest scriptures of ancient India, the Vedas, in contrast to *puja*, a later practice that may include image worship and other devotional practices. A *yajna* is always purposeful, even though the aim may be as general as sustaining the natural order of the universe (see Britannica, T. Editors of Encyclopaedia. "yajna." *Encyclopedia Britannica*, March 2, 2015. https://www.britannica.com/topic/yajna).

18. A particular caste group found in the Bengali Hindu section, who are in charge of cremation. It is their hereditary guild. This group stands right at the lowest end of the ladder of the Hindu ritual purity hierarchy. Considered to be untouchable because of the pollution they accumulated over the years because of their association with this particular occupation.

Chapter 4

The Craft of Handloom Weaving

Technology, Work Coordination, Products and Their Market

The term "technology" stands for several aspects such as (i) total material means employed to obtain desired objects or (ii) the bodies of skills, knowledge, and procedures for making, using, and doing useful things (Spier 1970; Lemonier 1986, 1989). Virtually every activity in human society involves interactions between people and one or more technologies. It is even true for acts like procuring raw materials and preparing food and so on (Schiffer 2004). Needless to say, the act of handloom weaving is no exception in this regard. Handloom weaving technology often involves many important aspects such as (i) looms and other implements, (ii) knowledge and skill involved in different stages of cloth production, (iii) work coordination and division of labor, and (iv) raw materials and products. Superficially it looks simple. Yet handloom weaving is quite labor intensive and involves an enchanting series of activities where one gets to see interaction between different work groups, who based on their skill perform different sets of roles within the system of production and marketing. Most importantly the intention of participation in the cloth making of these different work groups is different from one another which often fetches different outcomes for these different groups and puts them in different hierarchic positions within their society.

Historically, a number of weaving traditions are found in West Bengal. The scenario in Hooghly district where Begampur is located is very similar to the overall scenario in West Bengal. As touched upon in the previous chapter, there are both silk and cotton weaving traditions in the Hooghly district. Begampur is one of the cotton weaving traditions in the district. Barring the recent efforts for the upgradation of handloom weaving techniques, especially since 2010, handloom weaving technology and its adaptive mechanism in Begampur region was in a state of moderate development in comparison to other developed centers of cotton weaving traditions in West Bengal. The techniques, implements, and raw materials used for production were more or less inferior. Technologically, it comes only second or third to Dhaniakhali which is the most renowned cotton weaving tradition in the district.

In the first subsection of this chapter, I discuss about loom and other implements of Begampur region that are used for cloth production. Then, in the second subsection, I provide a detailed description of the knowledge and skills involved with different stages of cloth production. Then I provide an overview regarding the division of labor and the scenario of work coordination of this region in the third subsection. Finally, in the fourth subsection, I provide a description of raw materials, products, and their market along with their correlation that makes an impact on the handloom weavers of this region.

LOOM AND OTHER IMPLEMENTS

Looms in Begampur region in general are quite simple in structure. Up until the establishment of Karsarai Madhyampara Samabay Samiti in 2013, weavers of Begampur region generally used fly-shuttle-framed *dobby* looms. But nowadays the use of *dobby* is gradually being replaced by jacquard machines.

Framed Dobby Looms

Frame looms have the utility of moving from one certain place to another (as shown in figure 4.1). Usually, these looms are formed by four vertical wooden poles—each one of them is around six feet in height. At around one-third of its total height, four wooden pegs attach these four vertical poles to one another and form a box-shaped structure. Moreover, there are two nine-foot-long wooden beams—one in the front and the other one at the back side—which form the outer structure of these looms. The warp beam (*pati*) actually holds the warp threads. Meanwhile, the front beam (*guti*) holds the finished object. Besides, in the middle portion of these looms there are two harnesses (*ba*) and a rectangular wooden frame (*dokti*) that hang on the same level as the vertical threads. These two harnesses are often suspended by nylon threads and three flexible wooden pulleys (*pakhi*) from the top. Even they are attached to the three bamboo paddles (*tal-pa*) at the bottom which helps in the shedding of warp threads. And the two small wooden pieces—one on each side of the rectangular wooden frame—and the handle which are attached by nylon threads help in weaving. The rectangular frame also holds a groove and comblike attachment (*sana*) which directs the shuttle (*maku*) through warp threads and tightens the texture of woven items, respectively.

Altogether, this whole structure supports the process of weaving. As a weaver presses the paddle the particular arrangement of warp threads—where

Figure 4.1 Fly-Shuttle Frame Loom of Begampur Region. *Source*: Author's Photo

one thread is placed within the loop of a harness and pushed through a gap between the loops of the next one—creates the space among the warp threads, which is one of most basic requirements in any weaving mechanism. In the meantime, as the weaver pulls the handle, one weft thread passes through the gap within the warp threads.

Even the designing apparatus (*dobby*) of the Begampur region is also quite simple in structure. Along with this simple form of machine, often weavers use a particular kind of loopy iron stick (*tarer-ba* and *dangi*) for designing. This machine looks like a box and often rests at the upper portion of the loom. A number of cyclically arranged wooden plates of this machine—each one of which has several nails attached to it—help in design formation (as shown in figure 4.2). Actually, the successful coordination of these loopy iron sticks (which are placed in between the warp threads) and the nails of the wooden rids forms the design. These wooden rids revolve at the time of weaving and generate tension among the chords attached to the wooden rids at the upper portion of the machines. Again, these chords, because of their connection with the loopy iron sticks around the border and base (*jami*) area of warp threads, create different sorts of alignment every time weavers press

Figure 4.2 Wooden Plates of a *Dobby* Machine. *Source*: Author's Photo

the paddle. And as the weavers weave the weft threads through these warp threads repetitively it formulates design.

Jacquard Frame Looms

Except for jacquard machines that are attached over the frame loom for designing the jacquard frame looms are not quite different from the frame looms with dobby in terms of their structure. Jacquard frame looms have similar rectangular boxlike structures formed by six-foot-high wooden vertical poles connected to one another by four wooden pegs. It also has two nine-foot-long wooden beams—one in the front (weft beam/*guti*) and the other one at the back side (warp beam/*pati*)—that form the outer structure of these looms. Besides, the two harnesses (*ba*) and a rectangular wooden frame *(dokti*) that hang on the same level with the vertical threads much like as found in frame looms with dobby. The main difference however lies in the number of tinny threads from jacquard machines that are placed over different sections of the warp threads. Even though the working mechanism of the two harnesses of jacquard frame looms—which are suspended by the nylon threads and three flexible wooden pulleys (*pakhi*) from the top and attached with three paddles at the bottom—is quite similar as these are responsible for shedding of warp threads with their alternative upward and downward movements, the number of tiny threads from jacquard machines is much higher in number compared to dobby frame looms, which create different sets of alignment within the warp threads along with a continuous rotation of designed splices.

Though the basic working mechanism of these jacquard machines is not much different, the number of iron sticks that go along with these machines is quite higher compared to traditional frame loom. The process of designing in jacquard frame looms is more rigorous and complex. It requires a properly articulated movement of predesigned splices (*pata*s) and several iron sticks in the two jacquard machines (as shown in figure 4.3). Even the process of designing in this region often involves a higher amount of skill. Weavers often pierce each of the warp threads of both the border and base area through loopy iron sticks according to the design to be made on the finished object. A netlike structure (*jali-pata*) helps to project an optimum amount of force that pulls or releases the tension among these loopy iron sticks while facilitating their upward and downward movement. During the time of weaving, as a weaver presses the paddle, a constant rotation of predesigned splices of jacquard machines creates different forms of alignment among the warp threads. At this juncture, as the weaver slings the handle sidewise, the two small wooden pieces attached within the groove of the rectangular wooden frame direct the shuttle (*maku*) through warp threads.

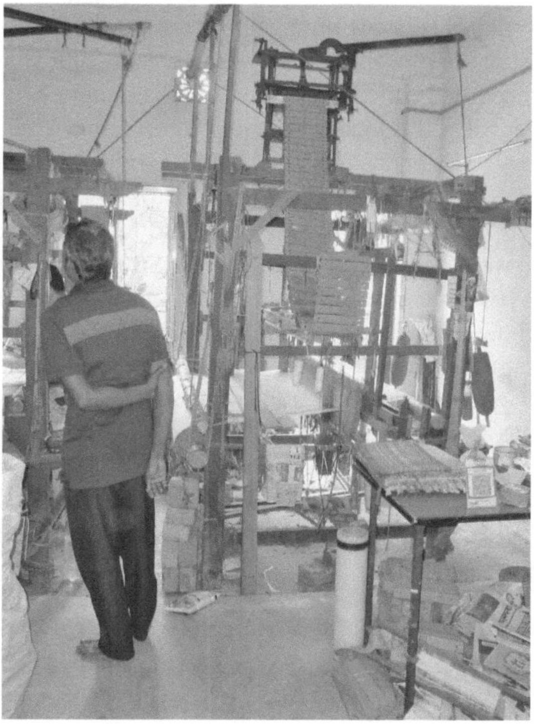

Figure 4.3 Jacquard Frame Loom. *Source*: Author's Photo

Shuttle

A shuttle is primarily made out of a wooden frame. It is around fourteen inches in length and elliptical in structure. The elliptical wooden structure has two iron caps at two opposite ends. There is a notch at the middle portion of the wooden frame where there is a separate place for attaching small reels containing the weft threads. Besides, there is a tiny little hole at one end of this wooden frame that serves as the outlet through which the weft thread from the small reels passes at the time of weaving.

Spinning Wheels

Weavers in Begampur use two different kinds of spinning wheels: (1) Starching wheel (*suto-bhatano-chakra*) which is used for starching the warp threads and preparation of big reels required during the process of drumming. This kind of spinning wheel is made of a wooden structure that consists of two wooden vertical poles at one end between which a wooden wheel is made of two circular wooden splices arranged beside one another in a perpendicular manner. These two circular wooden splices are attached to one another through a number of wooden rids which helps in the rolling of starched threads in an even manner. Besides, there is also a separate arrangement for attachment of a freely rotatable loopy structure (*charki*) made out of tiny threads from where raw colored threads are starched and rolled into the circular structure between these two wooden splices. Finally, this kind of spinning wheel also contains another separate pair of vertical poles on the other end of the wooden structure that holds the *latai*—from where the starched threads are rolled into the big reels. (2) Spinning wheels (*noli-pakano-charka*) which are used for the preparation of small reels required as weft threads within the shuttle. Structurally this kind of spinning wheel also has several wooden splices on one end specifically designed in a manner for holding and free rotation of the small reels. It has two separate cartwheels-like structures made out of several wooden rids and is attached to one another through a wooden pole at the center between them at the other end. This wheel rotates over two wooden vertical poles placed beside the two sides of the wheel through a handle. Finally, there is also a separate arrangement for the attachment of a freely rotatable loopy structure (*charki*) made out of tiny threads from where starched threads and rolled into small reels with the help of this spinning wheel.

KNOWLEDGE AND SKILLS IN DIFFERENT STAGES OF CLOTH PRODUCTION

The production itself has different phases like (i) designing, (ii) dyeing of thread, (iii) seizing and rolling of threads (*suto-bhatano* and *noli-bata*), (iv) drumming (*puruni-kara* and *naraj-gotano*), (v) denting and drafting and fitting of the loom (*ba-sana-gantha and tant-khatano*), and lastly, (vi) weaving (*banidari*). Each of these phases requires a specific skill. During each of these different phases, various participant members use relatively simple implements like different kinds of spinning wheels (*suto-bahtano-charka*, *nali-bata-charka*, and *charki*), shuttle (*maku*), wooden reel (*noli*), and quite complex one such as loom (*tant*). Furthermore, there are other important ingredients such as dye, starch, oil, and different varieties of yarn, which are used in both the body (*jami*) and border (*par*) of a saree. Often these different stages hold the basis for various roles and responsibilities within the handloom organization.

These investors generally provide different varieties of raw yearns[1] (i.e., usually the No. 80 and No. 60 variants as they are locally known) to the dyeing units. Most of the dyeing units in the Begampur region are independent and have a typical outlook. Usually, these dyeing work sheds contain a tiled roof that often has no walls and is supported by bamboo poles only. Even these units have a lot of open space which is used for drying already dyed bundles.

A number of skilled workers work under these tiled roofs—where they boil the raw threads with the solutions of chemical dye (see figure 4.4). In the beginning, they plunge these raw bundles of yarn into the solution of chemical dye and hot water, which are kept in a container (*kardai*). This process takes a little bit of time as this act is repeatedly performed until the raw

Figure 4.4 Dyeing of Raw Yarns in Begampur Region. *Source*: Author's Photo

bundles of threads do not soak the dye anymore. Then, the extra amount of dye is squeezed out from these bundles with the help of two bamboo sticks. Other people associated with these work sheds keep these dyed bundles over horizontally placed bamboo lines for drying. Often the time taken and treatment used in attaining a particular shade determine the cost of dyeing. Colors like orange and parrot green require additional treatment even after the initial stages of dyeing. For these particular shades, already dyed bundles are dyed all over again as soon as they absorb the primary coat of color. Naturally, the cost of dyeing for these particular shades is quite high in comparison to other common shades.

The completely dyed threads undergo subsequent processes of separation of threads, starching (*suto-bhatano*), drying, twisting, seizing, and rolling of threads into the bobbin and then into the pirns (*noli-pakano*). Initially, either the weaver himself or any of the women members from his family divides the dyed bundles into ten to fifteen equal units (*mora*). Then they plunge these small units of threads into the water kept in a container (either a bucket or earthen pot)—where these units absorb an optimum amount of water for over twenty-four hours. As these bundles absorb water the women prepare a pack of starch from readily available home ingredients like barley, rice paste, and cornflower. Next, they knead these moist bundles with the starch. Indeed, this is a tough job as it literally determines the nature and quality of threads, which determines the quality and durability of produced objects. Therefore, these people often use an optimum amount of starch while performing these jobs. Because a slightly lesser amount of starch generally withholds the spontaneous movement of the warp threads during weaving while too much starch often causes the breakage of warp threads. Both of them make the job of weaving quite difficult.

Due to this particular reason, often women workers starch these threads in small amounts. They starch only five to six units at a time. Often they roll these threads into the bobbins (*latai*) with the help of a particular kind of spinning wheel (*suto-bhatano-charka*). These wooden machines are medium in size and have a rectangular base. It has four pegs on each of its corners. On one side, two of these pegs form the grove which facilitates the free rotation of the bobbin. While the other two hold the wooden wheel which rotates the bobbins (as shown in figure 4.5). In general, women place these smaller units of threads over one to two *charki* which can rotate freely. They then rotate the handle attached to the wooden wheel. And then they just direct the starched threads from the two *charki* into the bobbins.

These bobbins are then kept in open sunlight for drying. Usually, one to two days later, the starched threads from these bobbins are rolled into two kinds of pirns (*noli*). This process uses a slightly different kind of spinning

Figure 4.5 Process of Rolling Starched Bundles into the Bobbins. *Source*: Author's Photo

wheel (*noli-pakano-charka*). Generally, women folks from weaver families perform these tasks. Even some women help the close neighboring families to complete the task. However, at present very few of them do so. There are few who do these jobs for their own family. But in most cases, weavers often hire specialists from another region. Due to the immediate requirement at the time of drumming/warping, these people produce bigger pirns (*tanc-noli*) prior to smaller ones. In fact, they produce smaller pirns (*poren-noli*) at a later stage—where these are attached to a particular notch within a shuttle and used as weft at the time of weaving.

The process of drumming is one of the most complex activities in weaving. Often a group of specialist workers perform this job in their own work sheds. These people assort warp threads in terms of predetermined design—which is absolutely vital for design formation. First, on the basis of the design, these people divide the entire width of warp threads (which varies between 1600 and 1900 threads) into small segments of 100 to 150 threads. Then depending upon the necessity of a particular color in specific places, they place the bigger pirns within specifically positioned wooden frames—which facilitates their free rotation. Generally, they take each color of threads one after another and then pierce them through a comblike structure attached to a wooden frame (*bar*). These frames contain several thick strands—arranged one after another with one perforation right at the mid portion. Usually, if they pierce one specific thread through the perforation of a strand, then they push the next one through the gap between these strands. The threads, therefore, form an "X"-like structure where either a thread or tiny piece of bamboo splice is placed to demarcate the shedding of warp threads. In fact, this is one of the most important parts which support the mechanism of weaving. Thereafter, both the threads (one which is pierced through the perforation and the other that is pushed through the gap) are cumulatively pierced through another small comblike structure just to spread these threads well.

This process continues till the very end up to the 100th or 150th thread. Then these people roll the warp thread into a circular wooden drum. In between, they even mark at specific intervals demarcating the length of each product. It also helps them in keeping track of the amount of thread that they have rolled into the drum. Meanwhile, with the completion of a particular segment, these people go to the next segment of 100 to 150 threads. In this way, consecutively they roll up to 1,600 to 1,900 warp threads depending upon the variety of an item (see figure 4.6A and B).

All of the warp threads that have been arranged in a specific manner are then rolled back into the warp beam (see figure 4.7). Usually one, sometimes even two people cumulatively perform this job. Initially, they set the wooden drum in tension, so that it releases the warped threads slowly. They also tie all warp threads with tiny bamboo split (*paluikathi*) and place it within the specific groove of the warp beam (*pati*) and then place this warp beam over a wooden stand that supports its free rotation. And lastly, with a constant

Figure 4.6A Different Activities in Drumming of Threads. *Source*: Author's Photo

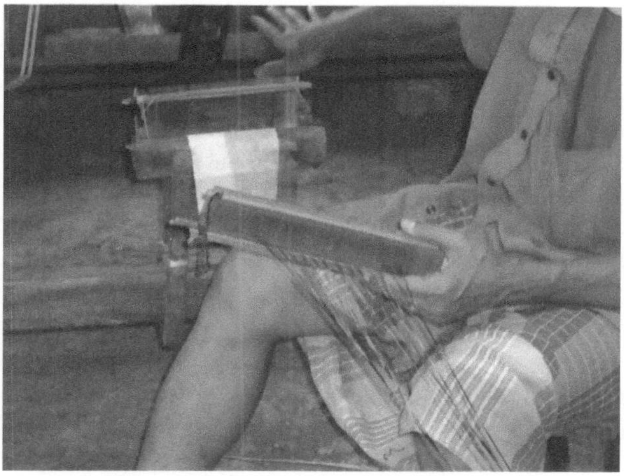

Figure 4.6B Different Activities in Drumming of Threads. *Source*: Author's Photo

Figure 4.7 Process of Rolling Arranged Threads into Warp Beam. *Source*: Author's Photo

rotation of the iron rod placed through the notch of the warp beam, they roll the warp threads into the warp beam in a slow and condensed manner. To save warp threads from twisting and tangling into each other, these people often place pieces of newspaper within a particular fold of warp threads. This in fact plays a very vital role in maintaining the quality of woven items.

The warp beams are then taken to the people who are specialized in the job of denting and drafting (*ba-sana-gantha*). These people minutely pierce all the warp threads through the two harnesses (*ba*) and a single comblike structure (*sana*) (as shown in figure 4.8A and B). While doing their job, they alternatively pierce each warp thread through a single loop and a gap between two such loops of another harness. For example, if they pierce a particular thread through a loop of a particular harness, then they push it through the gap between two such loops in another harness.

This arrangement supplements the shedding of warp threads at the time of weaving. Then they take each of the threads from the two harnesses and cumulatively pierce them through a single gap in the comblike structure. Needless to say, this process often requires a good amount of skill and immense concentration as they have to pierce 1,700 to 1,900 warp threads at a stretch.

With the completion of denting and drafting, the weavers reset their looms. In general, most of the weavers because of prolonged and close association are quite aware of the technicalities associated with every stage of production. In most cases, they perform this job on their own. However, on a few occasions such as setting up a new design—which requires special skill—they

Figure 4.8A Process of Denting and Drafting. *Source*: Author's Photo

Figure 4.8B Process of Denting and Drafting. *Source*: Author's Photo

often seek the assistance of specialists. On such occasions, often an expert (*ostad*) reallocates iron sticks (*tarer-ba*). Keeping in mind which and how many of the iron sticks are to be placed where, these people often translate the design into a workable form (as shown in figure 4.9A and B).

Otherwise, weavers themselves place the iron sticks for design formation. Usually, they place a number of iron sticks among the marginal warp threads. Each of these sticks has three holes—one in the middle and the other two with two terminals. They pierce each of the separate threads through the gap in the mid portion of these iron sticks. Then they place a slightly thicker iron rod (*dangi*) through the upper gap of a number of such iron sticks to keep these iron sticks vertically. With the help of thin nylon chords, they attach these slightly thicker iron rods with the small wooden rids of the designing apparatus (*dobby*) (as shown in figure 4.10A and B). At the time of weaving, these wooden rids facilitate their upward and downward movement. In fact, as each of the wooden plates—with their specifically placed screws—pushes some of the wooden rids above while leaving the other plates virtually at the same level, simultaneously they lift different iron sticks each time. It helps in design formation.

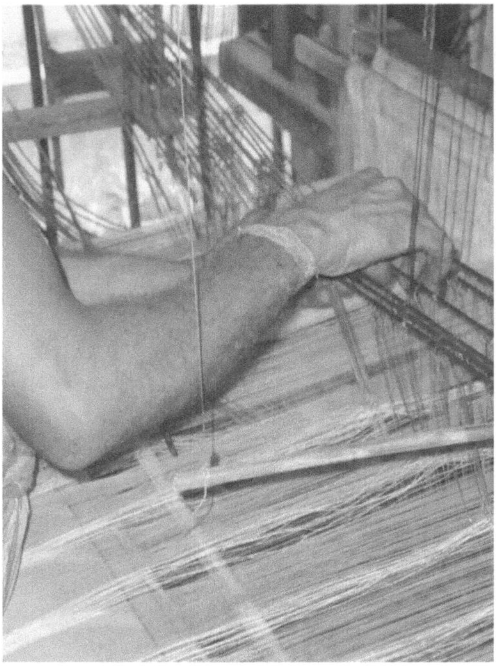

Figure 4.9 A Process of Reallocation (*penchano*). *Source*: Author's Photo

Figure 4.9B *Tarer-ba* and the *Dangi* which are Used for Design Formation in the Border Region. *Source*: Author's Photo

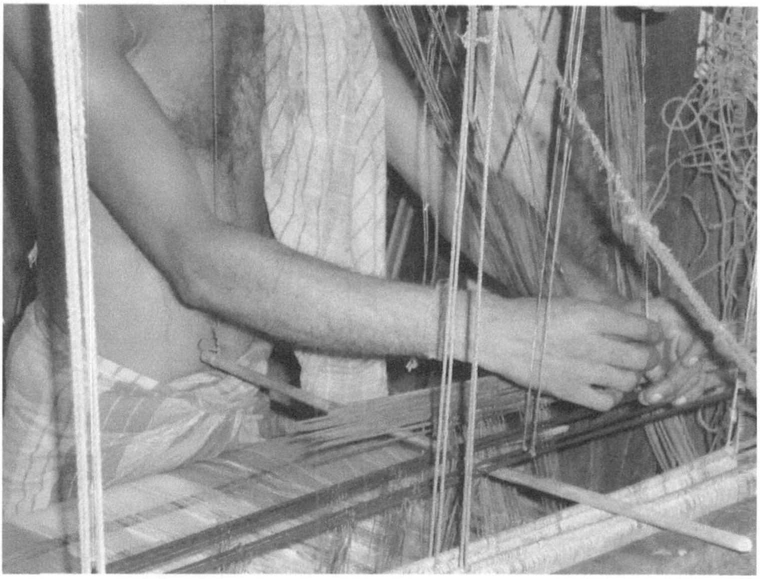

Figure 4.10A Attachment of Nylon Chords with Thick Iron Rods (*Dangi*). *Source*: Author's Photo

Figure 4.10B Attachment of Nylon Chords with Wooden Plates of Designing Apparatus. *Source*: Author's Photo

Figure 4.11 Weaver Working on His Loom in Begampur Region. *Source*: Author's Photo

After resetting their looms weavers start the actual job of weaving. The process of weaving involves a number of activities—most importantly a successful coordination between a weaver's mind, body, and several tiny little implements of a loom. In fact, during the process, weavers often illustrate a perfect orchestration of a series of complex activities. At first, weavers press the paddle which creates a gap among the warp threads. Then with an alternate swing of the handle, they direct the shuttle through the gap between warp threads. Then they release pressure in the paddle that brings the warp threads back to their normal position. And lastly, in order to maintain uniformity of texture they also pull the rectangular wooden frame inside. This is one cycle of weaving which weavers perform repeatedly all day long to produce a single item (see figure 4.11).

WORK COORDINATION AND DIVISION OF LABOR

Throughout the course of history, handloom weaving has been a caste-specific job. And the work coordination within the Begampur handloom industry has retained some of its typical characteristics to a large extent. The existing caste-wise division of labor in this region and the interrelationship among various caste groups has helped the local handloom industry to retain some of its core characteristics.

However, the situation in recent years started becoming considerably different as a number of people from other castes/communities have entered into weaving or its allied activities. Nonetheless, most of the people in the region still consider weaving to be the activity of the weaver caste people (*Tanti*s). One of the primary reasons is that the weaver caste people still constitute a sizable section of the population who are associated with the handloom industry of this region. They have accepted weaving as their community-specified job for a long time. The other sizable section is formed by either some of the blacksmith families who have gradually taken up weaving as their profession or the Muslim women who are engaged with seizing and rolling of threads and embroidery work. Furthermore, there are few carpenters (*Chhutar*) and blacksmiths (*Karmakar*) who often facilitate handloom weavers by producing shuttle and iron spare parts.

Apart from such caste-wise specifications, if we look at the number of people who are associated with weaving and its allied activities as a whole, it shows that different groups of people often perform their specific roles in productive processes. Proportionately the large chucks of these people are either involved with various allied activities or the act of weaving. A relatively small portion of the workgroup is associated with powerlooms and embroidery works. The roles of an entrepreneur or a dyer are relatively less common. Moreover, certain jobs such as seizing, rolling of threads into the bobbin, and even rolling them into the pirn mostly involve family labor, whereas other activities like drumming, denting, and drafting involve external labor. However, a new trend has come up in recent years where the local weavers don't involve family labor for the seizing and rolling of threads. Few of the weavers in fact often provide these jobs to experts as these ultimately affect the quality of produced objects.

One of the most important aspects of the allocation of responsibility is based on gender and age. There are certain works such as seizing, rolling of threads into the bobbins, and embroidery works which are traditionally performed by female folks. Even some of the respondents have mentioned the fact that "one doesn't need to teach a woman of the weaver (*Tanti*) family . . . . how to seize or how to roll the threads into the bobbin." Due to their upbringing and gradual participation from early childhood days, the female members often grasp these skills from a very tender age. Weaving, on the other hand, is often considered a job of men. Similarly, other jobs such as dyeing, drumming, and entrepreneurship mostly belong to the domain of men. My field observations also suggest that now women have gradually started to take part in works such as denting and drafting, sometimes drumming and even weaving. Meanwhile, their participation in seizing and rolling threads into the bobbin still continues to be quite high, though over the years the number has declined a little. The growing demand for earning more to sustain livelihood may have pushed female members to look beyond their traditional role of preparing finished fiber for cloth production.

PRODUCTS, RAW MATERIALS, AND THEIR MARKET

Today, almost all the states in India have their own unique weaving techniques, patterns, and designs. The vibrant *Banarasi* silk of Uttar Pradesh to the intricate *Ikat* of Telangana and Odisha's traditional *Sambalpuri* sarees, *Jamdani* and *Baluchari* sarees of West Bengal, *Kota* sarees of Rajasthan, *Patola* sarees of Gujarat, *Chanderi* sarees of Madhya Pradesh, *Paithan* sarees of Maharashtra, *Mysore* silks of Karnataka, *Kanjivaram* silks of Tamil Nadu, *Pashmina* from Kashmir, and *Phulkari* of Punjab are few prominent examples of this diversity. Interestingly, the captivating diversity of Indian handloom items, a key strength of this craft, has emerged from the dynamic shifts in market demand. Handloom weavers, driven by changing consumer preferences, have continuously experimented with a variety of raw materials, embraced technological innovations, and diligently passed down their consolidated knowledge through generations.

The scenario of handloom products in Begampur region has been quite mediocre compared to all these well-renowned traditions and designs across India and in West Bengal. Historically Begampur never became renowned for any distinct handloom item or design. A prolonged history of restricted clientele, lack of technological innovations, and the use of certain cheap varieties of raw materials all have played their part in this regard. Even if we leave the issue of technological innovation aside, simply the use of different varieties of yarns had significant implications in determining the quality of a woven item from Begampur region. The use of coarse and finer quality of yarn, for example, often determines the number of warp and weft threads in an woven item. Typically, handloom items show a greater count of warp and weft threads, ranging from 1,700 to 2,000, particularly when crafted from finer-quality yarn. But, due to the frequent use of coarser varieties of yarns, Begampuri handloom items often exhibited a reduced number of warp and weft threads, approximately ranging between 1,500 and 1,700. Eventually, this had a severe impact on the quality, neatness, and durability of the woven items of this region.

The handloom weavers of Begampur region were mostly known for the production of striped sarees in general (see table 4.1). Historically, some of the weavers of this region used to produce other items like *dhoti* and *gamchha* which one hardly gets to see nowadays. Up until the recent efforts of technological upgradation, handloom items in Begampur region didn't have a huge distinction in terms of quality and the designs of the product. The sole variations observed were either related to product quality, stemming from the utilization of diverse yarns, or the incorporation of relatively small- to medium-sized motifs in the woven items. However, with the incorporation of jacquard frame looms this scenario started to change as weavers started producing a finer variety of handmade items with a considerable amount of design. Subsequently, the production of complex designs with a finer variety of yarn (100s x 100s) is gradually becoming the new norm. Today, Begampuri sarees are generally woven in a balanced texture using dyed cotton yarn with contrasting borders in red, black, purple, orange, etc. emphasized by a serrated edge motif. Products of Begampur region can be categorized into the following categories;

However, despite all these efforts, the majority of the handloom items of Begampur region still fall under mediocre to low-range categories. The *Matapar* saree is the best example of the lowest-grade item of this region (see figure 4.12A, B, and C). *Matapar* means a simple border without any ornamentation. This particular variety of saree is woven with coarser cotton yarns (i.e., 40s x 40s & 40s x 60s) using a simple fly-shuttle frame loom. These

Table 4.1 Categories of Handloom Items of Begampur Region

Product Name	*Produced with*	*Yarn Variety Used*	*Aesthetic Elements*
Matapar	Simple Fly-Shuttle Frame Looms	40s x 40s & 40s x 60s	None
Mediocre Items	Fly-Shuttle Framed *Dobby* Looms	60s x 80s & 80s x 80s	Mediocre, mostly restricted to the border area
Kata-naksa or *Kotki* sarees	Fly-Shuttle Framed *Dobby* Looms	80s x 80s	Relatively good amount of designs in both Border and Body of the woven items
Chua-Pati	Fly-Shuttle Framed *Dobby* Looms	2/40s and 2/60s	Design shows influence of Manipur. These items contain designs in both Border and Body of woven items
Highest Quality Items	Jacquard Frame Looms	80s x 100s & 100s x 100s	Considerable amount of designs all over the woven item

Source: Author

Figure 4.12A A Plain (*Mata*) Saree of Begampur Region. *Source*: Author's Photo

Figure 4.12B Simple Forms of Design in the Border Region. *Source*: Author's Photo

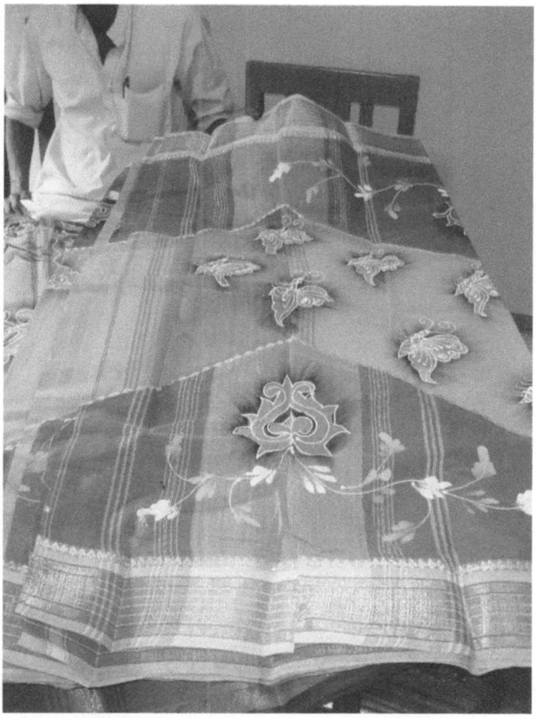

Figure 4.12C Plain Fabric and Embroidery Saree of Begampur Region. *Source*: Author's Photo

cheaper varieties of sarees are mainly loosely woven, lightweight, and translucent of colored stripes and check patterns. Historically, the majority of the local weavers were engaged with the production of a relatively lesser-known variety of cotton items. A few of the local weavers are producing this particular type of item even today. Similarly, the mediocre items of the Begampur region include items that are produced with relatively finer varieties of yarns (i.e., 60s x 80s & 80s x 80s) using fly-shuttle framed *dobby* looms. Generally, in order to curtail production costs, a few of the local weavers use No. 80 yarns as warp threads and No. 60 yarns as weft threads. These products are relatively coarse and have a lesser amount of design. Designs in these items are mostly restricted within the border region. Some of the mediocre items of this region also include items with fabric design or embroidery work.

Meanwhile, the *Kata-Naksa* or *Kotki* and *Chua-Pati* sarees of Begampur region are slightly different from the mediocre items in terms of the quality of raw materials and aesthetic content. Both, the *Kata-naksa* and *Kotki* sarees are produced with a relatively thinner diameter of yarns, but often thicker twisted varieties (i.e., 2/40s or 2/60s) of yarn are used for the production of *Chua-Pati* items (see table 4.1). A *Kata-naksa* saree (as shown in figure 4.12D)

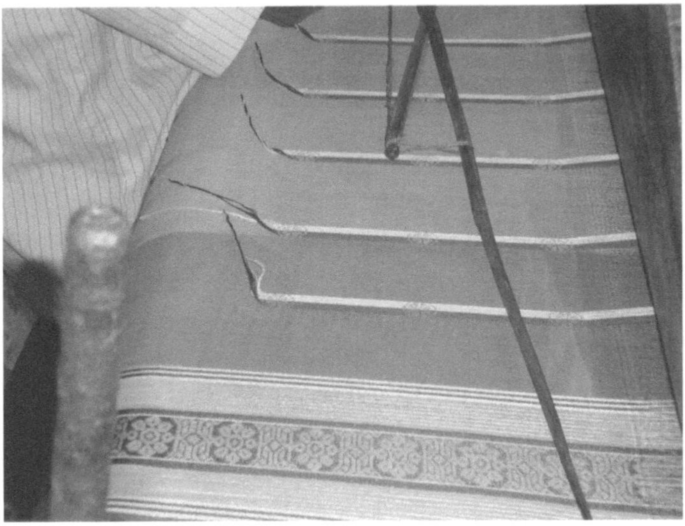

Figure 4.12D ***Kata-Naksa*** **Saree of Begampur Region.** *Source*: Author's Photo

often contains designs in both the border and base (*jami*) area. Weavers use different other varieties of yarn (mainly *zari*) in the border area. It separates these items from the rest of the products. The name has been adopted for the process of design formation—where weavers generally cut small segments of threads in between weaving. *Kotki* sarees on the other hand are entirely different kinds of products. For this particular type of product weavers often use a different variety of yarn brought in from Odisha. These bundles of yarns come in a specifically dyed form which supplements the particular pattern within a woven item (as shown in figure 4.12E). The *Chua-Pati* sarees on the other hand despite being made from coarser and thicker varieties of yarns contain quite a considerable amount of design. The name has been adopted from use of wooden splice (pati) for maintaining an optimum height between warp threads required for design formation.

The highest quality of broad border sarees in Begampur region are produced with the finest varieties of yarns (i.e., 80s x100s & 100s x 100s) using jacquard frame looms (see figure 4.12F and G). Both technology and use of finer variety of yarn have helped in increasing the count of warp and weft threads to its optimal range (i.e., 1,700–2,000). Moreover, these items are often woven in two contrasting colors—such as black and red and with simple floral motifs at the *jami* (body) with an extra warp of 2/100s or 2/80s cotton yarn. Due to these there has been a considerable amount of improvement in the quality of products.

Most of the handloom products of Begampur are quite simple and budget-friendly as they are produced with coarser varieties of yarns using fly-shuttle

Figure 4.12E ***Kotki*-Saree of Begampur Region.** *Source*: Author's Photo

Figure 4.12F Highest Quality Jacquard Loom Items of Begampur Region. *Source*: Author's Photo

Figure 4.12G Highest Quality Jacquard Loom Items of Begampur Region. *Source*: Author's Photo

frame looms. The unfussy and less aesthetic nature of items also makes them cheap in price. The low- and medium-grade products are available in the price range of rupees 160 and 650. Except for some of the highest-grade products, the rest of the Begampuri items do not have huge demand in the market. Due to the steep competition from the products of other major centers like Shantipur, Dhaniakhali, or Rajbalhaat, these people often sell their own products to their customers in the nearby marketplaces. Buyers of these items are mostly restricted to a few regions. Most of the products from this region generally go to several shop-floors in Chanditala and Srirampur (in Hooghly district), who sell them to both their well-known and floating customers. Most of these customers usually buy these products for their daily use. Only the high-quality products which range between rupees 1,500 and 2,000 go to places like Howrah and Barabazar of Kolkata.

CHAPTER SUMMARY

This chapter provides a comprehensive overview of the world of handloom weaving, exploring intricate complexities inherent to various aspects of the handloom weaving process in Begampur region. With four key sections of this chapter, each shedding light on different facets of handloom weaving, i.e., technology, production processes, work coordination, products, and their market, this chapter provides a well-rounded exploration of this age-old yet ever-evolving artisanal practice where the local weavers are struggling to straddle the realms of tradition and innovation.

The chapter starts with a comprehensive examination of the tools and equipment essential to handloom weaving. With a detailed description encompassing particular types of looms and other associated apparatus used for cloth production, this chapter has tried to paint a picture regarding the intricacies of the loom, its components, and other implements that play a pivotal role in the processes of handloom weaving and its evolution in the course of time. It shows that the local weavers have often worked in small, family-based units and utilized traditional tools and techniques that have been handed down to them through generations. Traditionally, weavers of Begampur region have used fly-shuttle framed dobby looms and have produced simple, mediocre, and above-average items. However, the handloom weavers of this region began to face tough competition from powerloom, especially since the post-independence period when powerlooms grew rapidly across the country.

Moving forward, the chapter delves into the diverse knowledge and skills required at various stages of cloth production. From the initial stages of yarn preparation to the final intricacies of fabric finishing, the expertise demanded at each step is explored. This section serves as a valuable resource for both novices and seasoned artisans, offering a nuanced understanding of the craft's intricacies. Findings reveal that the process of handloom weaving in Begampur, much like in any other center in the Hooghly district, was and perhaps still is a labor-intensive art, characterized by its precision and skill. However, the emerging powerlooms with their capability of earning more profit even with lesser labor requirements began to impact the existing scenario regarding labor market, skill, knowledge, work coordination, and the economy of the local weavers. Due to this, factors like infrequent supply of job assignments, low wage, and exploitation have severely impacted the perception of local weavers, especially the younger generation.

This chapter explores the significance of work coordination and the division of labor within weaving communities in the next section. It provided readers insights into how artisans often work in tandem, form relations in production, and contribute to the creation of finely woven fabrics. It shows how often caste, age, gender, and skill lay the rules of work coordination and division of labor within the handloom industry of Begampur region. For example, most of the tasks of handloom weaving were controlled by the weaver caste population, jobs such as seizing and rolling of yarns were exclusive domain of the women and children, meanwhile men perform the job of warping, weaving, and entrepreneurship. But the community of craftsmen in this region is gradually moving toward skill and specialization-based rules of work coordination. This not only highlights the communal aspect of the craft but also underscores its socioeconomic implications.

The final part of the chapter delves into the raw materials used in handloom weaving, the diverse range of products crafted, and the dynamics of their market. From the sourcing of high-quality yarns to the market trends influencing consumer preferences, this section provides a holistic view of the handloom industry's supply chain and market dynamics. It shows that the traditional Begampuri handloom items owing to the use of cheap quality raw material and less aesthetic contents were easily emulatable in powerlooms. Due to this reason, the cheap-priced powerloom products started providing tough competition to Begampuri handloom items. Invariably, the handloom weavers of Begampur region, who generally catered to the needs of a particular section of customers only, began to use finer varieties of yarns and adopt new tools and techniques to save themselves from this unfair competition. Eventually, this paved the way for the incorporation of technologically more capable and advanced jacquard looms in Begampur region, because jacquard looms with the opportunity of making handloom items with finer varieties of yarn and much higher aesthetic content, which is very hard to emulate in powerlooms, are able to provide certain levels of security to the local handloom weavers.

NOTE

1. Yarns are classified into No. 60, No. 80, and No. 100 based on their diameter. In comparison to No. 80 threads, No. 60 threads are thicker in diameter. And, the No. 100 thread is the finest.

Chapter 5

The Disjuncture and Juxtapositions of Cloth Production, Organization, and Marketing

Like in many other parts of our country, the life of handloom weavers in Begampur region is often epitomized by intricate choices between "tradition and modernity," "sustenance and struggle," and "artistry and economic challenges," which become the biggest source of disjuncture and juxtapositions. This disjuncture is characterized by a stark contrast between the artisanal traditions they represent and the challenges posed by technological advancements, economic shifts, and social transformations.

Artisans of Begampur often find themselves in a tricky situation of having to adjust according to the demands of a rapidly changing world. On the one hand, their life is deeply rooted in a particular cultural heritage and tradition. The traditional hand-woven items they produce are made through age-old techniques, skill, and artistry, which they have inherited from their predecessors. On the other hand, these artisans face the constant pressure of producing cheaper, mass-produced textiles owing to the process of mechanization and commercialization. This conflict between preserving tradition and meeting market demands creates a disjuncture that weavers have to grapple with daily.

Needless to say, juxtapositions emerge within this intricate interplay between tradition and modernity, creativity and commercialization, and empowerment and exploitation. For example, these artisans invest their time and skill in crafting handmade clothes with intricate designs and personal touches. Yet, the economic returns often are not commensurate with their effort. Globalization has brought opportunities, but it has also exposed them to competition from cheaper, mass-produced goods. Many weavers find themselves at a crossroads, where their artistry and economic sustainability are placed in stark juxtaposition. The prevalent informal system of cloth production and marketing in the Begampur region is another example, which empowers a particular group leaving the rest of the people at the margins. This paves the way for inequality, oppression, and massive disparity in income. Even though we often get to see successful coordination of "skills," "cloth weaving techniques," "intergroup-labour-coordination," and "vision and market network of the entrepreneurial classes" in the arenas of cloth production and marketing. But deep down these different groups of people, driven by the disjuncture[1] of their social life, come together with different sets of intentions that stand in stark juxtapositions.

In this chapter, I will look at some of the juxtaposition and the sources of disjuncture that deeply affect the life of handloom weavers of the Begampur region. In so doing I will first try to explain how the issue of individual creative identity and community-level collective production creates juxtapositions in the first subsection. Then, in the second subsection, I look closely into the dichotomy of traditional artisanal craft and technology-driven commercialized mass production which perhaps is one of the biggest sources of disjuncture among the handloom weavers of this region. Then I move my attention toward some of the organizational juxtapositions. In the third subsection, by looking into the informal and formal organization setups I explore how handloom weavers act upon the issue of dependence and relative independence. In the fourth subsection, I unravel some of the persisting types of contracts in which the weavers of this region engage themselves to understand the issue of empowerment and exploitation. Here I explain how and under what circumstances despite having different life experiences and intentions, these different sets of groups involved with cloth production and marketing come together to provide a character to cloth production and marketing in the Begampur region. Finally, in the last two subsections, I discuss some of the core juxtapositions that have haunted investors and philanthropists for a long period of time. In the fifth subsection, I explain how due to the persisting situation the local weavers, entrepreneurs, and philanthropists often face difficulty while making the choice between utility products and items with high aesthetic content. In the sixth subsection, I explain the dilemma that the local weavers encounter while retaining their local identity amid the ongoing process of homogenization.

INDIVIDUAL CREATIVE IDENTITY VS. COMMUNITY-LEVEL COLLECTIVE PRODUCTION

On the one hand, handloom weaving often involves exploration and expression of individual artistic ideas, emotions, and experiences. This independence provides artisans with ample room for experimentation, risk-taking, and the development of a distinctive artistic style. Again, on the other hand, the act of weaving often requires collaborative efforts, with family members and sometimes neighbors contributing their skills. By bringing together diverse perspectives, skills, and talents community-level collective production presents the possibility of shaping the cultural identity of a group, fostering a sense of shared heritage and belonging. The act, therefore, on the one hand, pushes individual weavers to create something unique to stand ahead in the competition, again on the other hand, weavers are bound to collaborate as a group due to their deep sense of togetherness, belonging to the community feeling and requirement of mutual support. This tension between maintaining individual creative identity and community-level collective production in handloom is quite an old phenomenon, perhaps as old as the act of handloom weaving itself. But the issue became more prominent especially when the handloom industry began to expand and cater to the growing demands while satisfying the diversified needs of the customers during the medieval period. Then in the late sixteenth century, the insurgence of European traders into the arena of India's cloth business increased this tension manifold, which perhaps has taken its worst form, especially since the beginning of commercialization and mass production of hand-woven clothes during the twentieth century. The external interventions in the form of specific demand have often forced handloom weavers to curtail their artistic liberty to earn their living amid market-driven mass production.

The situation of handloom weavers of Begampur is quite precarious in this regard. The handloom industry in Begampur region was originally developed to cater to the needs of specific niche of customers. Handmade items of Begampur region were not as aesthetically rich compared to other well-developed handloom weaving centers in the Hooghly district. Due to the restricted demand of the Begampuri handmade items the handloom weavers of this region historically had no solid reason for inclining toward the individual creative liberty with which they can bring innovation and product diversification. Instead, they mostly engaged themselves in mass production and sale of relatively mediocre handloom items that were capable of earning them their livelihood at that point in time. However, handloom weavers of this region found themselves in a lot of trouble as soon as powerloom products started grabbing a large share of their market and customers. Invariably, due to their less labor-intensive nature and the possibility of earning more profit, entrepreneurs started favoring powerlooms over their hand-driven counterparts. Needless to say, it resulted in low earnings, shrinkage of job assignments, and at times joblessness. Therefore, in order to maintain their existence, handloom weavers of this region had to come up with some sort of innovativeness as they became subject to much tougher competition. It is from this point onward, the tension between maintaining the individual creative identity and being a part of community-level mass production became prominent within the handloom industry of Begampur region. Though quite few and far between, some individual weavers felt the need and began to bring necessary changes in terms of technology and design. Handloom weavers' cooperatives and the handloom cluster of this region played a crucial role in this regard. During the course of time, the handloom weavers of this region have been able to make the required modifications and rekindle a separate identity along with the incorporation of jacquard frame-looms within their tradition. But the process of creation of a separate identity comes with a lurking danger of pushing handloom weavers under the same loop of being a part of mass market-driven production, invariably which has the potency of throwing Begampuri handmade products into oblivion again. Perhaps, due to this constant pressure to keep innovating, the handloom weavers of Begampur region will never be free from this innate tension.

TRADITIONAL ARTISANAL CRAFT VS. TECHNOLOGY-DRIVEN COMMERCIALIZED MASS PRODUCTION

The choice between traditional artisanal craft and technology-driven commercialized mass production is another juxtaposition that has haunted handloom weavers since the beginning of mechanization. On the one hand, the act of handloom weaving was and perhaps still to a large extent is a traditional artisanal craft production that relies on expertise in a specific craft and the mastery of individual skills that are passed down through generations. Craftsmen focus on honing their expertise in a specific craft. Each produced item therefore reflects a craftsman's skill and dedication involving a personal touch and meticulous attention to detail, resulting in high-quality, unique products. The technology-driven commercialized mass production on the other hand provides the opportunity for rapid and large-scale production of goods that results in cost efficiency, making products more accessible to a wider market. Moreover, machines and automation ensure a high level of consistency in product quality and specifications. The traditional crafts, therefore, often contribute to cultural preservation, while mass production pushes weaving practices toward cultural homogenization as standardized products permeate global markets.

The situation in Begampur is not much different. Today, framed dobby looms and jacquard frame looms, which are traditional artisanal equipment, stand in direct juxtapositions to the technology-driven commercialized mass production in powerlooms. Invariably, the choice between the existing competing forms of technologies available for cotton cloth production often puts the handloom weavers in a great dilemma because it often works as one of the biggest sources of disjuncture for the handloom weavers of the Begampur region. Apparently, this disjuncture of technological choice may appear to be a simple phenomenon from a shallow point of view. But in reality, it epitomizes the struggle that several groups involved with cotton cloth production in the Begampur region had to go through to be in tune with the "process of modernization" while "keeping alive their tradition." Furthermore, this technological transition has wider socioeconomic implications for different groups involved with cotton cloth production in the Begampur region. For example, despite having similarities regarding the involvement of the number of men and women for different preparatory activities, the mechanism of cloth production and the outcome in human-operated framed dobby-loom, jacquard frame looms, and machine-driven powerlooms are vastly different (see table 5.1).

Compared to powerlooms, the mechanism of cloth production in handlooms (i.e., in both the cases of framed dobby looms and jacquard frame looms) is highly skilled and labor-intensive. However, there are differences between the mechanism of cloth production in framed dobby loom and jacquard frame loom as well. Cloth-making activities in a jacquard frame loom are much more labor-intensive and highly skilled compared to that of framed dobby looms. Often weavers have to invest much more time and labor to produce a single item in jacquard looms. Meanwhile, the mechanism of cloth production in powerlooms is a machine-driven cost-effective process.

The product range in powerlooms is not as wide as found in the case of handmade items of Begampur region, that is, in both the cases of framed dobby looms and jacquard frame looms. But the rate of production in powerloom is much higher invariably which saves a lot of time. Hence, powerloom products of the Begampur region are cheap compared to handmade items. The cost of handmade items is much higher as production of these items usually requires a lot of time, skill, and manual labor. So powerloom products with their cheaper price range and higher rate of production provide tough competition to low-grade handmade objects. However, the situation of weavers persisting with jacquard looms in Begampur region is quite different in this regard. The jacquard loom products, because of their higher aesthetic content, stand relatively immune to such steep competition from powerloom products. Understandably, the practices of using jacquard frame looms and producing hand-woven items with much higher aesthetic content in the Begampur region have emerged as an adaptive mechanism not only to carve out a separate identity for Begampuri hand-woven items but also to regain some of the lost clientele and counter this particular problem as well.

This difference in the process of production often results in different outcomes, especially in terms of the "rate of production" and "profit margins."

Table 5.1 A Comparative Overview of the Productive Processes in Handlooms, Powerlooms, and Jacquard Looms of Begampur Region

			Type of Technology		
			Frame-Loom with Dobby	*Powerloom*	*Jacquard Loom*
Investment	**Buying of Raw Materials (Amount in Rupees)**	Warp [*tana*]	1,900–2,000	2,400–2,500	8,500
		Weft [*poren*]	1,700–1,800	2,100	8,000
		Border & Design [*par-o- paton*]	700–800	1,000–1,100	1,600–1,700
	Dyeing of Raw Yarns (Amount in Rupees)		750–850	1,000–1,200	1,500–2,000
	Preparatory Activity (Amount in Rupees)	Production of finished fiber	750–850	1,000–1,200	1,200–1,500
		Puruni-kara and *Naraj-gutano*	500–600	600–700	800–1,000
		Ba-sana-gantha	120–150	150–175	400–500
	Electricity Bill (Amount in Rupees)		0	300–400	0
	Cumulative Labor Charge for Weaving for a Set of Production (Amount in Rupees)		1,350–2,250 [i.e., 45–75/item]	450–600 [i.e., 15–20/item]	36,000–48,000 [i.e., 600–800/item]
	Total (Amount in Rupees)		7,500–9,000	9,000–10,000	58,000–71,000
Rate of Production (in Hours)			10–15	2–3	40–45
Output (Amount in Rupees)			10,000–12,000	18,000–20,000	90,000–120,000
Profit (Amount in Rupees)			2,500–3,000	9,000–10,000	30,000–48,000

Source: Author

Field observations reveal that a person persisting with the simple framed dobby loom in Begampur region often gets a profit of around rupees 2,500–3,000 per loom in comparison to rupees 9000–10000 against one powerloom (see table 5.1). The case of the jacquard frame loom is relatively different. Despite providing the chances of gaining higher profit of rupees 30,000–48,000, the rate of production in the jacquard loom is much lower, even lower than the framed dobby looms. Hence the amount of return is also moderate.

Such stark disparities in labor involvement and production outcomes have pushed these different groups to make their choice differently. For example, the entrepreneurial classes of this region, because of the higher chances of profit, started inclining toward cloth production through powerlooms. Setting up powerloom requires a high amount of money which is not as difficult for an entrepreneur to accumulate as for a resourceless weaver. Needless to mention, buying a jacquard loom also requires a hefty amount of money. Moreover, jacquard looms also require a total investment of rupees 58,000–71,000 for carrying out production. Due to their higher asset base, the entrepreneurial class (*mahajans*) can manage their own cloth business even without setting up such a powerloom unit, as they have 20–30 separate looms working under their fold, from which they can earn a monthly profit up to rupees 30,000–40,000. Even they had the capability of buying and setting up a jacquard unit as well. However, the common artisans were hardly able to manage their affairs, as they didn't have plenty of resources to carry out cotton cloth production on their own.

Thus, powerlooms in the Begampur region became a matter of concern for the resourceless weavers who up until a point were producing simple cheap-priced clothes for a particular clientele in their framed dobby loom using a moderate technique. The woes of the local artisans aggravated further as soon as the coexisting tradition of powerloom production units started replacing the skills and knowledge required in handloom cloth production by changing the role of a particular section of the population who used to associate themselves with different stages of cotton cloth production in a different manner altogether. This gradual takeover often resulted in underemployment among the handloom weavers of the Begampur region, for which many members from the younger generation have shifted to lucrative livelihood options. Eventually, this paved the way for some of the other problems and juxtapositions that weavers of this region are they are facing currently.

THE INFORMAL VS. FORMAL ORGANIZATIONAL SETUP: THE ISSUE OF DEPENDENCE AND RELATIVE INDEPENDENCE

The organizational aspect of cloth production in handloom epitomizes another important juxtaposition and perhaps one of the biggest sources of disjuncture in the life of the handloom weavers. Historically, activities of handloom weaving in India have always been carried out in informal terms since the time of its inception. It was more a subsidiary economic activity restricted to a particular geographical region only. However, gradually with the opening of maritime trade in the sixteenth century some of the exquisite Indian handmade items gained popularity in the west-Asian and European markets. Invariably it attracted many European traders to venture into the arena of Indian cloth business. To ensure a constant supply of their desired products, these traders started a system of advance payment[2] to the Indian artisans. The business prospect of Indian clothes in the foreign market has also allured the Mughal rulers to make structural reorganizations in India's cloth production. To scale up the rate of production Mughal rulers started establishing several native courts across different parts of India. Even they appointed supervisors to look after the affairs of cloth production in these native courts. Due to this gradual commodification and commercialization, Indian handloom weavers got trapped within an oppressive system where skilled artisans became mere laborers. The artisans had very little room to bargain for their own benefit. The situation got aggravated further along with the emergence of the Indian entrepreneurial class and *mahajani* system during the colonial period. This prolonged oppression and exploitation of the handloom weavers forced the then-British government to encourage the budding cooperative movement. This eventually resulted in the formation of formal institutional alternatives in handloom weavers' cooperatives during the post-independence period. Handloom weavers' cooperatives tried to provide weavers with an opportunity to escape poverty through the provision of fair wages, access to resources, and improved market linkages. Due to their clear hierarchical structure, well-established rules and regulations, clear job roles, and standardized processes and policies, handloom weavers' cooperatives soon gained popularity across different parts of the country. Looking at the popularity and role of the cooperatives for community development and poverty eradication, the newly formed Indian government started making special provisions for these institutions through three consecutive Five-Year Plans, especially during the first two decades after the independence. With opportunities, handloom weavers' cooperatives started improving the situation of the poor handloom weavers to a certain extent. Nonetheless, the path that handloom weavers' cooperatives have taken for the revival of Indian handloom is not free from challenges, obstacles, and corners. For example, the formal institutional structure which often ensured handloom weavers with a sense of security at times held them with their stringent institutional rules and bureaucratic nature of the decision-making procedures. Moreover, despite its well-developed credit framework and its vital role as an intermediary between the poor artisans and their customers in distant marketplaces, handloom weavers' cooperatives have often fallen behind in regard to the poor recovery of loans and high levels of over dues. Invariably, this has put handloom weavers in a dilemma of whether to continue with complete dependence on handloom weavers' cooperatives or to shift back toward relative independence under the informal system, even if it comes with the possibility of exploitation and oppression.

This dilemma was and perhaps still is quite evident among the handloom weavers of the Begampur region. Historically handloom weavers of this region have carried out cloth-making activities under informal terms and conditions of the *mahajani* system. Cloth-making activities under this system were often carried out on the basis of some informal rules of exchange. Such informal organizational setup often involved different groups such as (i) entrepreneurs—either in the form of big merchants (*mahajan*) or master weavers, (ii) laborers—which included both the resourceless weavers and the people who were engaged in several allied activities, and (iii) the distributors or the middlemen (*pikers*)—who used to accumulate different kinds of products from local production units and supply them to distant market places, constituted the hierarchy of this informal. Based on the role, responsibilities, and rank within the production and marketing system the *mahajans*, master weavers, middlemen (*pikers*), weavers, and the people associated with several allied activities constituted the hierarchy in descending order (as shown in figure 5.1). Except for the class of middleman involved with the marketing of products, the rest of the labor force engaged in "dyeing of threads," "drumming" or "production of back beam," and "denting and drafting," including the artisan weavers themselves ranked much lower than a big merchant or a master weaver. Usually, the middlemen used to work as subordinate employees under the big merchants or master weavers and ranked relatively higher than the rest of the labor force.

The working conditions for the resourceless weavers who usually had a single loom were never quite conducive, to say the least. These weavers mostly organized various activities of production with the assistance of their family labor. Apart from weaving, which they performed themselves, weavers took assistance from their own family members for preparatory activities such as seizing, rolling of threads into the bobbins, and rolling of threads into the pirns. And, for other specialized jobs such as drumming, preparation of warp beam, and denting and drafting the resourceless weavers have taken the assistance of outside laborers. However, these single-loom owners/petty producers failed to run their own enterprises as they often operated with a weak asset base. For that reason, they became vulnerable to the credit network of big merchants. The big merchants of Begampur region, on the other hand, were chiefly engaged in trade apart from providing a supply of raw materials,

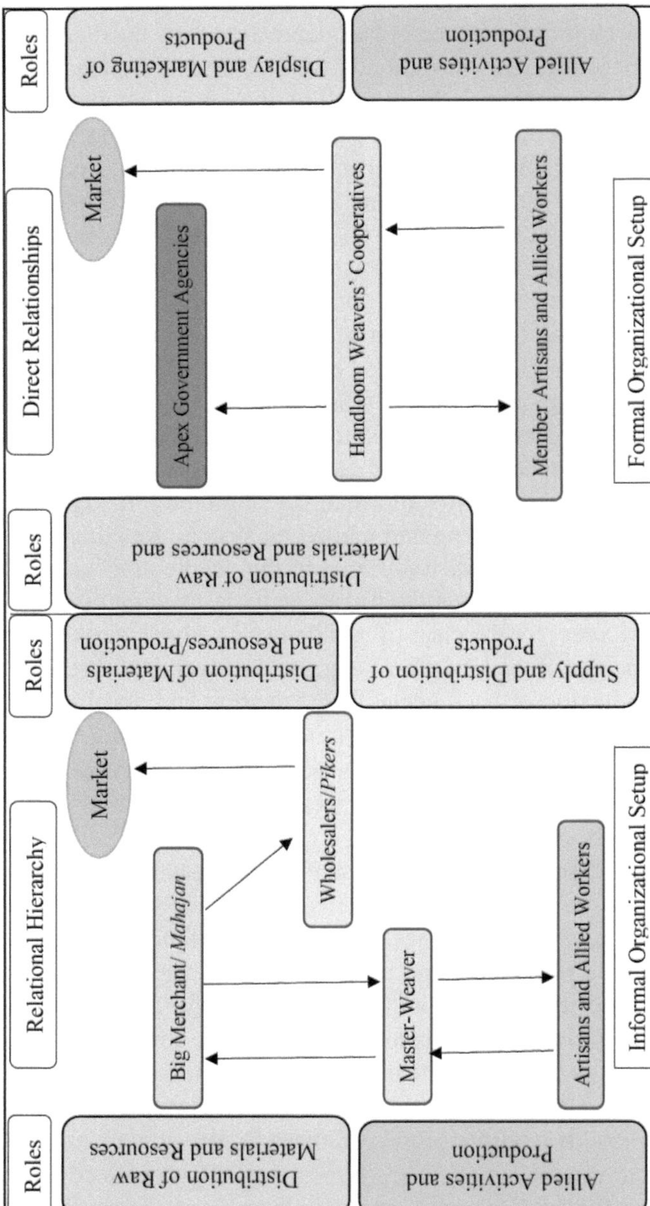

Figure 5.1 Informal vs. Formal Organizational Setup in Begampur Region. *Source:* Author's Photo

investing money in different stages, and marketing. Some of the big merchants have organized productive activities within their household premises. They mostly engaged loom-less weavers as wage laborers for this job. Sometimes, these big merchants even worked with these men, when they didn't have the time to hire a master weaver for supervision. Like big merchants, some of the master weavers at times have taken the burden of investing money in several stages of production. They even have employed some of these resourceless single-loom owners. Despite this, eventually, due to their lack of ability to take risks and necessary access to the market, master-weavers too had to sell their products through the big merchants, resulting in the curtailment in their share of profit. Interestingly, the single-loom owners or loom-less weavers hardly had any room to advocate for better wages.

To save these resourceless weavers from the clutches of such informal organizational setups, handloom weavers' cooperatives were introduced in the Begampur region during the 1970s. Much like elsewhere in the country, the handloom weavers' cooperatives of this region have also tried to provide the required support to each of their enrolled members. In terms of structure, the constitution of these handloom weavers' cooperatives in the Begampur region, much like in other parts of the Hooghly district, was pretty simple. There was a fixed number of enrolled member weavers who directly worked under these institutions. Member weavers often worked on the basis of formal contracts under which they are expected to produce a certain number of items without having to worry about sales and marketing of these items. Unlike in an informal organizational setup, there were no intermediaries between member weavers and these handloom weavers' cooperatives. The rest of the labor force engaged in several allied activities like "drawing the design," "seizing, rolling of threads into the bobbins," "rolling of threads into pirns," "drumming," "denting and drafting," and even "weaving of cloth" got their predetermined wage in return. Despite having relative success during the initial period, handloom weavers' cooperatives didn't get their intended success due to persisting issues like lack of working capital, lack of innovativeness and product diversification, corruption, and difficulties associated with the marketing of products. Invariably this has pushed a lot of the handloom weavers of this region of shift back to the informal *mahajani* system even if it is filled with loads of oppression and exploitation. Today, most of the weavers in the Begampur region work under the *mahajani* system. Only a very negligible number of people work under the formal setup of the handloom weavers' cooperative. Thus, the choice of whether to associate themselves with informal or formal organizational setups has been affecting the life of the handloom weavers of the Begampur region for a long time.

EMPOWERMENT VS. EXPLOITATION: TYPES OF CONTRACTS AND THE RELATIONS IN PRODUCTION

The juxtaposition of empowerment and exploitation that handloom weavers encountered was and still very much is a part and parcel of the choice where handloom weavers decided either to associate themselves with the formal or the informal system of cloth production. The Indian handloom weavers have been facing this dilemma since the emergence of handloom weavers' cooperatives after the independence. On the one hand, due to their clear job roles, well-defined rules, regulations, policies, and a definite hierarchical structure, the formal system of handloom weavers' cooperatives provided a considerable amount of security to the poor handloom weavers. Moreover, these institutions empowered them as they financed different cloth-making activities along with their definitive role in the marketing of the products. The informal cloth production system on the other hand has often oppressed and exploited poor artisans by capitalizing upon their economic condition and lack of access to the market. These artisans have often received unfair wages despite providing their immaculate skill and artistry for cloth production. This vicious cycle of becoming mere workers under an employer made handloom weavers even poorer. The emergence of handloom weavers' cooperatives certainly has provided weavers some opportunity to restrain themselves from falling prey to the vicious trap of indebtedness under the informal system of cloth production.

The situation in the handloom industry of Begampur region is not much different in this regard. Handloom weavers' cooperatives were introduced in the region to save weavers from oppressive unjust and unequal systems of profit and returns allocation under the informal organizational setup of cloth production. However, owing to the inability to provide work assignments to all members, corruption, and difficulties associated with the marketing of products most handloom weavers of this region have shifted back to the oppressive and exploitative informal system. Despite knowing all of these, most weavers in the Begampur region have no other alternative but to work under the same oppressive, unjust, and unequal organizational setup.

Interestingly, the degree of exploitation and oppression varies depending upon the type of contract between an employer and the worker. Currently, handloom weavers of Begampur region engage in three types of contracts under the informal organizational setup for cloth production, that is, (i) "system of taking prepared warp beam," (ii) forward contract system (*tana-ana*), and (iii) "system of taking direct credit from the market" (*nokta*) (see table 5.2). And the way relations in production were regulated and maintained in these types of informal contracts are some of the biggest forms of disjuncture

Table 5.2 An Overview of Informal Labor Contracts within the Handloom Industry of Begampur Region

Type of Contract	*Type of Weaver in Terms of Resource*	*Received Item/s*	*Tasks*	*Market Risk*	*Return*
"System of Taking Prepared Warp Beam"	Resourceless Artisans	Prepared Warp Beam from the Employers	i) Weaving Cloth	Nil	i) A fixed wage, depending on the complexity of the design ii) Typically, this wage ranges from rupees 50 to 70 per woven item
Forward Contract System (*Tana-Ana*)	Weavers with Relatively Better Asset Base	Dyed Yarns from the Employer	i) Processing of Finished fiber ii) Preparation of Pirns iii) Drumming/ Warping iv) Denting and Drafting v) Weaving	Relatively Higher	i) A share of the profit from each woven item ii) Typically around rupees 630 for a pair of woven cloths
System of Taking Direct Credit from the Market (*Nokta*)	Big-Merchants/ Master-Weavers	Buys Raw Yarn from the Market	i) Dyeing of Raw Yarn ii) Processing of Finished fiber iii) Preparation of Pirns iv) Drumming/ Warping v) Denting and Drafting vi) Weaving	Fully Exposed to Vulnerabilities of Market	i) Major share of profit from the sold woven items

Source: Author

that have tremendously affected the lives and livelihood of the handloom weavers of the Begampur region.

The majority of weavers in Begampur region have typically shown a preference for and have been engaged in the forward contract system. In contrast, both the "system of taking prepared warp beam" and the method of "obtaining direct credit from the market" have been less commonly adopted. The forward contract system is utilized by weavers who possess relatively more resources compared to their counterparts, the common artisans, whose primary asset is their looms. Today only very few weavers of this region with inadequate amount resources, take "prepared warp beams" from big merchants. In return depending upon the complexity of the woven design they get a pre-fixed amount of wage which varies between rupees fifty to seventy per woven item. The reason for the obscurity of this type of contract is its provision of such a meager wage that depends upon the volatility of the market situation, especially the prices of raw ingredients and the labor costs associated with the other allied activities, which are always on the rise. Generally, the big merchants (*mahajans*) fix labor charges based on their expenditures in buying raw yarn, dyeing, and other related processes right up to the preparation of the warp beam. The floating nature of labor charges has made the situation even tougher for the local weavers. Over the years, the situation has become so volatile for the local resourceless weavers that they hardly have any chance of meeting their requirements with their low earnings.

Due to the inconsistencies associated with the adoption of already prepared warp beams, the majority of common weavers tend to favor the forward contract system. In the Begampur region, weavers with a relatively stronger asset base, owning at least two looms, typically opt for the forward contract system. The standard practice under the forward contract system involves employers supplying the entire quantity of warp and weft threads to their workers. In return, the employees produce finished woven items, receiving a predetermined wage. Under this arrangement, the workers take on all responsibilities, including dyeing, seizing, rolling of threads, drumming, denting, and drafting, up to the final production stage. For this, they receive a share of the profit for each woven item, typically valued at around 630 rupees per pair of woven cloths as compensation. Clearly, it places them in a more advantageous position compared to those who receive an already prepared beam from their employer. However, due to the limited income generated from this system, weavers often find themselves compelled to make compromises, either on the width or the quantity of thread in a woven item to secure additional profit. Many a time, these weavers don't provide 1,700 or 1,800 warp threads as instructed by their *mahajan* (employer) and take advantage of the general ignorance of their customers. To secure additional income, these weavers occasionally sell some items produced from the residue threads directly to customers apart from fulfilling their contractual obligations.

Conversely, the "system of taking direct credit from the market" in Begampur region primarily involves two classes: the big merchants and the master weavers who historically had sufficient capital to operate multiple independent production units. Typically, these two classes, having procured raw materials and other essentials from the market, distribute them among their employees who lack resources. The master weavers usually often put in their tiny amounts along with the huge amount of these big investors which eventually results in the formation of a larger production umbrella that encompasses both resourceless weavers and those with limited resources.

A single independent production venture of such a big investor, therefore, involves many dependent units of both small-scale investors and resourceless weavers. Big investors provide weavers with pre-dyed bundles of warp and weft threads, other than overseeing the processing, weaving, and return of the finished products. To mitigate risks, these bundles are often supplied in stages. Initially, investors provide the total warp threads required for thirty-five to forty-five pairs of woven items, typically sarees. Once the weaver and their family complete the processing of warp threads, the investors supply the corresponding weft threads. Additionally, these investors invest in various related activities, primarily in post-processing. Generally, it's the weavers who cannot invest on their own who seek their assistance in this regard. Depending on the nature of the contract, these investors not only calculate the total investments and labor charges for each product but also monitor the contingent expenditures incurred by small investors or weavers with adequate resources. Finally, these investors determine the market price of a woven item after considering factors such as their own expenses, the labor and investment put in by specific employees, and the maximum profit achievable from each item.

Typically, the yield from each of their fifteen to twenty looms ranges from 15,750 to 24,750 rupees, contingent on the nature and qualities of the woven item. Remarkably, they only allocate approximately 3,000 to 4,500 rupees for labor charges and other processing costs for a single loom. It is evident that their earnings surpass those of the workers under them by a considerable margin. The big investors, benefiting from their advantageous position, frequently exert complete control over the entire production system. Weavers not aligned with these major investors, participating in various stages of the production processes, often find themselves entangled in the credit network and marketing links established by these big investors.

Evidently, the current scenario of Begampur region is not conducive to investment for those lacking substantial resources. In recent years especially, prices of raw cotton threads have inexplicably risen to a level where only a select few large investors (*mahajans*) can sustain independent operations. This has placed a stranglehold on artisan weavers, affecting not only them but also some of the investors in the process. The situation over the years has become so tricky that even small-scale entrepreneurs find themselves susceptible to the challenges of obtaining "direct credit from the market." Consequently, in the face of such challenges, a growing number of small-scale investors in this region have become hesitant to venture into entrepreneurship. It's not that these small-scale investors of this region cannot invest independently. However, the volatility of the market and the challenges in meeting large-scale market demands have often deterred them from conducting their trade solely through individual investments. In most cases, these investors had to contend with a modest amount of profit due to their inability to increase the price of woven items amid competitive market conditions. Due to this reason, many of these investors find themselves in a situation where they are not able to bear the added responsibility of providing adequate compensation to their workers.

With the escalating difficulties and risks, reducing the level of investment in handlooms has emerged as a predominant trend among handloom investors. Interestingly, a more notable adaptive mechanism has emerged in response to these adversities, where money lenders and master weavers have started to collaborate with the big merchants. A few of them have even started shifting their focus toward more lucrative livelihood avenues, such as manufacturing collars for t-shirts or distributing food items. It's only some of the more resourceful weavers of this region who have managed to hold on to their traditional business.

THE UTILITY PRODUCTS VS. ITEMS WITH HIGH AESTHETIC CONTENT

The juxtaposition surrounding the production and marketing of utility handloom products and items with higher aesthetic value has been haunting weavers, investors, and philanthropists for a long period. Barring the initial period, when cloth production in handloom was more of a subsidiary activity, Indian handloom items always had a steady clientele, especially since the opening of sea trade during the sixteenth century. Invariably as the customers determined the fate of some of the handmade items, the Indian handloom weavers always had to strike a balance by prioritizing artistic and visual appeal while keeping in mind some of the more basic aspects like functionality, durability, practicality, and affordability. These issues became more diversified and intense later on along with the beginning of mechanized mass production that resulted in diversification of India's textile sector. The establishment of mills and powerloom targeting a different section of customers is a prominent example. Today, the demands and needs of the customers have become so diversified that we often get to see the development of regional specialization, style, and tradition in different parts of India. *Pashmina* from Leh, Ladakh, and the Kashmir Valley, *Phulkari* from Punjab, *Kota* from Rajasthan, *Benarasi* of Uttar Pradesh, *Patola* of Gujarat, *Chanderi* of Madhya Pradesh, *Paithani* of Maharashtra, *Sambalpuri* from Odisha, and *Mysore Silk* of Karnataka are few of the prominent examples of such regional specializations.

The case of Begampur in this regard is a little bit different. Historically, the handloom industry of this region has never become well-renowned for the production of any such specialized items. Products woven in fly-shuttle framed dobby looms were more targeted toward the regional niche of clientele as they were hardly able to match the higher aesthetic contents of *Jamdani*, *Baluchari*, and *Tangail* products that flourished under the then-undivided Bengal. Begampuri sarees in general were crafted with a harmonious texture using dyed cotton yarn, featuring contrasting borders in vibrant hues like red, black, purple, and orange. These affordable sarees often exhibited colored stripes and check patterns, with minimal border designs highlighted by a serrated edge motif. However, due to constant steep competition from powerloom products, invariably the handloom weavers of this region felt that there was a definite need and ample scope for product diversification. And, from this point onward, the handloom industry of this region started witnessing some of the major changes in this regard. Occasional training of the local handloom weavers and the incorporation of jacquard frame looms within the existing cloth production tradition are a few examples of these efforts. This eventually led to the beginning of the production of some of the aesthetically rich Begampuri items that we witness today. Characterized by intricate serrated extra weft broader border designs, these items are produced using a finer variety of yarns such as 80s x 80s and 80s x 100s. These sarees often present a striking interplay of two contrasting colors, such as black and red, and feature simple floral motifs on the *jami* (body). Sometimes, the additional warp is created using 2/100s or 2/80s cotton yarn, which adds to the overall elegance of these sarees.

While this has helped the handloom weavers of Begampur region to regain some of their lost grounds, this also puts them under severe pressure as most of the handloom weavers of this region still don't have the access and training to operate a jacquard loom. Needless to say, the handloom industry of this region is hardly equipped to handle huge pressures of demand for their products. Moreover, with such technological advancement and the use of a finer variety of yarns, the cost of production has also gone up quite a bit, eventually which makes the Begampuri item less affordable to their regular customers.

THE ISSUE OF LOCAL VS. GLOBAL: LOCAL IDENTITY VS. THE PROCESS OF HOMOGENIZATION

Retaining local identity often involves preserving cultural traditions, values, and practices that define a community's unique heritage. The process of homogenization on the other hand refers to the emergence of standardized, globally recognized practices that often result in the loss of diverse cultural expressions, as standardized processes tend to create a uniform global culture. Even the field of economy isn't free from the effects of homogenization. The process of globalization most certainly has integrated local economies into the global supply chain. The constant pressure of the demands in the global market has led to the prioritization of global economic interests over local ones, potentially undermining the uniqueness of locally produced goods. Due to this reason, there is an existing juxtaposition between scholars who advocate in favor of retaining local identity while others see the process of homogenization as quite natural and inevitable. The reason for the latter belief is quite clear as it is almost impossible to imagine any secluded economic activity in this day and age.

The Indian handloom industry is not an exception in this regard. On the contrary, India's clothing materials have always enjoyed a steady demand in the west Asian and European markets. Despite the constant demand for Indian handmade clothes Indian handloom weavers have managed to retain a separate identity, which invariably kept their demand intact for a long period. But the scenario started to change along with the deindustrialization of Indian handloom which many scholars see as a result of the prioritization of the British economic interests and undermining the uniqueness of potentiality of India's handmade items. Due to the heavy tariff imposed on the export of Indian handmade clothes and tough competition from cheap-priced British mill-made clothes Indian cloth market started shrinking. The business opportunities for India's handmade clothes were reduced further along with the emergence of Indian mills as an inevitable part of the process of industrialization. It is from this point in time the Indian handloom weavers started to witness some of the ill effects of the processes of homogenization and globalization. Even the process of homogenization and globalization can be held responsible for so many product diversifications within India's textile sector that we get to see today. Some of today's Indian textile products include hand-woven sarees, traditional garments, embroidered fabrics, and hand-block printed textiles. However, despite its crucial role in the country's export earnings, the future of India's textile sector is heavily reliant on the demand for its products in the global market. The exact size of this market fluctuates annually based on global demand and trade dynamics.

The situation within the handloom industry of Begampur region was and perhaps still is quite intricate, to say the least. Unlike in many other developed handloom weaving centers in Hooghly district and in West Bengal, the handloom weavers of this region hardly had any separate identity to cherish. Because of the lack of innovativeness and a prolonged history of producing cheap-priced durable textiles for particular niches of clientele, they always stood on muddy grounds. The act of cloth making hasn't given them anything except their livelihood. Due to this, these weavers have fallen way behind as soon as the handloom industry of this region started witnessing some of the effects of the process of mechanization. Due to the changing demand the local weavers started adapting according to the needs of the customers. Many of the local weavers received training regarding the operation and handling of jacquard loom, dyeing, and design formation. However, despite understanding the role and requirement of the adaptive measures for securing their livelihood in the future, most of the weavers of this region stand in front of a great dilemma today. Often a question haunts them day in and day out—whether, this training, installation of a new form of technology, and inspiration from designs that are in demand will eventually push these weavers toward submerging themselves in the process of homogenization.

CHAPTER SUMMARY

This chapter sheds light on some of the prime disjuncture and juxtapositions that govern the life of the handloom weavers of Begampur region. First and foremost, it shows how the local weavers, much like in any other handloom weavers centers across India, often face one of the most integral dilemmas regarding "maintaining the individual creative identity or participating in community-level collective production." Then the chapter shows how their dilemma increases due to ongoing technological transition and how these local weavers often struggle to "associate themselves with traditional artisanal craft or technology-driven commercialized mass-production." Meanwhile, with a comprehensive examination and comparison between the two different types of organizational setups, types of contracts between employer and the employee, and more particularly the relations in production and marketing, this chapter then sheds light on issues like "dependence and relative independence" and "empowerment and exploitation," which perhaps act as some of the most prime sources of disjuncture and juxtapositions.

Findings show how due to the issue of dependence and independence associated with these two different kinds of organizational setups the local weavers often struggle to associate themselves with either of the two types of organization of production. Because both types of cloth production systems come with their own sets of benefits and limitations. While the informal system of cloth production, because of its openness, provides independence to its workers, the formal system often binds its workers under stringent and well-established rules. Again, on the other hand, the formal system of cloth production provides much more security to its members compared to what members enjoy under the informal system. Findings further show the dynamics of labor relationships among various groups surrounding the production and marketing systems in Begampur region are not solely contingent on the distribution and capitalization of technological expertise. Instead, narratives surrounding labor contracts between different stakeholders demonstrated that these contracts are also formed based on disparities in resources (capital) and access to market networks. Another key factor is the considerable dependence on entrepreneurs for crucial resources, which frequently limits the choices available to weavers. Most weavers in this region are acutely aware that success in the cloth-making business hinges on a precise amalgamation of control over economic resources, concurrent technical skills, and access to market networks. These factors highlight the significance of trust, loyalty, mutual understanding, and the advantages of forging long-term bonds with employers. Individuals proficient in all these facets, more specifically resourceful individuals and their family members, often position themselves favorably amid technological transformations. Conversely, those who provide their labor and services in exchange for a fixed wage often fall on the wrong side of the system of capital accumulation that alienates them further from the products they manufacture and, more significantly, denies them the opportunity to amass sufficient capital to invest in technologies that could improve their situation. Due to this reason, despite possessing technical expertise, the resourceless artisans fall behind in the dynamics of class relationships. Consequently, resourceless weavers in this region often find themselves working under the umbrella of resourceful entrepreneurs due to their reliance on these entrepreneurs for essential resources.

Finally, this chapter shows how due to the aforementioned factors like ongoing technological transition persisting exploitative relations in production and precarious working conditions, the woes of the local weavers increase manifold as they find themselves under the compulsion of making more dilemmatic choices of either "producing utility products or items with high aesthetic content" and "retaining their local identity despite the allure of homogenization". Eventually, all of these have played a crucial role in shaping the trajectory of this particular handloom weaving tradition of the Begampur region.

NOTES

1. Disjuncture refers to a point of "discontinuity or contradiction" (Moore 2011, 291), points at which different logics or processes go in different directions and cause ruptures, tensions, or conflicts.

2. Advance payment is a system where an investor in order to secure the purchase of products provides money to the producers or the artisans in advance. Even though it is a kind of informal contract, the investor can drag producers into a legal suit in case of violation.

Chapter 6

Handloom Weavers' Cooperative Societies in Begampur

A Failed Experiment?

The term "cooperative society" stems from the term "cooperation," in which members of this society will form a voluntary association with the motive of the welfare of the members. Members of a cooperative society are often driven by the need to protect their economic interests in the face of possible exploitation at the hands of middlemen. Characterized by its open membership, democratic setup, limited liability, and service motives, cooperative societies can be of many types. "Producer cooperatives," "marketing cooperatives," "consumer cooperatives," "credit cooperatives," and "housing cooperatives" are a few of the prominent examples. However, to function as legal entities these societies needed to be registered under the Cooperative Societies Act, 1912.

Handloom weavers' cooperative societies are basically the producer cooperative societies that contribute in regard to the empowerment of marginalized groups of handloom weavers and promote inclusive growth among them. Handloom weaving is primarily a rural-based industry. The development of cooperatives in rural areas can lead to rural employment generation, improved infrastructure, and the overall development of rural communities. Many handloom weavers come from economically disadvantaged backgrounds. Handloom weavers' cooperatives offer them opportunities to escape poverty by providing fair wages, access to resources, and improved market linkages. These cooperatives often act as intermediaries between weavers and markets, helping handloom weavers access broader consumer bases and gain recognition for their products.

Similarly, these cooperative societies were also known for fostering a rural-urban linkage as they provided urban consumers with access to unique, handmade products while benefiting rural artisans. Moreover, handloom weavers' cooperatives encourage a sense of solidarity among weavers and ensure social welfare benefits, including healthcare, education, and housing.

Apart from its primary level of concern for maintaining the economic well-being of cloth producers, these cooperative societies are also renowned for their multifaceted roles in society such as the promotion of cultural preservation, gender equality, and sustainable practices. For example, handloom weavers' cooperatives, because of their association with the handloom weavers, eventually play a vital role in preserving the cultural and artistic traditions that have been passed down through generations. Besides, many cooperatives focus on empowering women weavers as handloom weaving is a labor-intensive industry that often involves a significant number of female weavers. They try to empower women by providing them with financial independence and a voice in decision-making. Finally, handloom weavers' cooperatives often promote eco-friendly practices and sustainable sourcing of materials compared to mass-produced textiles.

However, despite all its promise, handloom weavers' cooperatives in many handloom weaving traditions have failed miserably. From an ideological standpoint, the objectives with which handloom weavers' cooperative societies were introduced in India are quite immaculate, to say the least. For obvious reasons, the number of weavers' cooperatives, their membership, and the amount of their working capital throughout the country has increased, especially since the independence. In fact, as a policy, this was, perhaps still is, one of the best measures that the Indian government has adopted for the well-being of the poor artisans. However, this policy has also faced serious challenges concerning its implementation in a pan-Indian scenario. The social, economic, cultural, and political situations in many of the handloom weaving traditions across India were not conducive to the establishment of handloom weavers' cooperative societies.

Historically, Begampur has been one such instance where handloom weavers' cooperative societies haven't attained that much success. Even though the situation started to turn around in the last ten years, especially since the inception of Begampur Handloom Cluster, most of the handloom weavers' cooperatives in Begampur region today still stand on the muddy ground. In this chapter, I will look to provide a brief history of handloom weavers' cooperative societies in India through the first subsection. This will help readers understand the reasons and causes for which handloom weavers cooperatives were formed across the country. In the second subsection, I will look into the specific reasons and the factors based on which handloom weavers' cooperatives in the Begampur region came into existence. Here I will also try to provide a brief overview of the institutional structure, primary objective, and proceedings of the handloom weavers' cooperatives in the Begampur region. And then I will look to unravel the causes behind the stalled growth of handloom weavers' cooperatives in this region. Finally, in the third subsection, I will shift my research attention toward the Begampur Handloom Cluster and try to evaluate how with the introduction of the Begampur Cluster society the situation started to turn around for these poor artisans through the second subsection. First, I will look into the existing perceptual differences among groups of people responsible for setting up the Begampur Handloom Cluster. Here I will also try to understand the component-wise funding and support difference that the handloom cluster of this region continues to receive compared to handloom weavers cooperatives. Needless to say, invariably the proceedings, structural, operational, and fundamental differences between handloom cluster and handloom weavers' cooperatives come into contention. For this, I look into some specific areas such as "technology and production," "weavers" training," and "promotion and marketing" where Begampur Handloom Cluster has been able to bring the required changes.

A BRIEF HISTORY OF HANDLOOM WEAVERS' COOPERATIVE IN INDIA

The history of handloom weavers'' cooperatives in India is closely intertwined with the country's rich tradition of handloom weaving, which has been a source of livelihood for millions of people for centuries. The seeds of cooperatives were sown perhaps during the pre-independence period, especially with the enactment of the Cooperative Credit Societies Act 1904 and the establishment of industrial cooperatives in India (Venkatasewarlu and Sathish Babu 2017). Thereafter, the cooperative movement in India began to flourish since the year 1923 as the British Indian Government started providing financial assistance to industrial cooperation that included handloom weavers' cooperatives.

Prior to this, handloom weaving was a vital part of India's rural economy and Indian handloom weavers mostly operated as individual artisans in small, decentralized clusters. But, it all started to change when Mughal rulers started establishing the Native Courts and cast the whole "organization of production" into a different mold altogether between the early sixteenth and the mid-eighteenth centuries. The system of finance, involvement of the state, and role of peasant families in production never remained the same since that period. Gradually, the active role of the weavers in the creative field was curtailed. Weavers no longer remained as independent artists. With a State-sponsored system of production, weavers became merely skilled and hired workers under the State (Das 2001). The entry of European traders into the arena of the Indian clothing business made things much worse for Indian artisans as they began to face several challenges like "injustice" and "deprivation," mostly inflicted by exploitative middlemen based on their limited access to the markets. As a result, weavers began to unite for the demand of fair wages and better working conditions.

Nonetheless, the condition of the handloom weavers in India didn't improve much with such demands. Instead, the Indian handmade clothes, which retained an edge in the domestic market up until the first decade of the twentieth century, began to face stiff competition due to the growth and consolidation of the mill sector. Handloom weavers' growing dependence on mill-made yarn proved detrimental as the inter-sectorial competition reached its pinnacle along with the outbreak of the First World War. Some of these problems were even recorded by the Royal Commission on Agriculture in the year 1928. The Royal Commission on Agriculture reported that the development of the village industry on cooperative lines was essential to the survival of weavers in the face of increased competition from organized industry (GOI 1986–87, 1).

Meanwhile, the condition of handloom weavers continued to worsen even after the independence in the year 1947 as the insurgence of the new breed of cloth production techniques altered the configuration of the Indian cloth market and decreased demands for Indian handmade items. Soon, the independent Indian government began to recognize the requirement to support traditional crafts and the livelihoods of handloom weavers as these artisans came across other correlated problems such as sturdy inequality, low wages, loss of jobs, unemployment, etc. (Roy 1993; Basu 2001; Murshed 2004, 312).

To tackle some of these issues the Government of India started adopting several policies, schemes, and initiatives. This was the time when the cooperative movement in India began to receive fresh impetus from the newly formed Indian government during the first two decades of India's independence. Three consecutive Five-Year Plans, that is, First Five-Year Plan (1951–1956), Second Five-Year Plan (1956–1961), and Third Five-Year Plan (1961–1969), have provided crucial guidelines and made significant contributions in this regard. A detailed vision of the cooperative movement in India is outlined in the First Five-Year Plan (1951–1956), which encouraged the adoption of the cooperative method for community development, in many aspects such as setting up of urban cooperative banks, industrial cooperatives of workers, consumer cooperatives, housing cooperatives, etc. The Second Five-Year Plan (1956–1961), based on the recommendations of the All India Rural Credit Survey Committee (AIRCS) emphasized "building up a cooperative sector as part of a scheme of planned development" as being one of the central aims of National Policy, and the Third Five Year Plan (1961–1969) stressed that "Cooperation should become, progressively, the principal basis of organization in branches of economic life, notably agriculture, minor irrigation, small industries and processing, marketing, distribution, rural electrification, housing and construction and provision of essential amenities for local communities" (Tiwari and Ahirwar 2017, 880–881). As a result, handloom weavers' cooperatives started to emerge in different states across India. These cooperatives were often formed with the assistance of government agencies and nongovernmental organizations. They provided weavers with access to credit, raw materials, training, and marketing support.

Meanwhile, the Fourth (1969–1974), Fifth (1974–1979), and Sixth (1979–1985) Five-Year Plans continued to advocate for a reorganization of cooperatives; especially for the direct benefit of the underprivileged or the downtrodden section of India's rural population, the National Bank for Agriculture and Rural Development (NABARD) Act was passed in 1981 to provide financial support to Cooperative Banks and to supplement the resources of Commercial Banks and Regional Rural Banks to enhance credit flow to the agriculture and rural sector (Tiwari and Ahirwar 2017, 881). Then the National Handloom Development Corporation (NHDC) was established in the year 1983 to provide financial and technical assistance to handloom weavers and weavers' cooperative societies. The All-India Handloom Board was established in the year 1992 to coordinate and support the promotion of handloom weaving and encourage the formation of cooperatives. Needless to say, all these initiatives have played an indirect but significant role in the development and promotion of handloom weaving in India as they helped weavers' cooperatives in improving the income of the handloom weavers, preservation and revival of traditional Indian weaving techniques and designs, and promotion of indigenous textiles.

Despite the positive initiatives taken by the cooperatives, handloom weavers continued to face various challenges. Competition from power looms and mechanized textile industries, fluctuations in demand, and issues related to access to credit and marketing remained significant hurdles for these cooperatives. Even there were issues concerning the proceedings of cooperatives as well. As the Seventh Five Year Plan (1985–1990) pointed out while there had been all-round progress in the provision for providing credit, poor recovery of loans, and high levels of overdues were matters of concern. Eventually, this led the Indian government to make slight alterations in the Eighth Five-Year Plan (1992–1997), which encouraged the cooperatives to develop a more autonomous and democratic environment in order to become self-managed, self-regulated, and self-reliant institutions. In 2002, the Government of India established a National Cooperative Policy. The objective of the Policy is to facilitate an all-round development of cooperatives in the country. The government of India periodically announces schemes and programs to support handloom weavers and cooperatives, including financial incentives, training, and marketing support.

HANDLOOM WEAVERS' COOPERATIVE SOCIETIES OF BEGAMPUR REGION

For a long period, especially before India's independence, the situation of the handloom weavers across India and in West Bengal was deemed to be unfair for those poor artisans who didn't possess anything other than their innate skill set and at times one single loom. The task of accumulating the required money for investment in different stages of cloth production, coordinating, organizing, and paying for the entire production and auxiliary activities, and eventually selling the woven items to its customers proved to be too hazardous for these poor artisans time and again. In most cases, the common artisans in general lacked the entrepreneurial skills required for running and coordinating all these activities successfully.

The situation in Begampur region was not much different in this regard. Over the years, much like in other handloom weaving traditions across the country, the handloom weavers of Begampur region faced many problems which I will explain one after another in the following subsection that has led to the inception of handloom weavers' cooperative societies in Begampur region.

The Inception: Historical Causes

Unlike in many other parts of our country, where handloom weavers' cooperatives began to emerge after the independence, handloom weavers' cooperatives in the Begampur region came into prominence during the late 1970s. The then-communist government of West Bengal played a crucial part in their development as the group of poor artisans began to realize the importance of comradery and cooperation. Bara-Begampur Samabay Samity (Cooperative Society of Bara-Begampur) was one of the first weavers' cooperative societies that was set up in this region. It was very successful during the early years. Gradually, many others began to emerge. Chhototajpur Samabay Samity (i.e., Cooperative Society of Chhotatajpur) and Kharsarai Madhyampara Samabay Samity (i.e., Handloom Weavers' Cooperative of Kharsarai) were two prominent examples.

(i) *Technological Stagnancy and Unfair Competition from Powerlooms*: For a long time, up until the inception of the handloom cluster society, which has taken considerable steps toward technological upgradation in recent years, handloom weaving technology in Begampur region was in a state of moderate development. The techniques, implements, and raw materials local weavers use for cloth production are comparatively inferior to other developed centers of handloom weaving in West Bengal. The handloom weavers of Begampur region in general mostly operated in the framed dobby loom. Due to the restricted clientele and relatively low demand, handloom weavers of this region generally preferred a coarser variety of yarns (i.e., No. 40 or No. 60) and produced relatively simple form woven items. Traditionally, handloom weavers of Begampur region were renowned for a particular brand of simple woven item. Except for exquisite items produced through jacquard frame loom, the handloom sarees in Begampur region are usually made from the coarser quality of yarn and with relatively less warp threads. Therefore, products of this region, in general, fell way behind in the competition as they hardly provided any competition to products from other prominent centers of cotton weaving in the Hooghly district like Dhaniakhali or Rajbalhat.

This long period of stagnancy regarding technological upgradation made Begampuri hand-woven items more susceptible to the growing competition in the market. On the one hand, where handloom weavers in many of the handloom-weaving traditions were upgrading their skill sets and adopting new cloth-making techniques, the handloom weavers of Begampur region stuck to their old way of making cloth. This has proved to be quite detrimental to the growth and prospect of the handloom industry in Begampur region. However, the situation in Begampur region became drastically different along with the expansion of cloth cloth-making business. Because of the lack of aesthetic content within the hand-woven items of Begampur region, and the possibility of gaining more amount of profit from the technology-driven, less labor-intensive cloth production process of powerlooms, the entrepreneurs began to view powerlooms as a more lucrative option for investment. As a result, powerloom products have emerged as one of the major competitors during the last twenty years.

Obviously, loopholes in textile policies have also helped these machine-driven looms to take unfair advantage of handloom items. Powerlooms in Begampur region, much like in other parts of the country, often ripped all the benefits of small-scale industry without having to follow the obligations imposed on mills. For example, instruction regarding the installation of a certain number of powerlooms within a work shed has often been bypassed. In most cases, powerloom owners installed more of these machines than they are actually permitted. In place of the stipulated two to three, which they have originally requested in their applications, these owners have often installed five to six powerlooms. At times, power loom owners haven't followed the particular rule either that debars the powerloom from copying the designs of handmade items. Many such deviations are found in practice in the Begampur Region.

Obviously, handloom weavers of this region have protested against this unfair growth and illegal practices, which has curbed the illegal installation of the powerlooms in Begampur region to some extent. But, even after such protests, powerloom products, because of low price, high production rate, and relatively less labor-intensive nature of production system, managed to capture a major share of the cloth market. Looking at the opportunities of making more profit, many local entrepreneurs became more inclined toward cloth production through powerlooms. And, this shift from labor-intensive to capital-intensive productive processes has badly affected the labor force of Begampur region. Nonetheless, this hasn't made much difference to the proceedings of the big investors. Because with slight adjustment they continued to enjoy full control over the marketing mechanism. In most cases, these investors used the local weavers for the production of cheap but relatively attractive cloth aimed at a particular section of the population. In case of low demand in the market, they often decreased their rate of production, and that ultimately led the common weavers to face its consequences. Either way, the weavers of Begampur region suffered from underemployment or the problem of low wages. Due to this, many young members of the weaver caste families have shifted to the production of collars for t-shirts in search of better livelihood options.

(ii) *Unorganized and Exploitative System of Production and Marketing*: The unorganized system of production and marketing—where a few entrepreneurs because of money and control over the marketing mechanism oppressed the majority of the poor resourceless artisans—is one of the biggest problems. Under this unorganized system, there is no fixed rule or system of formal contracts between an employer and employee. Moreover, such a system didn't really provide resourceless weavers an opportunity to get their due share of earnings, subsequently making them poorer to suffer even more at the hands of the investor class.

Most of the handloom weavers of Begampur region were very poor. As per the historical references these artisans mostly used to cater to the needs and demands of local customers. These poor artisans didn't have anything other than their innate skill sets which they had inherited from their forefathers. The scenario began to change along with the overall changes that have taken place across India and in West Bengal. These poor artisans needed to scale up their cloth production owing to the growing demand for handmade clothing items. But with their meager amount of resources, these poor artisans were hardly capable of making a series of investments for essential activities like buying raw yarn, dyeing, preparation of finished fiber, warping, denting and drafting, fitting, and finally weaving, all of which required substantial amounts of money. Invariably, this pushed most of these artisans of Begampur region to go to the local resourceful people or entrepreneurs who are capable and willing to fund these activities of cloth production. Otherwise huge number of these artisans would have become jobless all of a sudden. Taking money from the investors for carrying out cloth-making activities soon became a new norm in Begampur. In due course, a few of the local weaver caste men with adequate among of money for making investments in these different stages of cloth production started seizing the opportunity and formed their own networks of cloth production within and outside Begampur. Sensing the opportunity of making money from such ventures a few other non-weaver caste residents also jumped into the cloth-making business. Even though these non-weaver caste people didn't have the money, they because of their prolonged stay in Begampur region had the necessary contacts and knowledge of markets and customers. Even though less in number, these non-weave caste men by fetching money from investors residing in distant places started building their own network of funding and investment for the local resourceless artisans. This increased competition among the investors to make more money out of their investment sowed the bedrock of exploitation and oppression of the poor artisans. Slowly, the investor class of Begampur region started marginalizing the interest of these poor artisans which resulted in either curtailment in the share of profit or stagnation of the wages.

The woes of those weavers who operated with a moderate amount of resources were quite different. Despite investing in all these stages of cloth production, the act of selling their woven items soon became a challenge along with the entry of these entrepreneurial classes in the arena of cloth-making business in Begampur region. Up until the scaling up of cloth production activities in Begampur region, these petty investors were catering to the minuscule demands of their local and regional clientele. All of a sudden, the growing and diverse range of demands from different sections of West Bengal and the country put them under immense pressure. They could not afford to carry on in their old way of production due to the changing demands and customers. Invariably, they also needed to form alliances with these newly emerging entrepreneurial classes (*mahajans*) in Begampur region who often control the activities of production and marketing.

Institutional Structure, Primary Objective, and Proceedings

Even though the institutional structure of handloom weavers' cooperatives in India varies from one cooperative to another, the handloom weavers' cooperatives across India in general follow and fall within a well-defined institutional framework. Handloom weavers' cooperatives in general have a typical structure: (i) General Body, (ii) Board of Directors, (iii) Executive Committee, and (iv) Weaver Members. The general body is the highest decision-making authority of the cooperative and consists of all the weaver members. Each member typically has one vote, regardless of the number of shares they hold. The general body meets periodically to discuss and make decisions on various cooperative matters, such as electing the board of directors, approving annual budgets, and setting cooperative policies. Elected by the general body and usually consist of experienced weavers or individuals with expertise in cooperative management who look after and manage the day-to-day affairs of the cooperative. The board often oversees the cooperative's operations, makes key decisions, and represents the interests of the weaver members. Often a subset of this board is formed in the form of an executive committee, which typically includes key office-bearers such as the president, vice-president, secretary, and treasurer. These individuals play important roles in the administration and financial management of the cooperative. Sometimes, managers are appointed and finance, procurement of raw materials, training, marketing, and social welfare subcommittees are formed in cases of larger cooperatives to oversee the operational and administrative functions other than implementing the policies and decisions of the board and streamline the operations by focusing on various aspects of the activities of handloom weavers' cooperatives, respectively. Needless to say, the weaver members work as the main driving force of these institutions as they actively participate in the production of handloom textiles and are key beneficiaries of the cooperative's activities. Weaver members typically have the opportunity to purchase shares in the cooperative, which entitles them to various benefits and a say in the cooperative's governance. In addition, handloom cooperatives sometimes employ staff for administrative, marketing, and operational roles. These employees help in the day-to-day functioning of the cooperative and the implementation of various programs.

Structurally, the handloom weavers' cooperatives of the Begampur region are not much different. These weavers' cooperatives have a general body, a board, an executive committee, a manager, and weaver members (see figure 6.1). The board members are selected by the general body in the same manner who oversee the cooperative's operations, make key decisions, and represent the interests of the weaver members. The executive committee or the "office" again is the subset of this board which typically includes a secretary, a manager, and a cashier. These three individuals cumulatively look after the entire proceedings right from the buying of raw yarn, dyeing, distribution of work assignments among the member weavers, receiving and scrutiny of woven items, and finally marketing or selling of woven items. Just like in other handloom weavers' cooperatives in the country, all the member weavers of

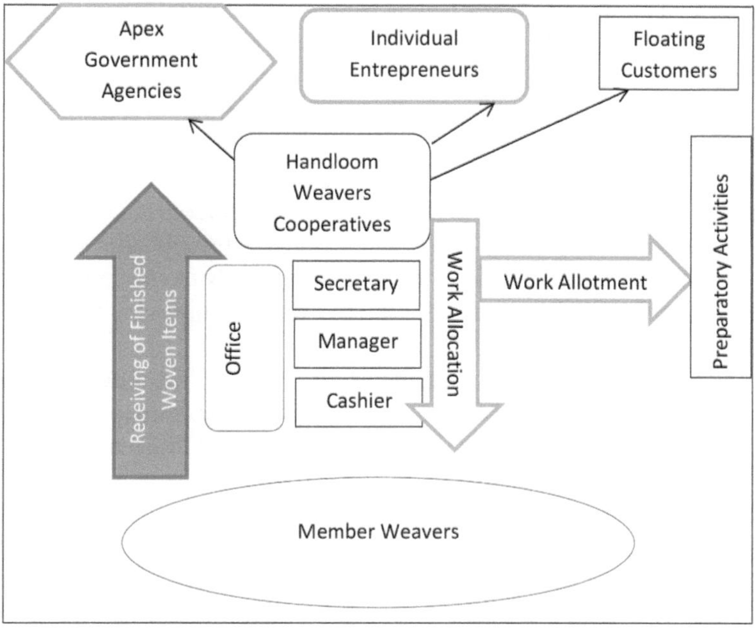

Figure 6.1 Intuitional Structure of Handloom Weavers Cooperative Societies in Begampur Region. *Source*: Author's Photo

these institutions accumulate and sit together after a certain interval to discuss the progress of the cooperative, resolve issues, and update members on the cooperative's activities, decide on the future course, and to take important decisions. These meetings provide transparency and accountability in the functioning of the cooperative.

Handloom weavers' cooperative societies across India, in general, were introduced mainly to serve two primary goals, i.e., (i) to provide infrastructural facilities and (ii) to strengthen the economic conditions of the resourceless weavers. Most of the handloom weavers' cooperatives of this region tried to reorganize different activities of handloom cloth production and marketing by bringing the resourceless weavers of Begampur region under a formal setup as members of these institutions, where they don't have to worry about anything else except for technical aspects of cloth production. Other than improving the overall scenario of the Indian handloom industry, which held an important place in the Indian economy as a major provider of employment next only to agriculture,[1] handloom weavers' cooperatives are formed to support and empower weavers with a view that these institutions would ensure various benefits, including access to credit, training, and marketing support especially because of their liberal structure.

The primary objective with which handloom weavers' cooperative societies were introduced in different regions in India and West Bengal is not much different in Begampur either. Much like elsewhere in the country, the proceedings of these institutions in Begampur region revolved around some of the core tasks like (i) safeguarding the interests of the resourceless weavers from the exploitation and clutches of the middlemen; (ii) supplying raw materials, equipment, and other facilities to the members according to their capability of production; and (iii) regular disposal of reasonable wages to the weaving members to enable them to continue in the weaving profession and thereby improving their standard of living as well as improving the handloom production (Kshetrimayum 2011, 67).

However, despite having similarities in terms of the intent, "ways of fund accumulation," "supply of raw materials," their principle of distribution work assignment, wage, and other facilities, few differences have been observed in terms of the proceedings of these institutions compared to other handloom weavers' cooperatives across India and West Bengal. Handloom weavers' cooperatives of Begampur region much like in different places across India often provide raw materials like yarn, dye, and other materials to the local weavers at a cheaper price. Moreover, these institutions finance various stages of cloth production for which funds are accumulated from (i) the enrolled members, (ii) working capital provided by the State Government against each of its enrolled members, and lastly, (iii) the fund provided by the Government of India for the State's participation. These institutions even left no stone unturned with the better marketing of the hand-woven items of this region. By imposing strict rules on their member-weavers, these intuitions have even tried their level best to maintain the quality and texture of the hand-woven items in the Begampur region. However, despite the strong requirements most of the handloom weavers' cooperative societies have failed to capitalize upon the technical assistance and training aid that they have received from government agencies, NGOs, and other organizations for raising the standard the woven materials and developing new and sophisticated designs that have high demand. Lack of innovative measures in the marketing

Factors Responsible for Its Stalled Growth

Despite having similar objectives, intent, and proceedings, the handloom weavers' cooperative in the Begampur region hasn't been a success. Even though it is very hard to single out any particular factor as responsible for this apparent failure, cumulatively many broad factors can be pointed out for its stalled growth which I will discuss one after the other.

(i) Lack of Capital and Less Coverage: Today, most of the handloom weavers in Begampur region suffer from the problem of insufficient working capital. Despite having the provision of a prescribed way of fund accumulation where these institutions are likely to receive financial support from both the state and the central government, the board members of these institutions often complain about not having sufficient amount of capital to cloth-making activities of all the members at the same point in time. Providing uninterrupted investment for each of our enrolled member weavers is often the biggest problem for handloom weavers of Begampur region. The board members, especially the managers have often expressed their inability and dissatisfaction regarding their lack of coverage of distributing work assignments to their enrolled members. The handloom weavers' cooperatives in the Begampur region on average usually provide a yearly work assignment to only 30 to 50 members among the total 100 to 300 of their enrolled member weavers. Their reasons are quite obvious. One single loom of an enrolled member weaver requires a start-up investment of 8,000 to 10,000 rupees for a single set of production (*charan*) which contains forty to forty-five pieces of saree. Moreover, this loom will require similar investments of 8,000 three to four times to keep the loom running throughout the year. Additionally, investments of at least rupees 5,000 to 6,000 are required for the initial preparatory processes as soon as a weaver completes 50 percent of production. Otherwise, the member weaver will have no job for about twenty to thirty days, as he/she will have to sit out during the period of initial processing that includes dyeing, production of finished fiber, *puruni-kara*, *ba-sana-gantha*, etc. Understandably, the money required for facilitating all the enrolled members becomes quite a challenge. Cyclically, this lack of coverage results in the curtailment or decrease in the number of member weavers, which in turn makes the task of accumulating funds further difficult for these institutions as the government often provides funds based on the number of member weavers. In this way, a number of the handloom weavers' cooperatives have become dysfunctional.

(ii) Corruption: Due to this reason, only a very negligible number of weavers are associated with these institutions. Even the members who are associated with these institutions are not very optimistic about their ability to bring the required transition. Despite this frank admission of the inability to provide work assignments to all its enrolled members, the general feeling among the local resourceless weavers about these handloom weavers' cooperatives in Begampur region is not pleasant. Unlike the handloom weavers' cooperative officials of this region, the resourceless weavers don't consider the inadequacy of funds to be one of the crucial factors. Rather, they mostly point toward the innate corruption that has hindered the progress of these

institutions in this region. These people often speculate and at times openly admit about the misappropriation of governmental funds and facilities. This can be understood from the following remark:

> Weavers' cooperatives exist only in paper. Over the years, a few of these institutions have managed to keep their existence . . . and a few others, those are repeatedly being shown are merely a reflection of a corrupt system . . . Apart from the annual meet to sign on the paper where each member gets a packet of food there are no facilities for the actual weavers. . . . and the irony is that most of the members (weavers) are satisfied with that.

The local weavers often accuse these institutions of "fraud," because, in most cases, these agencies are run by the local *mahajans* themselves who deliberately put the names of relatives and other kinsmen as members of handloom weavers' cooperatives for accumulation of funds and facilities. Some of the idle member weavers often accuse these people of using these funds and facilities for their own benefit instead of using them for the well-being of these resourceless weavers. A few of the member weavers have gone a step further by accusing the cooperative officials of forgery, dodging, and faking. One of the most important examples of this is when *mahajans* are accused of collecting the products from independent production units and showing them as the products of the handloom weavers' cooperatives as soon as government officials come for inspection during the time of annual audit. Understandably, cases of alleged bribing of government officials coming for such visits have also been reported as accumulating a bulk number of different variety products is quite difficult within such a short time period.

(iii) Hurdles of Marketing Mediocre Hand-Woven Items: Due to the non-inventiveness and lack of adaptability to the ongoing technological transition across the world of weaving, the products of Begampur region always had a restricted clientele. For a long time, weavers of this region have fallen way behind in this competition compared to the other developed centers in the district and the state. It has obstructed in expansion of the customer base across the state and the country. With the emergence of powerloom products and the sharing of client-base the lives of simple poor artisans of the Begampur region became dreadful. Soon, this restricted demand closed the option of selling items to the open market. Even though the handloom weavers' cooperatives in Begampur region had the safety net of their well-established network with apex governmental agencies, the task of selling mediocre hand-woven items of this region remained quite a challenge for these cooperatives as they failed to capitalize upon the opportunity of technological upgradation given by both the state and central government. The apex governmental agencies also felt the brunt of this ill-adjustment as buying without assessing the demand of

their prospective buyers led to the stacking of the unsold handloom items of this region. Looking at the diminishing prospect of business, these apex agencies also gradually started curtailing their orders to these agencies.

(iv) Ground-Level Politics and the Influence of Mahajans: The lack of coverage of the handloom weavers' cooperatives especially has increased the intensity of other related problems manifold. The local investors of this region have often used their familiarity, money, and the loopholes with the working mechanism of the handloom weavers' cooperatives to their advantage. On the one hand, the inability to provide a continuous yearlong work assignment to all the enrolled members has left many poor artisans on the verge of joblessness. The funds and facilities often did not reach the resourceless weavers which eventually sowed the seed of doubt in the minds of these resourceless weavers concerning the credibility, functionality, and relevance of these institutions in general on the other hand. The limited marketability of mediocre hand-woven items has also played its part in this regard. Due to such insecurities associated with the handloom weavers' cooperative, the local investors have been able to easily allure the resourceless weavers by making lucrative offers that they could not be able to refuse. This ultimately entailed the local weavers to work under the individual entrepreneurs as the situation didn't provide them with any other option. However, the situation was not that grave always, especially during the days of the inception of handloom weavers' cooperatives in the Begampur region. A number of these institutions were quite successful in providing raw materials at a cheap price and successful marketing of the hand-woven products of this region. In fact, due to this early success, a few of the local investors (*mahajans*) started to feel threatened by the establishment of handloom weavers' cooperatives in Begampur region. Invariably, they started to use their influence to stop the progress of these institutions. Invariably with continuous resentment from local investors, many of these handloom weavers' cooperatives did not survive. Bara-Begampur Samabay Samity was one of the prime examples which was allegedly burnt out by the influence of the local investors. Since then, no other handloom weavers' cooperative societies in Begampur region have ever reached that level of success. This incident clearly reflects the reason why local weavers are still persisting with *mahajani* system despite several of its disadvantages.

RISE OF BEGAMPUR HANDLOOM CLUSTER SOCIETY

The situation in many handloom weaving centers in West Bengal and across the country invariably pushed the Indian government to look for an alternative policy or scheme that could alter the situation. Needless to say, the handloom weavers' cooperative despite having credulous objectives were falling behind in several aspects. Stringency in rules and regulations, lack of success regarding technology and skill upgradation, and product diversification according to needs in the market are a few examples. Understandably, to chart out sustainability for handloom weavers across the Indian government has begun to encourage those weavers who remained outside the fold of the handloom weavers' cooperative to form handloom clusters.[2]

Invariably, with the constant encouragement from the Weavers Service Centre (WSC) in Kolkata, the handloom weavers of Begampur decided to apply for a cluster development scheme in 2008. However, due to the lesser number of members (400 approximately), these weavers have applied for the formation of a mini-Handloom Cluster only. As stipulated in the guidelines of the scheme, a baseline survey was conducted. Officials from the Directorate of Handloom, Government of West Bengal, visited each household of those weavers whose names were enlisted in the application. Their criterion of evaluation was based on an association of these individuals with the job of handloom weaving along with the prospect of the handloom weaving tradition in terms of technological upgradation and product diversification. Upon receiving a satisfactory response from the baseline stakeholders, the scheme was sanctioned in the year 2010.

The Structure and Consortium

Handloom clusters are structurally and fundamentally much different from handloom weavers' cooperatives. Unlike handloom weavers' cooperatives, handloom weaving clusters are often registered under the Society Registration Act 1860. The consortium of handloom weaving clusters often involves stakeholders from Self-Help-Groups (SHGs), cooperative societies, master weavers, private entrepreneurs, nongovernmental organizations (NGOs), etc. including government officials who play the role of key office bearers during the initial implementation period. The case of Begampur Handloom Cluster was not much different as it mostly involved resourceless weavers who remained stuck in the middle of formal proceedings of the handloom weavers cooperative and the oppressive *mahajani* system. Besides, it involved many cooperative officials and individual entrepreneurs who also felt the need for revival.

Funding and Support

Usually under a handloom cluster scheme a group of weavers receives funding under several heads right from the very beginning. For example, the funding and support in cluster development programs often include the cost incurred for conducting the "baseline survey," "diagnostic study," and "formation of consortium." In most cases, a service charge is provided to a designated agency that carries out the first two tasks. Moreover, other than the "project management cost," "cost for engaging a textiles designer", and "wage compensation to the trainees for skill upgradation", handloom clusters also receive funding for carrying out awareness programs, "product development," "exposure visit," "participation in exhibitions," and "documentation of cluster activities." Because of the application as a mini handloom cluster, Begampur Cluster Society has received rupees fifty-five lakh as a fund, fifty thousand of which has been received for conducting the baseline survey, carrying out the diagnostic study and the formation of a consortium, five lakh of which has been received for building dyeing unit, ten lakh as margin money or working capital, and the rest of the amount as project management cost that includes employing a designer, providing wage compensation to trainees involved in skill upgradation, building awareness, exposure visit, and conducting buyer-seller meet. The officials involved with Begampur Cluster Society have been diligent enough in terms of their utilization of the space provided by Handloom Weavers' Cooperative of Kharsarai (Kharsarai Madhyampara Samabay Samity) and their vision for technological upgradation. However, due to the difficulties associated with getting the pollution permit, the money received for building of dyeing unit has been returned unutilized.

Activities and Proceedings

Understandably, the activities and the proceedings of Begampur Handloom Cluster are relatively different. Even though there are similarities in terms of activities like collection of raw yarn, dyeing, work allocation to its members, scrutiny, collection of products, provision of wages, and sales and marketing, there is no concept of membership or buying of shares. For this reason, members cannot claim their share in profit. The scale of cloth production in Begampur Handloom Cluster is much higher compared to handloom weavers' cooperatives. Therefore, the handloom cluster often purchases raw yarn from the open market as the fixed stipulated amount of five-kilogram yarn per weaver member in subsidized Mill Gate Price doesn't suit the production requirements. Moreover, as discussed earlier the consortium of the handloom cluster is relatively different. Unlike in a handloom weavers' cooperative, several stakeholders from Self-Help Groups (SHGs), members of cooperative societies, master weavers, and private entrepreneurs come together for a business purpose. SHGs under a handloom cluster are often formed to fetch financial assistance to the cluster weavers through banks apart from fund allocation. Currently, there are ten SHGs under Begampur Cluster. However, that doesn't mean that handloom clusters do not provide facilities and welfare measures to their members. And Begampur Cluster is not an exception in this regard, they provide subsidiary loans to all the member weavers, facilities of Provident Fund (PF), wage compensation for holidays, and days of training.

Efforts and Initiatives for Revival

Begampur Handloom Cluster has taken considerable steps for the revival of handloom weaving in Begampur region. Right from bringing in infrastructural development to bringing innovation and providing training to the local weaver for skill upgradation, to building awareness, and finally their effort regarding policy advocacy and sales and marketing welfare initiative of the Begampur Handloom Cluster has been multifaceted. I will discuss them one after another.

(i) Infrastructural Development: Begampur Handloom Cluster has been associated with a considerable amount of infrastructural development. The office and work shed of Begampur Handloom Cluster is located on the first floor of the Handloom Weavers Cooperative Kharsarai. This was the place from where this cluster began its journey in the year 2010. To reduce individual costs and invest money in improving the quality of their products, Begampur Cluster still uses this common infrastructure facility as an office, common workspace, finishing, and storage unit. This old office includes office furniture, internet facility, desktop computers with printers, scanners, and tablets along with CATD software—"SWATHI Textile Designer Release 4.0." Digital facilities also enabled improvements in design execution for the weavers. However, during the course, it has built another common training facility center, especially for training. This "Common Facility Centre" comprises a work shed, office cum meeting room, design studio with CAD facility, yarn storeroom, and a toilet. It was constructed for the benefit of weavers. A yarn bank was set up to cater to their needs. An effort has also been noticed regarding the incorporation of new technologies. There are thirty-two dobby looms, two jacquard looms, and six plain looms functioning in the cluster. Ten frame looms, ten dobbies, and five jacquards were provided to the weavers, and fifty weavers were given loom accessories at a subsidy of 90 percent (Press Information Bureau 2017).

(ii) Innovation, Training, and Skill Development: Begampur Handloom Cluster has taken part in several initiatives concerning the innovation of weaving techniques, training of the handloom weavers and their skill development. For example, Begampur Cluster has actively taken part in a sample development program, financed by the state government, which was carried out in September 2012. Under this program, the looms used for making sarees

were upgraded to frame looms. Stoles were woven on narrow-width looms. Changes like better reeds and picks, dobby with extra levers, and 100-hook jacquards were introduced to the local weavers. Several small design shuttles along with the main one were used to improve the aesthetic element. Besides, steel reeds and finer cotton yarn were introduced for a smoother texture. Crucially, new designs with appealing color combinations were added. In this regard, the cluster officials have also encouraged their member weavers to make innovations. The development of *Chua-Pati* designs is one of the prime examples (see figure 6.2), the design elements of which contain influences of weaving patterns of Manipur. Often 2/40 or 2/60s thicker twisted yarns are used for making these particular designs. Moreover, in place of a cheaper arbitrary one, a new costlier technique of yarn dyeing was introduced to improve the quality and colorfastness. With the initiative from Weavers Service Centre (WSC), Kolkata, more than 260 handloom weavers have received training on designing, dyeing, preparatory processes like drum warping and sizing, and more importantly, in dobby and jacquard weaving. The goal was to provide the weavers with motivation and tools to break the monotony in design and proceed toward product diversification. Additionally, soft skills

Figure 6.2 *Chua-Pati* Design of Begampur Handloom Cluster. *Source*: Author's Photo

were imparted to these trainee weavers to enhance their confidence along with production.

(iii) Exposure and Awareness Building: Besides Begampur Cluster has not been far behind in terms of building awareness toward their efforts and their products. A buyer-seller meeting was organized to invite patrons and buyers to introduce the redefined *Mathapard* handloom products to the world with the range having expanded to include stoles (see figure 6.3A). Moreover, the Begampur cluster has introduced the practice of labeling their products with a unique barcode readable handloom tag to facilitate their buyers in differentiating the authentic and copied handloom items (see figure 6.3B). This has helped the products of Begampur region to acquire a rekindled identity in the world of weaving up to a certain extent. The designs gained popularity and have been in high demand since then. In the last few years, Begampur Cluster has formed linkages with significant organizations and aims to increase their business even further, that is, 40 percent of their present annual sales of rupees one crore (Press Information Bureau 2017).[3]

(iv) Sales and Marketing: Concerning the sales and marketing of their product, the approach of Begampur Handloom cluster has been quite different compared to the handloom weavers' cooperatives. To resolve the problem of inadequate exposure to the market it has taken considerably innovative strategies and formed alliances with even private business organizations and retail brands like "Fabindia," "Kamala" of Crafts Council of India, "By Loom" in Kolkata, "Shilpi," and "Red Sanders" in Chennai. Besides, the cluster also maintains contacts, connects, and delivers products to their customers

Figure 6.3A ***Matapard*** **Saree with Serrated Boarder Produced in a Framed Dobby Loom.** *Source*: Author's Photo

Figure 6.3B Process of Tagging Sarees with Handloom Mark. *Source*: Authors Photo

through websites which has increased their reach and business prospect manifolds across the country and the globe.

(v) Policy Advocacy and Collaboration: Other than the aforementioned efforts Begampur Handloom Cluster has also been quite active in their advocacy regarding the needs and prospects of the handloom weavers of Begampur region. Protection against unfair competition, especially from powerlooms, has been a chronic problem in Begampur region for a long time. And now that the local handloom weavers have been able to rekindle their identity to a certain extent, government officials including the District Magistrate (DM), Hooghly, and officials of Begampur Cluster are now looking forward to Geographical Indication (GI) registration as one of the measures of protection, which would eventually restrict other from blatantly copying their design. In the process, Begampur Handloom Cluster has drawn collaboration from the Department of Law National University of Juridical Sciences (NUJS), Kolkata. An application has been submitted in April 2022 which is under consideration.

CHAPTER SUMMARY

This chapter, to begin with, sheds light on how the constant oppression and marginalization of resourceless artisans have led to the consolidation of cooperative movement among the handloom weavers across the country.

Handloom weavers' cooperatives were envisioned as a means to uplift and empower relatively less privileged handloom weavers. It also shows how due to the intricacies and myriad challenges associated with developing handlooms, the welfare initiatives aimed at the advancement or revival of the handloom industry often revolved around enhancing the physical products created through specific technological processes, which, in turn, depended upon various external factors and influences such as funding availability, market demands, and ever-evolving fashion trends and apt navigation through the divergent perspectives of development agents, institutions (including government bodies and NGOs), and the state itself. And, then it shows that the handloom industry of Begampur region is not an exception in this regard. It reveals some of the factors responsible for the establishment of handloom weavers' cooperatives in Begampur region and the subsequent challenges faced by these institutions.

Findings show that the handloom weavers' cooperatives were introduced in the Begampur region to (i) tackle the issue of technological stagnancy, (ii) address the inequalities and hardships stemming from the informal system of production and marketing, and (iii) most importantly save handloom weavers from unfair competition. However, due to the intricate complexities inherent in their formal institutional structure and some of the stringent institutional rules, the handloom weavers' cooperatives of this region took a considerable amount of time to fully grasp and comprehend the exact nature of disparities and gauge the prospect and the actual requirements for nurturing a rich craft tradition while being at par with other facets of development. Furthermore, with persisting issues of lack of capital, corruption, difficulties in marketing, and ground-level politics, the handloom weavers' cooperatives in the Begampur region have not provided significant attention to addressing related issues, including (i) the moderately advanced cloth-making techniques that hardly aligned with the emerging market trends and (ii) the dominance of particular social classes within the unorganized or informal system of production and marketing. Consequently, due to this reason, the handloom weavers' cooperatives in this region, as a welfare measure, failed to transform the handloom sector into a more structured and sustainable model. As a result, these institutions have not been able to achieve any notable success during the initial stages.

Then the chapter shows how the Begampur Handloom Cluster was formed based on the initial failure of handloom weavers' cooperatives. Then it sheds light on the structural and proceedings-wise differences between the handloom weavers' cooperative and the handloom cluster. In fact, by focusing on the initial failure of handloom weavers' cooperatives and the recent success through cluster development program in this region, this chapter perfectly epitomizes the changing attitude and the growing awareness about the actual requirements that have ultimately drawn some of the required changes for the betterment of handlooms in this region. Infrastructural development, training and skill upgradation of the local weavers, incorporation of jacquard looms within the handloom weaving tradition of this region, exposure and awareness building, and inception of web platforms for better sale and marketing may appear to be a simple effort on the part of Begampur Cluster Society. But in reality, these efforts certainly have brought much wider socioeconomic implications. For example, the opportunity to upgrade their skills provided to the handloom weavers of this region proved to be a means through which they can compete with the handloom weavers of other major centers in the Hooghly district and West Bengal. Again, skill upgradation is directly correlated with the improvement in the product range, simultaneously which provides a feasible possibility to increase the earnings of these handloom weavers. But most importantly, these efforts epitomize the struggle of a bunch of handloom weavers who otherwise did not have their share of recognition in the world of handlooms. Improvement within the aesthetic elements of the woven items, on the one hand, renewed the interest of the customers toward Begampuri handloom items. Meanwhile, it has presented the weavers of this region an opportunity to resurrect their situation from the ill effects of mechanized mass production on the other hand.

NOTES

1. The handloom sector accounts for a large proportion of employment, of which the participation of women and children in both the weaving and related activities is quite significant. In terms of the 1987–1988 Handloom Census, the estimated figure of the population which was directly or indirectly dependent on a handloom is 2 to 2.5 million and another 1 million, respectively (Srinivasulu 1996, 3198). And this number has increased over the years, as the Annual Report (2007–2008) of the Ministry of Textile reports about the engagement of 6.5 million people who are directly or indirectly engaged in either weaving or in any of its allied activities contributing to over 22 percent of total cloth production (Sinha et al. 2006).

2. A handloom cluster may be defined as a place or territory in which a large number of handloom weavers (at least 800–1200) are involved with the activities of cloth production in tune with market demand.

3. For more information see Press Information Bureau. 2017. "Begampur-Mathaparh Saris." August 3, 2017. https://pibindia.wordpress.com/2017/08/03/begampur-mathaparh-saris/#:~:text=Rise%20of%20Begampur%20as%20a,cotton%20yarn%20was%20never%20practiced.

Conclusion

With this book, I take both the general readers and those particularly interested in studying the functioning of a craft tradition that is in the process of transition on a journey through the intricate tapestry of a relatively lesser-known handloom industry of Begampur region, situated in the Hooghly district in the Indian state of West Bengal. Other than projecting the profound significance of this age-old tradition within the broader contexts of India's economic, cultural, and social fabric, I have tried to delve into an exploration of the multifaceted aspects that have defined the essence and determined the course of the handloom weaving in this region by addressing the historical, technological, economic, and sociocultural dimensions of the transformation. In essence, through this book, I have tried to offer a comprehensive exploration of the handloom heritage in Begampur region by tracing the course of the handloom industry through different historical phases, the changing social-cultural dimensions of this particular group of artisans, the disjuncture and juxtapositions resulting from the processes of technological innovation, particular forms of work coordination, and the relational politics surrounding the acts of cloth production, marketing, welfare measures and development. The study shows how the unique setting of Begampur, particularly its history, geography, and cultural heritage, played vital roles in shaping the course of this handloom weaving tradition. Therefore, it would not be wrong to claim that my effort throughout this exploration may illuminate the intricate interplay and the uneasy balance between issues of technology, disjuncture, and development in Begampur region, which might have similarities with many other handloom weaving traditions in India and other parts of the world.

The current situation of the handloom industry of Begampur region is quite precarious as most of the local artisans stand amid a mosaic of contradictions. On the one hand, the local weavers often recapitulate their roots within the handloom industry's glorious past during the period of Mughal Emperors and in a period even before that, when labor contracts were often maintained through kinship ties or at best by the patron–client relationships. Again, it would be very hard to overlook that these artisans are now grappling with forces like industrial capitalism and labor commodification (Castree et al.

2004, 28; Hart 1982, 39). And, precisely this has pushed me to explore the areas of transformation induced by the process of technological transformation within the handloom industry of Begampur region. The findings of this study show that there has been a significant shift in the social division of labor. Previously centered around a weaver caste group, this division within the handloom industry of Begampur region has now moved more toward technical specializations. Today, each task of production has become specialized, and often specific groups of individuals perform them. Consequently, weaving no longer remained an exclusive domain of the weaver caste population. Even the patron–client relationship—which has been one of the prime characteristics of the cloth production system—has shifted more toward paid services, contracts, or market-regulated relationships. In place of a sense of loyalty with which weavers and their employers have often pursued their role in the productive process, the laborers and their employers in Begampur region today often proceed based on economic gain, profit, and loss (Banerjee 2016). This shift aligns with Goody's (1982) perspective on the role of technology in this transition. He elucidates how the increased flow of capital within craft production systems has accelerated technological innovation, thereby influencing labor relationships. The growing prevalence of powerlooms, collar machines, and now jacquard looms in the Begampur region, for instance, serves as compelling evidence supporting this assertion. Nevertheless, a comprehensive analysis of cloth production and marketing mechanisms in the Begampur region does not leave room for such rigid technological determinism, because findings also show that traditional kinship ties still retain a regulatory role within the cloth production system. The role of kinship hasn't been entirely supplanted by new forms of trade relationships induced by technological innovation or the influences of industrial capitalism. The handloom weavers of the Begampur region have managed to preserve some of their customary norms, where family and kin members continue to hold significance in coordinating labor relationships.

Meanwhile, the examination of the interplay and interrelationship between technology, capital, and labor relationships revealed that the situation in the Begampur region is considerably more intricate. Technological choices and operations in this region are deeply rooted in the community context, where artisans frequently leverage their skills and draw upon their knowledge, expertise, and networks. Furthermore, within this community context, numerous stakeholders with interdependent perspectives collaborate and enter into various forms of agreements driven by a multitude of requirements. This aligns perfectly with the concepts put forth by Law (1987) and Pfaffenberger (1992, 498), who describe it as a "socio-technical system" operating within significantly more intricate circumstances and is interconnected through intricate networks that encompass manual labor, expertise, artistic creativity, precision, entrepreneurial abilities, and the effective mediation of numerous actors. The findings of this study showed that the handloom tradition in Begampur region has functioned within a complex web of socioeconomic dynamics, where trust, loyalty, and inequality were interwoven into the fabric of the everyday life of this particular group of artisans. And, how handloom weavers of this region navigated through these multifaceted landscapes where personal relationships and economic interests often coexisted and sometimes collided with one another.

The study shows that the process of transformation in Begampur region hasn't taken place in a straightforward linear progression. The emergence of the coexisting tradition of powerlooms and incorporation of jacquard looms in Begampur region, for example, has not been entirely autonomous. Rather, these decisions regarding technological innovations have been taken based on different social, cultural, and economic contexts. Especially in the first instance, technological innovation has functioned as a strategic tool in the struggle for control over the labor process. The situation in the Begampur region mirrors the phenomena observed by Smith (1976), Roseberry (1976), and Russell (1987), wherein they elucidate how class relations stem not only from unequal access to the means of production but also from disparities in access to the means of exchange. It is in this regard the findings of this study go much closer to Marglin's (1974, 62) assertion, as they highlight that the social division of labor within the hierarchical cloth production system in Begampur doesn't hinge as much on technology or technological efficiency as it does on the interests of a specific class. Due to this, some of the effects brought about by the emergence of powerlooms within the handloom weaving tradition of Begampur region haven't been entirely self-contained. The process of technological "polarization' (e.g., Sørensen 1985, 139) in this region has indeed favored certain individuals while leaving others in dire straits. For instance, petty capitalists or entrepreneurs, by virtue of their exclusive access to the intricate networks of exploitative relationships that govern marketing channels, often capitalize upon their advantageous position to perpetuate a specific cycle of power dynamics. This cycle has further marginalized the resourceless weavers of the region. The second instance of incorporation of jacquard looms within the handloom weaving tradition of Begampur region however presents an entirely different picture. The decision regarding the incorporation of jacquard looms has been taken as part of a real meaningful welfare measure as the members of Begampur Handloom Cluster were keen to carve out a separate identity for Begampuri items while counteracting the process of polarization brought in by earlier technological innovation.

Furthermore, the study shows how these instances of technological innovation, welfare measures, and the efforts of development, with their differential impact on different groups of people, have put the local weavers in front of several dilemmatic choices. And how eventually, these have become prime sources of disjuncture and juxtapositions in the life of this particular group of artisans. Findings show that the local artisans often struggle to make technological choices in either clinging to their old techniques of handloom cloth production or accepting technological innovation. Because, while the first one, due to the lack of required technical efficiency for producing aesthetically rich handloom items, appeared as a roadblock to creating a separate identity for Begampuri handloom items, the second one, despite all the possibilities of making aesthetically rich handloom items, presented the potency of alluring the local weavers under the same loop of being a part of mass market-driven production and eventually pushing the entire industry toward homogenization. Similarly, findings also show that the wages are quite low and the working conditions are quite exploitative for weavers working under the informal system in Begampur region they enjoy relative independence. The weavers working under the formal system on the other hand enjoy a more progressive and empowered working environment at the cost of a complete dependence. Due to this, the local weavers often struggle to choose whether to associate themselves with the informal and informal systems of cloth production and marketing.

The study also shows how barring the recent efforts of Begampur Cluster Society most of the welfare measures due to their inadequacy in understanding some of these nuances have failed terribly in bringing transition within the existing socioeconomic situation of local artisans. In fact, the situation of the handloom weavers of this region is much closer to what Venkatesan (2009, 268) has referred to as the "heterotopia" of the Indian craft world—where artisans, development agents, the state and philanthropists, patrons, consumers, and the concerned individuals and institutions sometimes act in harmony while many times show coerciveness in their proceedings. Thereby, the "network," encompassing all these intermediaries with its "messiness," "hierarchies," and "inequalities," is simultaneously a source of hope and profound concern for resourceless artisans due to its continuous exposure to the dynamics of precolonial, colonial, and postcolonial perspectives. As we envision the future of the handloom heritage in Begampur, it is crucial to recognize the importance of preserving and revitalizing this invaluable cultural legacy. The challenges are real, and the path forward may be complex, but the potential for renewal and growth remains ever-present. It is a tapestry waiting to be woven, a story waiting to be told, and a tradition waiting to be cherished by generations to come. Hopefully, the handloom heritage of Begampur is not just a part of its past; it is a promise for its future.

With all of these, I hope that the insights garnered through this book will contribute not only to a deeper understanding of the intricate dynamics within the handloom industry in India and elsewhere in the world in general but also draw more efforts for the preservation and revitalization of this invaluable cultural legacy of Begampur as well. It is evident that the Begampur handloom industry is more than just a means of cloth production; it is a living testament to the creativity, resilience, and interconnectedness of individuals, communities, and their surroundings. While the challenges faced by the local handloom weavers are undeniable, the spirit of innovation, tradition, and the potential for revitalization remains steadfast.

Glossary

Apatani—Usually the term refers to the particular tribal group living in the Zora valley of Arunachal Pradesh. With relatively advanced weaving techniques compared to other tribal groups in the state, this group weaves their own textiles inscribed with nature-inspired geometric designs. It is carried out on a semi-curved bamboo tube set which is indigenous in every household of this tribe.

Arani silk—A particular variety of traditional silk saree made in Arani, Tamil Nadu, India. *Arani* saree is a strip of unstitched cloth, ranging from four yards to nine yards in length.

Ba—Harness, one of the essential parts of a loom. It is made up of two bamboo splits and a series of tiny nylon threads which have several loops. These loops often help in shedding warp threads at the time of weaving.

*Balu*chari—One form of saree, which is mostly produced in Bankura and Murshidabad districts of West Bengal. This item is popular for its exquisite designs, which often encompass motifs of mythological character or an event.

Banidar—Group of people who work in exchange of predetermined labor charge.

Barujibi—One of Bengali Hindu caste groups of West Bengal whose traditional occupation is cultivation and trading of betel leafs.

Basak—A weaver community that migrated from Bangladesh and settled down in particular parts of West Bengal.

Ba-sana-gantha—One of the stages of production which is also known as denting and drafting. A group of specialists perform this act before the actual job of weaving. They minutely pierce each single warp thread through the two *ba* and one *sana*.

Begum Bahar—A particular variety of saree commonly found in Bengal province. Originally became renowned for using silk warp and cotton weft. This practice of using mixed fiber later on transformed into the practice of using both cotton warp and weft.

Benarasi—A saree made in Varanasi, an ancient city which is also called Benares (Banaras), situated in the Indian state of Uttar Pradesh. *Benarasi* saree is among the finest in India and known for its gold and silver brocade or zari, fine silk, and opulent embroidery. *Benarasi* sarees are made of finely woven silk, are decorated with intricate designs, and, because of these engravings, are relatively heavy.

Bhagalpuri—As the name represents, these sarees originated from the city of Bhagalpur, Bihar, and are made from Bhagalpuri tussar silk. The fabric is known for its fine texture and amazing drape. Usually, heavier than the silk fabric itself because of the extra weft threads used to decorate its pallu. They also differ from the checked or striped silk fabric in the colors and motifs used.

Brahman—One of the caste groups whose rank is the highest as per the Hindu Varna system. Traditionally, people from this group are often found engaged in occupations of a priest, a spiritual teacher, or a scholar.

Chadar—One form of garment which is used for covering the upper body.

Champa Silk—Produced from a variety of tussar silk cultivated in various regions of Chhattisgarh, including Raigarh, Bilaspur, and Janjgir-Champa—*Champa silk* is produced in shades of brown, cream, and dull gold.

Chanderi—A particular kind of lightweight silk fabric that has glossy transparency and has a sheer texture. The name of the fabric came from the small place "Chanderi" which is situated in Madhya Pradesh.

Charan—Term used for referring to a set of production where forty to forty-five items are made at a stretch.

Charka—An implement used for processing warp and weft threads. It is made out of four vertical wooden pegs, two of which hold a circular wooden wheel and the other two encompass a grove for free rotation of the bobbin.

Charki—An implement used for processing warp and weft threads. It is hexagonal in structure and often made out of bamboo splits and tiny pieces of threads.

Chit—Starch.

Dadan—System of making advance payment. European traders used to fix a trade contract with this system.

Dangi—Iron rod which bears the weight of a number of small iron sticks (*tarer-ba*).

Dhoti—One form of garment used for covering the lower body.

Dokti—One of the parts of a loom. It is made up of rectangular wooden frame. This wooden frame encompasses a *sana* and a grove which directs the shuttle through warp threads at the time of weaving.

Drum—An implement which is made out of big circular wooden frame. It is used for assortment and rolling of warp threads into the warp beam.

Eri silk—Made from cocoons of *Eri* silkworm, it is popular as peace silk or "Ahimsa," as it is processed without killing the silkworm. The ancient slow method of spinning silk with a spindle is predominantly practiced by weavers throughout the villages of Meghalaya. *Eri* is the most respected fabric of the local tribal people of Meghalaya.

Farasdanga—An old name of modern-day Chandannagar, located in the district of Hooghly in the Indian state of West Bengal. The name originated from infusion of the two Bengali terms, that is, *farasi* (French) and *danga* (land), a name that recalls its long French connection.

Gamcha—Bathroom napkin.

Guti—Front beam.

Ikat—is a resist dyeing technique in which the yarn is "tied" and "dyed" before the fabric is dyed and woven. *Ikat* means "to bind" in the Indonesian language (country of origin). Since the pattern is created in the yarn itself, both sides of an *Ikat* saree are patterned. The art of making *Ikat* sarees is currently practiced in three states, namely, Odisha, Andhra Pradesh, and Gujarat. While Odisha *Ikat* is mostly cotton sarees, the Pochampally *Ikat* originating from Telangana/Andhra Pradesh are silk sarees.

Jacquard—One form of mechanical loom which was invented by Joseph Marie Jacquard. It was first demonstrated in the year 1801. Nonetheless, some of the products at times carry the name as they epitomize the finesse and skill associated with the process of weaving in these looms.

Jamdani—A renowned variety of saree produced in undivided Bengal. These sarees are typically woven using a mixture of cotton and gold thread. In 2013, the traditional art of weaving *Jamdani* was declared a UNESCO Intangible Cultural Heritage of Humanity. In 2016, Bangladesh received geographical indication (GI) status for *Jamdani* saree.

Kanjivaram silk—An exquisite silk item produced in the Indian state of Tamil Nadu. Authentic *Kanjivaram* sarees are made from high-quality silk, which is soft, smooth, and has a subtle shine. These items have a smooth glossy finish, so when rubbing your hands on the saree, it should feel soft and a difference in the temperature of your palm.

Kardai—Pan.

Karmakar—One of the Bengali Hindu caste groups whose traditional occupation is blacksmithy.

Kata-naksa—One form of saree which is commonly found in Begampur and Dhaniakhali regions.

Kayashyas—One of the Bengali Hindu caste groups who were traditionally associated with clerical and administrative works.

Kinnauri—A particular variety of shawl produced in the Indian state of Himachal Pradesh. Known for its intricacies and finesse, *Kinnauri* shawls are truly a fine work of perfection. Its geometric designs are heavily influenced by the Central Asian culture and consist of motifs that usually symbolize religions and cultures.

Kol-naraj—Front beam.

Kota Doria—A particular form of woven fabric produced in the Indian state of Rajasthan, *Kota Doria* fabric is a combination of cotton and silk woven in a square check pattern. The silk in it gives shine to the fabric whereas cotton gives strength. The checked pattern on it is known as "*Khat*" which is the distinguishing element of *Kota Doria.*

Kotki—One form of saree produced in Begampur region. However, this design originated in Odisha and often the raw threads for this item come from there.

Kullu—A particular variety of shawl produced in the Indian state of Himachal Pradesh. *Kullu* shawls are known for their sharp geometrical patterns and vibrant colors. Apart from the neat geometric patterns, these shawls can also be seen with floral motifs that can be both in the center and the corners. Color range generally consists of one to eight different colors of yarns.

Kumor—One of the Bengali Hindu caste groups who met their livelihood activity through production of clay pots and idols.

Kunbi weaves—A simple cotton item produced in the Indian state Goa. Traditionally, Kunbi is a cotton chequered saree in red and white with a sturdy weave good enough to be worn for farming. A dobby border, which is essentially a silken flat inset in the original Kunbi, can be found.

Kuthampully—Kuthampully is a small town situated in Thrissur District in Kerala. Kuthampully saree is usually manufactured in gray style with Kasavu (Zari). This traditional product is woven with 80s, 100s fine-count cotton yarn. These sarees are manufactured at Kuthampully, Thiruvilwamala, Eravathody, and Kondozhi regions.

Latai—Bobbin.

Lepcha durry—It is a traditional attire of the Sikkim. Generally, it is thick cotton fabric woven on loin loom. 2/20s cotton yarn used for weaving. They use geometrical patterns to ornament the cloth.

Mahajan—Entrepreneur or investor.

Maku—Shuttle.

Mangalgiri—A particular variety of saree produced in the Indian state of Andhra Pradesh. The Mangalagiri fabric is produced by weaving with the help of pitlooms from combed yarn by warp and woof interlacing. The fabric then undergoes the process of dyeing. The Nizam design is another characteristic of the fabric.

Mar—Starch.

Mata—Simple item.

Matapar—Simple bordered.

Meghdambru—A particular variety of saree which has its origin in Balasore, Odisha.

Mera—One of the parts of a *dokti*. It is made out of small rectangular wooden block which directs the shuttle through the warp threads.

Mizu Puan—a traditional textile item of the Indian state of Mizoram. One of the traditional attire worn by Mizoram women is the traditional dress called "Puan." Beautifully intricated design with perfect fit makes it the most preferred dress for the people of Mizoram.

Moirang Phee—A particular form of cotton textile produced in the Indian state of Manipur. *Moirang Phee* is a textile fabric which has a specific design called the "Moirang Pheejin" which is woven sequentially on both longitudinal edges of the fabric and oriented toward the center of the cloth, with cotton or silk threads.

Mora—It is a unit by which weavers often quantify the requirement of yearn for a particular set production. They also use this as a measuring unit while calculating labor charge. Usually, a *mora* contains ten separate bunches of threads, and *noli* is prepared from three such bunches.

Muslin—One form of silk saree which originated in the then Bengal. In the seventeenth century, it was introduced to Europe from the Middle East.

Mysore Silk—Another silk saree produced in the Indian state of Karnataka. Mysore silk is famed for its gleaming appearance and one-of-a-kind luster. The fabric's quality is remarkable, especially with its desirable historical significance. Mysore silk is known for its relatively heavier weight compared to other silk fabrics. The weight adds a sense of substance and opulence to the fabric, making it suitable for creating structured and tailored garments with a regal appearance.

Naga weaves—Due to the ethnic diversity the variation in the fabrics found from the Indian state of Nagaland is immense. Almost all the tribal groups have their own types. Furthermore, the production of fabric directly coincides with their usage and occasion. For example, *Vihe-ashak* is the ordinary white cloth and *Nempong-ashak* is the dark blue cloth meant for casual wear. *Phom fanet* is the cowrie shawl which is worn by a man who has offered feast of merit. *Henyu* is a handsome cloth and is a red shawl having narrow white horizontal bands at regular intervals.

Napit—One of the Bengali Hindu caste groups of West Bengal. The traditional occupation of these people is barbery.

Nilambri—The *Nilambari* saree originates from Shantipur in Nadia District of West Bengal. The unique selling points of this famous saree lie in the quality of dyeing and the fineness of the yarn.

Nokta—One form of contract where big investors take direct credit from the market.

Noli—Pirn.

Noli-pakano—Rolling of threads into the pirn.

Noli-pakano-charka—Implement used for rolling of threads into the pirns.

Pachhra—A particular variety of woven fabric produced in the Indian state of Tripura. Woven on loin loom and worn by women as bottom wear which extends just below the knee, it has colorful stripes and intricate embroidery.

Paithani—A particular variety of silk fabric found in Maharashtra. This variety is renowned for exquisite designs and luxurious fabrics made of silk threads and gold threads. This item can be distinguished by its intricate designs and motifs. *Paithani* sarees usually have distinctive designs such as parrots, peacocks, and flowers. Additionally, you can also check the quality of the fabric to ensure that the saree is made of pure silk and zari.

Pakhi—One of the parts of a loom. It is circular in structure and works as a pulley. This is an essential part of any loom as three to four of such pulleys help in the upward and downward movement of the two harnesses (*bo*) at the time of weaving.

Palui-kathi—A wooden stick where warp threads are tied and placed within the specific groove of warp beam before rolling threads into the warp beam.

Panchachuli—A particular pattern of weaving associated with residents of Almoa, Uttarakhand. Women weavers of this particular region use sheep and merino wool, in addition to pashmina and silk—all of the wool is woven and knitted by hand and only natural ingredients are used in the dyes.

Par—Border.

Pashmina—A particular variety of saree produced in Leh, Ladakh, and Kashmir Valley. The term originated from Persian word Pashma. *Pashmina* is the fabric that is woven out of the pashma. Because of its warmth and lightness, this exquisite fiber fetches a more excellent price than all-natural fibers.

Pata—It means splices, and one of the most important parts of a jacquard machine. These splices contain the specifications of the intended design.

Pati—Back beam or Warp beam.

Patola—is a luxurious and intricate saree made using a double ikat weaving technique, traditionally from the Patan region of Gujarat, India. These sarees are made using silk threads that are first dyed with natural colors and then woven together to create intricate patterns and designs.

Penchano—Means reallocation of iron sticks. It is one of the most essential activities concerning fitting of loom.

Phore—Distributor or agent.

Phulkari—A traditional embroidery art form of Punjab. It is also produced in neighboring states of Haryana and Delhi. *Phulkari* is renowned for its vibrant and intricate floral patterns. The use of soft chiffon fabric ensures a lightweight and delicate feel, draping elegantly on the body.

Pikers—Middleman, wholesalers.

Poren—Weft thread.

Poren-noli—Small pirns where weft threads are rolled. These are fitted within the specific channel of a shuttle.

Sana—It is a comblike structure, formed by a huge number of very thin splices which are arranged serially beside one another. The number of gaps between these very thin splices determines the quality of the woven item.

Sualkuchi—It is a well-known silk textile of the Indian state of Assam. Produced only in Assam, from both Mulberry and Muga silk or "the golden fiber," this silk fabric has also tremendous export potentiality.

Sunto-bhatano—It is one of the phases of cloth production. The process involves smearing starch with the dyed threads.

Suto—Thread.

Suto-bhatano-charka—An implement with four wooden poles, two of which hold a circular wooden structure and another two hold a specific grove for the bobbin.

Tana—Warp.

Tana-ana—One form of labor contract, where weavers with relatively mediocre asset base work under a resourceful investor. Here weavers invest in different stages of production and get a predetermined share of profit from the sold item.

Tana-noli—Means bigger pirns, where warp threads are rolled and provided to the drumming work sheds for the process of warping.

Tangail Saree—is famous for its extra-weft buits, tiny, repeated motifs, all over the ground of the saree, worked like embroidery on the loom. Originally this saree was produced in Tangail district (presently in Bangladesh) of undivided Bengal. But the popularity of this sarees gradually spread across to the adjacent Nadia districts which is now a part of Indian state of West Bengal.

Tant—Loom.

Tant-Baluchari—One form of saree found in Dhaniakhali region. These sarees have a reasonably good amount of design, most of which are either a motif of a flower or an animal. This item is one of the latest entrants to the cotton weaving tradition of this region.

Tanti—One of the Bengali Hindu artisan caste groups of West Bengal. These people are weavers by tradition. Their position in the social hierarchy is higher than that of untouchables.

Tarer-ba—Implements which help in design formation. These small iron sticks have three holes, one in the middle and the other two at its two terminals.

Tili—One of the Bengali Hindu caste groups of West Bengal. These people are oil pressers as per their tradition occupation.

Tussar Silk—is also known by its Sanskrit name *Kosa Silk*. It is produced mainly in Jharkhand, India. *Tussar* is valued for its rich texture and natural deep gold color.

Udupi Cotton—A particular variety of saree produced in the Indian state of Karnataka. This particular kind of cotton item got its name from the place Udupi. Udupi sarees started being woven around 150 years ago from the Malabar Frame Looms, introduced by the Basel Mission of Germany. They are woven using fine forty, sixty, and eighty-count single-ply combed cotton yarns, making them durable.

Venkatagiri Saree—is saree style woven in Venkatagiri of Tirupati district in the Indian state of Andhra Pradesh. It was registered as one of the geographical indications from Andhra Pradesh by Geographical Indications of Goods Act, 1999. Venkatagiri sarees are known for their fine weaving.

Zari—One form of raw material used mainly for the design formation in the border region of woven items.

References

Abdul, N. "Handlooms in Distress." *Economic and Political Weekly* 31, no. 23 (1996): 1384–1386.

Antlöv, H. "Review: Untitled." *The Journal of Asian Studies* 56 no. 4 (1997): 1172–1173.

Appadurai, A. (Ed.). *The Social Life of Things: Commodities in Cultural Perspective*. UK, Cambridge: Cambridge University Press, 1986.

Appadurai, A. (1990). "Disjuncture and Difference in the Global Cultural Economy." *Theory, Culture & Society* 7, no. 2–3 (1990): 295–310.

Argenti, N. "People of the Chisel: Apprenticeship, Youth, and Elites in Oku (Cameroon)." *American Ethnologist* 29 (2002): 497–533.

Bagchi, A.K. "Deindustrialization in India in the Nineteenth Century: Some Theoretical Implications." *The Journal of Developmental Studies* 12, no. 2 (1976): 135–164.

Banerjee, A. *West Bengal District Gazetteers, Vol. Hooghly*. Calcutta: Sree Saraswati Press Ltd, 1972.

Banerjee, A. "*The Changing Cotton Weaving Tradition in West Bengal: An Anthropological Case Study*." MSc diss., University of Calcutta, 2005.

Banerjee, A. "*Craft, Culture and Economy of the Traditional Weaving in West Bengal*." PhD diss., University of Calcutta, 2014.

Banerjee, A. "Understanding Some of the Key Factors Responsible for Transformation within an Indian Cotton Weaving Tradition". *Asian Journal of Social Science* 44, no. 4–5 (2016): 571599.

Banerjee, A., Chakrabarti, G.K. and A. Das. "Weavers and Their Woes: A Study of the Problems of the Traditional Weavers Living in the Margins of Kolkata Metropolis." *Journal of The Department of Anthropology* 12–13 (2010): 51–73.

Banerjee, A., Charkabarti, G.K. and A. Das. "A Study on the Dimensions of Marginalization among the Handloom Weavers of Begampur." *Journal of Indian Anthropological Society* 46, no. 1 (2011): 31–46.

Banerjee, A., and G. Chakrabarti. "Exploring the Effects of Globalization on Silk Weaving Tradition of Bishnupur Region in West Bengal, India." *The Oriental Anthropologist* 20, no. 1 (2020): 60–81.

Banerjee, D. "Market and Non-Market Configurations in Rural West Bengal: Local Organisations and Silk Weaving." *Economic and Political Weekly* 30, no. 47 (1995): M135-M137+M139- M142.

Barnes, R. (edt.) *Textiles in Indian Ocean Societies*. London: Routledge, 2005.

Basu, K. *Marginalization in Globalizing World: Some Plausible Scenarios and Suggestion for Measurement.* Asia and Pacific Forum on Poverty: Reforming Policies and Institutions for Poverty Reduction, held at the Asian Development Bank, Manila, 5–9 February 2001.

Baudrillard, J. *The System of Objects.* London and New York: Verso, 1996.

Bernard, H.R. *Research Methods in Anthropology: Qualitative and Quantitative Approaches*. United Kingdom: Altamira, 2011.

Bernstain, B. *Pedagogy, Symbolic Control and Identity*. London: Taylor and Francis, 1996.

Bhattacharya, Sukumar. *The East India Company and the Economy of Bengal from 1707–1740,* Calcutta: Farma KLM Private Ltd, 1967.

Birdwood, G.M. *The Industrial Art of India. South Kensington Museum Art Handbooks*. London: Chapman and Hall, 1880.

Burawoy, M. *Manufacturing Consent. Changes in the Labor Process under Monopoly Capitalism.* Chicago: University of Chicago Press, 1979.

Cable, V., Weston, A. and L.C Jain. *The Commerce of Culture: The Experience of Indian Handicrafts*. Lancer International for ICRIER, 1986.

Castree, N., Coe, N., Ward, K. and M. Samers. *Spaces of Work: Global Capitalism and Geographies of Labour*. London: Sage, 2004.

Chatterjee, R. "Cotton Handloom Manufactures of Bengal, 1870–1921." *Economic and Political Weekly* 22, no. 25 (1987): 988–997.

Chambers, T. *Networks, Labour and Migration among Indian Muslim Artisans*. United Kingdom: UCL Press, 2020.

Chaudhry, G. "On the Great Indian Handloom Traditions." https://culturalsamvaad.com/on-the-great-indian-handloom-traditions/accessed May 16, 2023.

Clammer, John. (ed.). *The New Economic Anthropology*. London: Basingstoke, 1978.

Clingingsmith, D. and J.G Williamson. "Deindustrialization in 18th and 19th Century India: Mughal Decline, Climate Shocks and British Industrial Ascent." *Explorations in Economic History* 45 (2008): 209–234.

Cohn, B.S. *Colonialism and Its Forms of Knowledge: The British in India*. New Jersey: Princeton University Press, 1996.

Cook, S. "Craft Commodity Production, Market Diversity and Differential Rewards in Mexican Capitalism Today." In *Crafts in the World Market: The Impact of Global Exchange on Middle American Artisans*, edited by J. Nash, 59–84, Albany: State University of New York Press, 1993.

Coomaraswamy, A.K. *The Indian Craftsman*. London: Probsthain, 1909.

Coy, M. *Apprenticeship: From Theory to Method and Back Again*. Albany, NY: State University of New York Press, 1989.

Creswell, J. *Qualitative Inquiry and Research Design: Choosing Among Five Approaches* (2nd edn.). Thousand Oaks, CA: Sage, 2006.

Crowfoot, G.M. "Textile Basketry and Mats." In *A History of Technology Vol . 1: From Early Times to Fall of Ancient Empires,* edited by A. R. Hall, Charles Singer, E. J. Holmyard, 413–455. United Kingdom: Clarendon Press, 1954.

Dant, T. *Materiality and Society*. Berkshire: Open University Press, 2005.

Das, S.K. *Warp and Woof: An Enquiry into Handloom Industry in West Bengal*. Kolkata: K.P. Bagchi and Company, 2001.
Das, T.K. "Itihase Begampur." *Chanditala Sangbad*. September 1st, 2002a.
Das, T.K. "Itihase Begampur." *Chanditala Sangbad*. September 16th, 2002b
Das, T.K. "Itihase Begampur." *Chanditala Sangbad*. October 1st, 2002c.
Das, T.K. "Itihase Begampur." *Chanditala Sangbad*. October 16th, 2002d.
De Neve, G. "Towards an Ethnography of the Workplace: Hierarchy, Authority and Sociability on the South Indian Textile Shop-Floor." *South Asia Research* 21 (2001): 133–160.
DeNicola, C.M. and A.O. Wilkinson-Weber. (ed.). *Critical Craft: Technology, Globalization and Capitalism*. New York: Bloomsbury Academic, 2016.
Dormer, Peter. (ed.). *The Culture of Craft: Status and Future (Studies in Design)*. Manchester: Manchester University Press, 1997.
Downey, G.L. "Human Agency in CAD/CAM Technology." *Anthropology Today* 8, no. 5 (1992): 2–6.
Dykeman, M. "Building a Strong Family: The Importance of Family Functioning." *Marriage & Family Review* 55, no. 3 (2019): 244–266.
Editors of Encyclopaedia Britannica. "Yajna." Encyclopedia Britannica. March 2, 2015. https://www.britannica.com/topic/yajna.
Ember, C., Ember, M. and P.N. Peregrine. *Anthropology* (12th edn.). Delhi: Pearson, 2007.
Ennew, J. "Harris Tweed: Construction, Retention and Representation of a Cottage Industry." In *From Craft to Industry,* edited by E. N. Goody, 166–199. Cambridge, UK: Cambridge University Press, 1982.
Ferguson, James. *Expectations of Modernity: Myths and Meanings of Urban Life on the Zambian Copperbelt.* Berkeley: University of California Press, 1999.
Fishel, L.A. "The Important Role of Families in Society." *Social Education* 82, no. 6 (2018): 325–329.
Gatha. "Photoloomic-Baluchari." July 3, 2014. https://gaatha.com/baluchari-saree-bangal.
Gell, A. *Art and Agency: An Anthropological Theory*. Oxford: Clarendon Press, 1998.
Gluckman, Max. "Anthropological Problems Arising from the African Industrial Revolution." In *Social Change in Modern Africa*, edited by Southall, Aidan 67–82. London: Oxford University Press, 1961.
GOI. *Report of the Working and Living Conditions of Workers in the Handloom Industry in India.* New Delhi: Ministry of Labour, 1986–1987.
GOI. *Report on the Working and Living Conditions of Workers in the Powerloom Industry in India.* New Delhi: Ministry of Labour, 1988.
Goody, E. "Daboya Weavers: Relations of Production, Dependence and Reciprocity." In *From Craft to Industry: The Ethnography of Proto-industrial Cloth Production* edited by Esther Goody, 50–84. Cambridge: Cambridge University Press, 1982.
Goody, E.N. (ed.). *From Craft to Industry: The Ethnography of Proto-Industrial Cloth Production.* Cambridge, UK: Cambridge University Press, 1982.
Goody, E.N. "Anthropology of Craft." *International Encyclopaedia of the Social & Behavioral Sciences, 2nd edition* 5 (2000): 108–112.

Goswami O. "Sickness and Growth of India's Textile Industry: Analysis and Policy Options." *Economic and Political Weekly* 25, no. 45 (1990b): -2496-2501+2503- 2506.

Goswami, O. "Sickness and Growth of India's Textile Industry: Analysis and Policy Options." *Economic and Political Weekly* 25, no. 44 (1990a): 2429–2439.

Goswami, O. 1985. "Indian Textile Industry, 1970–1984: An Analysis of Demand and Supply." *Economic and Political Weekly* 20, no. 38 (1985): 1603-1605+1607-1614.

Greiner, C. and Pröpper, M. "Hands, Skills, Materiality. Towards an Anthropology of Crafts." In *Migration-Networks-Skills: Anthropological Perspectives on Mobility and Transformation*, edited by A. Wonneberger et al., 209–230. Transcript Verlag. 2016.

Guha-Thakurata, T. *The Making of New 'Indian' Art: Artist, Aesthetics and Nationalism in Bengal, 1850—1920.* Cambridge: Cambridge University Press, 1992.

Gupta, Y. "Weaves of India." Accessed May 16, 2023. https://www.memeraki.com/blogs/news/weaves-of-india

Hann, Chris and Keith Hart. *Economic Anthropology*. Cambridge, UK: Polity Press, 2011.

Harnetty, P. "Deindustrialization Revisited: The Handloom Weavers of the Central Province of India." *Modern Asian Studies* 25 (1991): 455–510.

Hart, K. "On Commoditization." In *From Craft to Industry: The Ethnography of Proto-industrial Cloth Production,* edited by Esther Goody, 38–49. Cambridge: Cambridge University Press, 1982.

Havell, E.B. *The Basis of Artistic and Industrial Revival in India*. Delhi: Usha, 1986. Original Edition 1912.

Haynes, D. The Logic of Artisan Firm in Economy Capitalist: Handloom Weavers and Technological Change in Western India, 1880–1947. In *Institution and Economic Change in South Asia*, edited by B. Stain and S. Subrahmanyam, 173–205. Delhi: Oxford University Press, 1996.

Holstein, J.A. and J.F Gubrium. "Active Interviewing." In *Qualitative Research: Theory Method and Practice*, edited by David Silverman, 140–161. New Delhi: The Thousand Oaks, 1997.

Holzberg, Carol S. and Maureen J. Giovannini. "Anthropology and Industry: Reappraisal and New Directions. *Annual Review of Anthropology* 10 (1981): 317–360.

Hossain, H. *The Company Weavers of Bengal: East India Company and the Organization of Textile Production in Bengal (1750–1813)*. Delhi: Oxford University Press, 1988.

Hymes, D.H. *Reinventing Anthropology*. Ann Arbor, Michigan: University of Michigan Press, 2002 [1972].

ILO. *Handloom Weaving Industry in India with Specific Reference to Madras State*. New Delhi: Indian Branch, 1960.

Industrial Development Services (IDS). Handicrafts: 1955–1985, 'A Review Paper'. *Indian Council for Research on International Economic Relations*, Working Paper 33, 1985.

Jain, L.C. "1985 Textile Policy: End of Handloom Industry." *Economic and Political Weekly* 20, no. 27 (1985): 1121–1123.

Jain, L.C. "Development of Decentralised Industries: A Review and Some Suggestions." *Economic and Political Weekly* 15, no. 41/43 (1980): 1747–1749+1751+1753-1754.

Jain, L.C. "Handlooms Face Liquidation: Powerlooms Mock at Yojana Bhavan." *Economic and Political Weekly* 18, no. 35 (1983): 1517–1526.

Kashyap, S. *National Policy Studies*. New Delhi: Tata Mcgrowhil Publishing Company, 1990.

Keller, Charles M. "Thought and Production: Insights of the Practicioner." In *Anthropological Perspectives on Technology*, edited by Michael Brian Schiffer, 33–46. Dragoon, AZ: Amerind Foundation, 2001.

Khasnabis, R. and P Nag. "Labour Process in the Informal Sector: A Handloom Industry in Nadia District." *Economic and Political Weekly* 36, no. 52 (2002): 4836–4845.

Kluge, Friedrich. *Etymologisches Wörterbuch der deutschen Sprache*. Berlin/ New York: Walter de Gruyter, 1999.

Krishnamurty, J. "Handicrafts in the Indian Economy: A Study of the Handloom Industry from 1800." In *Imperialism, Nationalism and Regionalism in Canadian and Modern Indian History*, edited by Aparna Basu, 138–139. New Delhi: Manohar Publications, 1989.

Kshetrimayum, O. "Rethinking Cooperatives in Rural Development: A Case Study of Handloom Weavers' Cooperatives in Manipur." *Labour & Development* 18 (2011): 65–79.

Kumar Vivek, Pratishtha Kumari, Pooja Yadav, and Madan Kumar. "Ancient to contemporary—The Saga of Indian Handloom Sector." *Indian Journal of Fibre & Textile Research* 46 (2021): 411–431.

Kundu, A. 1980. "Pattern of Organization of the Handloom Industry in West Bengal: Part One." *Social Scientist* 9, no. 1 (1980): 18–32.

Lang, Hartmut. *Systeme der Wirtschaftsethnologie. Eine Einführung*. Berlin: Reimer, 2010.

Law, J. "Technology and Heterogeneous Engineering: The Case of Portuguese Expansion." In *The Social Construction of Technological System: New Direction in the Sociology and History of Technology,* edited by W. Bijker T. Huges and T. Pinch, 111–34. Cambridge: MIT Press, 1987.

Lemonnier, P. "Bark Capes, Arrow Heads and Concorde: On Social Representation of Technology." In *The Meaning of Things: Material Culture and Symbolic Expression,* edited by I. Hodder, 156–171. London: Unwin Hyman, 1989.

Lemonnier, P. "The Study of Material Culture Today: Towards an Anthropology of Technical System." *Journal of Anthropological Archaeology* 5 (1986): 147–186.

Liebl, M. and T. Roy. "Handmade in India: Preliminary Analysis of Crafts Producers and Crafts Production." *Economic and Political Weekly* 38 no. 51/52 (2004): 5366–5376.

Linton, D. S. "Industrialization and Intergenerational Social Mobility in a Rhenish Textile Town." *Journal of Interdisciplinary History* 18, no. 1 (1987): 107–126.

Majumdar D.N. and T.N Madan. *An Introduction to Social Anthropology*. Noida: Mayoor Paperbacks, 1999.

Mandara, J., C.B. Murray, and Joyner, H. "Family Interaction, Exposure to Poverty, and Parenting as Predictors of the Social Competence of African American Preschoolers." *Journal of Black Psychology* 35, no. 4 (2009): 387–406.

Marchand, Trevor H.J. *The Pursuit of Pleasurable Work: Craftwork in Twenty-First Century England.* United States: Berghahn Books, 2021.

Marcus, George E. and Fred R. Myers. (eds.) *The Traffic in Culture: Refiguring Art and Anthropology*. Berkeley: University of California Press, 1995.

Marglin, S. "What Do Bosses Do? The Origins and Functions of Hierarchy in Capitalist Production." *Review of Radical Political Economics* 6 (1974): 60–112.

Mark Kenoyer, J. "Ancient Textiles of the Indus Valley Region." 2004. https://www.harappa.com/sites/default/files/pdf/Kenoyer2004%20IndusTextilesfinal.pdf

McCarthy, J. and P. Wright. *Technology as Experience*. London: The MIT Press, 2004.

Mehta, S.D. *Indian Cotton Textile Industry*. Bombay: The Textile Association (India), 1953.

Miller, D. (ed.). *Material Cultures: Why Some Things Matter*. London: Taylor and Francis Group, 1998.

Miner, H.M. "Traditional Mobility among the Weavers of Fez." *Proceedings of the American Philosophical Society* 117, no. 1 (1973): 17–36.

Miner, H. *The Primitive City of Timbuctoo*. New York: Anchor Books, 1965 [1953].

Ministry of External Affairs. "India in Business." 2009. http://www.indiainbusiness.nic.in/industry-infrastructure/industrial-sectors/textile.htm Accessed on 01.07.09.

Ministry of Textile. "Annual Report." 2007-08. http://texmin.nic.in/annualrep/AR07-08-index.pdf, Accessed on 01.07.09.

Ministry of Textiles. "Annual report." 2017-18 http://texmin.nic.in/sites/default/files/Textiles-AnnualReport2018-2019%28English%29.pdf Accessed on 02.04.2020.

Ministry of Textiles. "4th All India Handloom Census." 2019-20. http://handlooms.nic.in/writereaddata/3736.pdf Accessed on 02.04.2020.

Ministry of Textile. "Annual Report." 2020-21. http://texmin.nic.in/sites/default/files/AR_Ministry_of_Textiles_%202020-21_Eng.pdf Accessed on 18.11.23.

Mitra, S.K. *Hooghly Jelar Itihash O Bongosomaj*. Calcutta: Mitrani Prakashan, 1975.

Mishra, S. *India's Textile Sector: A Policy Analysis.* New Delhi: Sage Publications, 1993.

Mishra, Shruti and Das Mohapatra Arka. "Handloom in India: An Overview." *Strad Research* (2021) 7. https://doi.org/10.37896/sr7.8/016

Mitter, P. *Art and Nationalism in Colonial India, 1850–1922*. Occidental Orientation. Cambridge: Cambridge University Press, 1997.

Mohamad, M. *The Mayan Handloom Weavers: A Study of Rise and Decline of Traditional Manufacture*. Singapore: Institute of South-East Asian Studies, 1996.

Mollona, Massimilano, Geert De Neve, and Jonathan Parry. (eds.). *Industrial Work and Life: An Anthropological Reader*. Oxford: Berg, 2009.

Moore, H. *Feminism and Anthropology*. Minneapolis: University of Minnesota Press, 1988.

Moore, Patrick. Review of *We Are Our Language: An Ethnography of Language Revitalization in a Northern Athabaskan Community*. *Anthropological Linguistics* 53, no. 3 (2011): 291–292. https://doi.org/10.1353/anl.2011.0018

Morphy, Howard and Morgan Perkins. "The Anthropology of Art: A Reflection on its History and Contemporary Practice." In *The Anthropology of Art: A Reader*, edited by Howard Morphy and Morgan Perkins, 1–32. Oxford: Blackwell Publishing, 2006.

Mukund, K. and B. Syamasundari. "Doomed to Fail? 'Handloom Weavers' Co-Operatives in Andhra Pradesh." *Economic and Political Weekly* 33, no. 52 (1998): 3323–3332.

Murdock, G.P. *Social Structure*. New York: The Macmillan Company, 1949.

Murshed, S.M. "Globalization and South Asia: A Perspective." *South Asia Economic Journal* 5 no. 2 (2004): 311–326.

Nadel, S.F. *A Black Byzantium*. London: Oxford University Press, 1942.

Narotzky, Susana. *New Directions in Economic Anthropology*. London: Pluto Press, 1997.

Nash, J. "Traditional Art and Changing Market in Middle America." In *Crafts in the World Market: The Impact of Global Exchange on Middle American Artisans*, edited by J. Nash, 1–24, Albany: State University of New York Press, 199[illegible].

Nath, P., N. Mrinalini. and G.D Sandhya. "National Textile Policy and Textile Research." *Economic and Political Weekly* 36, no. 5/6 (2001): 489–496.

Nehru, J. *The Discovery of India*. London: Meridian Books, 1947.

Niranjana, S. "Thinking with Handlooms: Perspectives from Andhra Pradesh." *Economic and Political Weekly* 39, no. 6 (2004): -553–563.

Niranjana, S. and S. Vinayan. *Report on Growth and Prospect of the Handloom Industry*. Andhra Pradesh: Planning Commission, 2001.

O'Malley, L.S.S. and M. Chakravarti. *Bengal District Gazetteers. Hooghly*. Calcutta: Bengal Secretariat Book Depot, 1912.

Ong, Aihwa. *Spirits of Resistance and Capitalist Discipline: Factory Women in Malaysia*. Albany, New York: SUNY Press, 1987.

Oxford Advanced Learners Dictionary (OALD). Oxford: Oxford University Press, 1987.

Parel, A.J. (ed.). *Gandhi: Hind Swaraj and Other Writings*. Delhi: Foundation Books, 1997.

Parry, Jonathan. "Industrial Work." In *A Handbook of Economic Anthropology*, edited by James G. Carrier, 141–159. Cheltenham: Edward Elgar, 2005.

Pfaffenberger, Bryan. "Fetishised Objects and Humanised Nature: Towards an Anthropology of Technology." *Man* 23 (1988): 236–252.

Pfaffenberger, B. "Social Anthropology of Technology". *Annual Review of Anthropology* 21 (1992): 491–516.

Pinch, T.J. and W.E. Bijker. "The Social Construction of Facts and Artifacts: Or How the Sociology of Science and the Sociology of Technology might Benefit Each Other." *Social Studies of Science* 4 (1984): 399–441.

Pinch, T.J. "The Social Construction of Technology: A Review." In *Technological Change: Methods and Themes in the History of Technology*, edited by Robert Fox, 17–35. Australia: Harwood Academic Publishers, 1996.

Plattner, Stuart. (ed.). *Economic Anthropology*. Stanford, California: Stanford University Press, 1989.

Prasad, A. "Review of Traditional Industry in the Economy of Colonial India." *Studies in History* 17 (2001): 281–283.

Press Information Bureau. "Begampur-Mathaparh Saris." August 3, 2017. https://pibindia.wordpress.com/2017/08/03/begampur-mathaparh-saris/#:~:text=Rise%20of%20Begampur%20as%20a,cotton%20yarn%20was%20never%20practiced. Accessed November 9, 2023.

Ramagundam, R. "Khadi and Its Agency: Organizing Structures of Philanthropic Commerce." *Social Scientist* 32, no. 5/6 (2004): 51–68.

Raniwala, P. 2020. "Everything You Need to Know about the Bengal Cotton Handloom Tant Sari." https://www.vogue.in/fashion/content/bengal-cotton-tant-sari-everything-you-need-to-know-about-the-handloom-weave#:~:text=The%20earliest%20record%20of%20sari,patronage%20alongside%20muslin%20and%20jamdani. Accessed May 16, 2023.

Ray, B. *District Census Handbook, Hooghly*. Calcutta: Ganges Printing Company, 1962.

Ray, H.P. "Far-flung Fabrics – Indian Textiles in Ancient Maritime Trade." In *Textiles in Indian Ocean Societies*, edited by R. Barnes, 16–34. London: Routledge, 2005.

Riello, G. and T. Roy. (eds.). *How India Clothed the World: The World of South Asian Textiles, 1500–1850*. Leiden: Brill, 2009.

Risley, H.H. *The Tribes and Castes of Bengal: Ethnographic Glossary*. India: Printed at the Bengal Secretariat Press, 1892.

Roseberry, W. "Rent, Differentiation, and the Development of Capitalism among Peasants." *American Anthropologist* 78 (1976): 45–58.

Rössler, Martin. *Wirtschaftsethnologie: Eine Einführung*. Berlin: Reimer, 1999.

Roy, T. "Relations of Production in Handloom Weaving in the Mid-1930s." *Economic and Political Weekly* 24, no. 4 (1989): PE21-PE25+PE28-PE34.

Roy, T. 1998. Development or Distortion? 'Powerlooms' in India, 1950–1997. *Economic and Political Weekly* 33, no. 6 (1998): 897–911.

Roy, T. *Artisans and Industrialization: Indian Weaving in Twentieth Century*. Delhi: Oxford University Press, 1993.

Roy, Tirthankar. (ed.). *Cloth and Commerce: Textiles in Colonial India*. India: SAGE Publications, 1996.

Roy, T. *Traditional Industry in the Economy of Colonial India*. Cambridge: Cambridge University Press, 1999.

Roy, T. "Economic History and Modern India: Redefining the Link." *Journal of Economic Perspectives* 16 (2002): 109–130.

Russell, S.D. "Middlemen and Moneylending: Relations of Exchange in a High-Land Philippine Economy." *Journal of Anthropological Research* 43, no. 2 (1987): 139–161.

Saha, S.N. "Trends in the Textile Industry and the Dilemma in Indian Cotton Textile Policy." *Economic and Political Weekly* 17, no. 9 (1982): M23+M25+M27+M29- M30.

Schiffer, Michael Brian. (ed.). *Anthropological Perspectives on Technology*. Albuquerque: University of New Mexico Press, 2001a.

Schiffer, Michael Brian. "Toward an Anthropology of Technology." In *Anthropological Perspectives on Technology* edited by Schiffer, Michael Brian, 1–16. Albuquerque: University of New Mexico Press, 2001b.

Schiffer, M.B. "Studying Technological Change: A Behavioral Perspective.' *World Archaeology* 36, no. 4 (2004): 579–585.

Schneider, J. "The Anthropology of Cloth." *Annual Review of Anthropology* 16 (1987): 409–448.

Schnieder, J. "Cloth in the Organization of Human Experience." *Current Anthropology*, 27, no. 2 (1986): 178–184.

Scholte, B. "Toward a Reflexive and Critical Anthropology." In *Re- Inventing Anthropology*, edited by Dell Hymes, 430–457. New York: Pantheon, 1972 [1969].

Seddon, D. (ed.). *Relations of Production: Marxist Approaches to Economic Anthropology*. London: Frank Cass, 1978.

Simpson, Edward. "Apprenticeship in Western India." *Journal of the Royal Anthropological Institute* 12 (2006): 151–171.

Sinha, A., P. Munjal, K. Basu, and S. Singh. *Examining Employment Figures in the Handloom Sector*. New Delhi All India Artisans and Craftworkers Welfare Association, 2006.

Sinha, S. "Development Impact of Silk Production: A Wealth of Opportunities." *Economic and Political Weekly* 24, no. 3 (1989): 157–163.

Smith, C.A. "Exchange Systems and the Spatial Distribution of Elites: The Organization of Stratification in Agrarian Societies." In *Regional Analysis, Vol. 2- Social Systems* edited by C. Smith, 309–374. New York: Academic Press, 1976.

Sørensen, K.H. "Technology and Industrial Democracy: An Inquiry into Some Theoretical Issues and their Social Basis." *Organization Studies* 6 (1985): 139–160.

Specker, K. "'De-Industrialisation' in Nineteenth century India: The Textile Industry in the Madras Presidency, 1810–1870." In *Arrested Development in India: The Historical Dimension*, edited by Clive Dewey, 341–377. New Delhi: Manohar Publications, 1988.

Spier, R. *From the Hand of Man: Primitive and Preindustrial Technologies*. Boston: Houghton-Mifflin, 1970.

Srinivasulu, K. "1985 Textile Policy and Handloom Industry: Policy, Promises and Performance." *Economic and Political Weekly* 31, no. 49 (1996): 3198–3206.

Srinivasulu, K. 1994. "Handloom Weavers' Struggle for Survival." *Economic and Political Weekly* 29, no. 36 (1994): 2331–2333.

Stromberg-Pellizi, G. "Coyotes and Culture Brokers: The Production and Marketing of Texaco Silverwork." In *Crafts in the World Market: The Impact of Global Exchange on Middle American Artisans*, edited by J. Nash, 85–102, Albany: State University of New York Press, 1993.

Suchman, Lucy A. "Building Bridges: Practice Based Ethnographies of Contemporary Technology. In *Anthropological Perspectives on Technology* edited by Michael Brian Schiffer, 163–178. Albuquerque: University of New Mexico Press, 2001.

Sur, A. *Bangla O Bangalir Bibartan*. Calcutta: Sahityalok Prakashani, 1986.

Tarlo, E. *Clothing Matters: Dress and Identity in India*. United Kingdom Hurst, 1996.

Tedlock, B. 1991. "From Participant Observation to the Observation of Participation: The Emergence of Narrative Ethnography." *Journal of Anthropological Research* 47, no. 1 (1991): 69–94.

Thorner, D. "De-industrialization in India 1881–1931." In *Land and Labour in India,* edited by Daniel Thorner and Alice Thorner, 70–81. Bombay: Asia Publishing House, 1962.

Tiwari, M. and G.S. Ahirwar. "Origin and Development of Cooperatives in India." *International Journal of Academic Research and Development* 2, no. 5 (2017): 878–889.

Ulin, R.C. 1991. "Critical Anthropology Twenty Years Later: Modernism and Post-modernism in Anthropology." *Critique of Anthropology* 11 (1991): 63–89.

Venkatesan, S. *Craft Matters: Artisan, Development and the Indian Nation.* New Delhi: Orient Blackswan Private Limited, 2009.

Venkateswarlu, B. and Sathish Babu A. "Handloom Weaver's Co-operative Societies in Prakasem District, Andhra Pradesh: A Case Study." *International Journal of Research in Social Sciences and Humanities* 7, no. 1 (2017): 63–70.

Victoria and Albert Museum. "Arts and Crafts: An Introduction." 2013. http://www.vam.ac.uk/content/articles/w/what-is-craft. Accessed 31 January, 2024.

Washburn, D.K. 1991. "Style, Classification and Ethnicity: Design Categories on Bakuba Raffia Cloth." *Transactions of the American Philosophical Society* 80, no. 3 (1991): i–157.

Weiner, A.B. and J. Schneider. *Cloth and Human Experience*. Washington, DC: Smithsonian Institution Press, 1989.

Wendt, I.C. "Four Centuries of Decline? Understanding the Changing Structure of the South Indian Textile Industry." In *How India Clothed the World: The World of South Asian Textiles, 1500–1850*, edited by G. Riello and T. Roy, 193–215. Leiden, Boston: Brill, 2009.

Wherry, F.F. *Global Markets and Local Crafts: Thailand and Costa Rica Compared.* Baltimore, MD: Johns Hopkins University Press, 2008.

Wild, J.P. and F. Wild. "Rome and India: Early Indian Cotton Textiles from Berenike, Red Sea Coast of Egypt." In *Textiles in Indian Ocean Societies*, edited by Ruth Barnes, 11–16. London and New York: Routledge, 2005.

Wilk, Richard R. *Economics and Cultures: Foundations of Economic Anthropology.* Oxford: Boulder / Colorado, 1996.

William, A.G. and L.D. Pearce. *Mixed Method Data Collection Strategies*. Cambridge: Cambridge University Press, 2007.

Index

About the Author

Abhradip Banerjee works as assistant professor of anthropology (W.B.E.S.) under the Higher Education Department, Government of West Bengal. Currently, he is posted at the Government General Degree College, Singur, Hooghly, India. He has worked as research investigator in the Cultural Research Institute, Backward Classes Welfare Department, Government of West Bengal. He also worked as a UGC-NET research fellow in the Department of Anthropology, University of Calcutta, from where he pursued his PhD research on three handloom weaver communities of West Bengal. He received his PhD in anthropology from the University of Calcutta in 2015. He is a life member of many professional organizations including the Indian Anthropological Society, Kolkata, and the Indian Science Congress Association. He has been on the editorial board of reputed international journal *The Qualitative Report* since 2018 and has recently been promoted to the role of editor. Additionally, he has played quite an active role as a peer-reviewer in many reputed international journals including *Social Science and Medicine*, *Journal of Contemporary Ethnography*, *Journal of Ethnographic Theory*, *International Journal of Qualitative Research*, and so on. His research interests include the Indian handloom industry, economic anthropology, pharmaceutical anthropology, material culture, rock art, the history of anthropology, and sustainable development. He has published several research articles in journals of both national and international repute. Finally, he jointly edited *Anthropological Research in India: Retrospect and Prospect* (Lexington Books, 2023). Correspondence regarding this book can be addressed directly to abhraanthro@gmail.com.

www.ingramcontent.com/pod-product-compliance
Ingram Content Group UK Ltd.
Pitfield, Milton Keynes, MK11 3LW, UK
UKHW041837031026
15587UKWH00002B/830

9 781666 960587